"An Empire of Ideals"

"Garrison has produced the most penetrating and finest analysis of Ronald Reagan's rhetoric. His findings are bound to surprise many and even shock some."

—**George W. Carey**, Georgetown University

"Justin Garrison's highly original work explodes conventional categorizations about Ronald Reagan's politics and governing philosophy. Using Reagan's own words, Garrison makes the provocative, yet ultimately convincing, case that the icon of modern conservatism was actually an adherent of the ideas of a variety of thinkers, including even leading progressive ones. I commend this work to scholars and students of the presidency, rhetoric, and political philosophy."

—**Mark J. Rozell**, George Mason University

"An Empire of Ideals" provides an original and groundbreaking analysis of Ronald Reagan's imagination as it was expressed mainly in his presidential speeches. The book argues that the predominant strain of Reagan's imagination is "chimeric"—that is, imbued with a high degree of optimism, romantic dreaminess, naiveté, and illusion. Justin D. Garrison challenges a number of existing assumptions about Reagan. Among other things, he draws into question Reagan's self-proclaimed status as a conservative and as a faithful adherent to the ideas of the American Founding. The book concludes that Reagan's vision contains many dubious elements that present dangers for practical politics. It also claims that the popularity of Reagan's imagination among Americans suggests a problematic self-understanding.

Surpassing existing works on Reagan's ideas and speeches, the book systematically explains the general quality and major components of Reagan's vision, and it draws upon political theory, aesthetics, and American political thought to analyze his imagination. Although the book is a rigorous work of scholarship, it is not a highly "technical" study accessible only to academic specialists. It will be of deep interest to general readers as well as scholars.

Justin D. Garrison earned his doctorate in political theory from Catholic University. His research and teaching interests include political theory, American political thought, literature and politics, and aesthetics and politics. He will be joining the faculty at Roanoke College as an assistant professor of political science in the fall of 2013.

Routledge Research in American Politics and Governance

"An Empire of Ideals"
The Chimeric Imagination
of Ronald Reagan

Justin D. Garrison

Routledge
Taylor & Francis Group

NEW YORK AND LONDON

First published 2013
by Routledge
711 Third Avenue, New York, NY 10017

Simultaneously published in the UK
by Routledge
2 Park Square, Milton Park, Abingdon, Oxfordshire OX14 4RN

First issued in paperback 2015

*Routledge is an imprint of the Taylor & Francis Group,
an informa business*

Library of Congress Cataloging in Publication Data

Garrison, Justin D.
"An empire of ideals" : the chimeric imagination of Ronald Reagan /
    Justin D. Garrison.
       pages cm. — (Routledge research in American politics and
governance ; 5)
    1. Reagan, Ronald—Language.   2. Reagan, Ronald—Rhetoric.
3. Rhetoric—Political aspects—United States—History—20th
century.   4. Communication in politics—United States—History—20th
century.   5. National characteristics, American—Political aspects—
History—20th century.   6. Optimism—Political aspects—United
States—History—20th century.   7. United States—Politics and
government—1981–1989.   I. Title.
    E877.2.G38 2013
    973.927092—dc23
    2012039929

ISBN13: 978-1-138-94300-1 (pbk)
ISBN13: 978-0-415-81848-3 (hbk)

Typeset in Sabon
by Apex CoVantage, LLC

To my wife, Laura

Contents

Permissions

Acknowledgments

I would like to thank Routledge and its staff for all their help during the editing, production, and publishing stages of this book. The independent reviews of the manuscript commissioned by the publisher were particularly valuable. I would also like to thank the academic journal *Humanitas* for granting me permission to reprint parts of my article "A Covenant with All Mankind: Ronald Reagan's Idyllic Vision of America in the World" and Palgrave Macmillan for granting me permission to reprint parts of my book chapter " 'The Land of Limitless Possibilities': Ronald Reagan, Progress, Technology, and the Modest Republic."

In conceptualizing, researching, and writing this book, I have drawn upon the wisdom of a number of people, including Michael P. Federici of Mercyhurst University, Phillip G. Henderson of the Catholic University of America, George W. Carey of Georgetown University, and David Richards. Michael Federici introduced me to political theory as an undergraduate. He made many astute observations on different chapters in this book and directed my attention to a number of ideas, texts, and thinkers relevant to explaining and analyzing Reagan's imagination. Phil Henderson's scholarship and advice gave me a better understanding of the American presidency, which, in turn, allowed me better to interpret Reagan. George Carey's scholarship has shaped to a great extent my understanding of American political thought and the American Framing. His comments on various parts of this book enabled me to explore more effectively the American historical resonances of Reagan's intuitive vision. David Richards gave me many keen insights into Reagan and his significance for understanding American culture. I am thankful for all of the assistance rendered by these colleagues and friends.

I owe a special debt of gratitude to Claes G. Ryn of the Catholic University of America. Claes Ryn introduced me to the writings and ideas of a number of important thinkers, including Irving Babbitt, Peter Viereck, and Benedetto Croce. His scholarship, on these thinkers as well as on constitutional democracy and on politics and the imagination, has had a profound impact on my understanding of political theory and on my analysis of Reagan's imagination. He made many perceptive comments on the conceptual and stylistic aspects of the manuscript, and all his efforts on these fronts are deeply appreciated. This book would not have been possible without his guidance and support.

My parents, Doug and Debra, provided me with a great deal of assistance and encouragement as I worked to complete my undergraduate and graduate degrees as well as this book. I am thankful for all their help, and I am proud to be their son.

Last, but certainly not least, I would like to thank my wife, Laura. I began working on this book shortly after we were married. She and I frequently discussed various aspects of the book. Laura read large portions of the manuscript, and she gave me a great deal of useful advice on how to make my writing as clear and concise as possible. She also suffered gracefully through the many frustrations and setbacks I experienced during the research and writing of the book. For her patience and encouragement, I will always be grateful.

Although I have taken many suggestions from a number of people as I have worked to complete this book, responsibility rests solely with me for any and all of its shortcomings.

There was a time when empires were defined by land mass, subjugated peoples, and military might. But the United States is unique, because we are an empire of ideals.

—Ronald Reagan

In the long run democracy will be judged, no less than other forms of government, by the quality of its leaders, a quality that will depend in turn on the quality of their vision. Where there is no vision, we are told, the people perish; but where there is sham vision, they perish even faster.

—Irving Babbitt

Introduction

The Enduring Appeal and Importance of Ronald Reagan's Imagination

> The greatness of Reagan was not that he was in America, but that America was inside of him.[1]
>
> —Lou Cannon

A solemn church bell rings out as rain gently falls upon the Washington National Cathedral. On the morning of June 11, 2004, many people, including members of the U.S. government, former American presidents, and foreign dignitaries, start taking their seats inside. A chamber orchestra begins to play a beautiful, mournful melody. Woodwinds fade away, and a lone tenor's voice fills the cathedral. He is singing *Ave Maria*. As the music continues, a hearse arrives outside bearing the body of an important man. With solemnity and grace, eight soldiers remove a coffin draped with the American flag. They begin to carry it up to the cathedral entrance followed by the family of the deceased. The procession stops in front of the Right Reverend John Bryson Chane, bishop of Washington and dean of the cathedral. He pauses for a moment, then says: "With faith in Jesus Christ, we receive the body of our brother Ronald for burial."[2] The national funeral for Ronald Wilson Reagan begins.

Former Canadian prime minister Brian Mulroney gives the second eulogy at the service. As do many people inside the walls of the great cathedral, Mulroney feels fortunate to have counted Reagan as a friend. Reagan's friends have much to say about him as a political leader and human being. Mulroney describes him as a man who inspired America and "transformed the world."[3] He praises Reagan for his determination to reinvigorate the West with a sense of mission and confidence in the midst of Soviet aggression, and he expresses appreciation for the former president's efforts to promote free trade between their two countries and within the Western hemisphere.

Former British prime minister Margaret Thatcher's declining health prevents her from giving her eulogy in person, but Reagan's express desire that she be at the funeral inclines her to provide prerecorded remarks that are played during the service. She too praises Reagan for standing firmly against the Soviet Union while leaving open genuine possibilities to discuss and make peace. She locates the source of his political success in his personal qualities including magnanimity, optimism, an unyielding belief in his core political ideals, and an unashamed love of country. She explains that these traits are evidence that Reagan embodied the American spirit. She says, "[He] carried the American people with him in his great endeavours because there was perfect sympathy between them. He and they loved America and what it stands for—freedom and opportunity for ordinary people."[4] She continues her remarks with one of the more memorable comments made about Reagan that day: "We here still move in twilight. But we have one beacon to guide us that Ronald Reagan never had. We have his example. Let us give thanks today for a life that achieved so much for all of God's children."[5]

A few minutes later, President George W. Bush makes his way to the lectern. Like Mulroney and Thatcher, he praises Reagan for his steadfast determination and patience during the close of the Cold War. He links Reagan's political success to Reagan's firm faith in a number of ideas. Bush states:

> Along the way, certain convictions were formed and fixed in the man. . . . He believed that people were basically good and had the right to be free. He believed that bigotry and prejudice were the worst things a person could be guilty of. He believed in the Golden Rule and in the power of prayer. He believed that America was not just a place in the world but the hope of the world.[6]

Bush reminds the mourners that Reagan came to the presidency in a time of national uncertainty and growing despair. Like many other people, Bush commends Reagan for imparting a genuine sense of hope in the midst of such anxieties. He pays tribute to Reagan for seeing a light in the darkness, for conveying his optimism to others, for working to free the American economy from excessive regulation, for cutting taxes for all Americans, and for reasserting American strength abroad. Bush expresses his hope that the separation between Reagan and all the people who love him is temporary. He says, "And we look to that fine day when we will see him again, all weariness gone, clear of mind, strong and sure and smiling again, and the sorrow of this parting gone forever."[7] Bush has delivered the last eulogy.

The service continues. Prayers of benediction are read over the coffin that holds the man many people at the funeral mourn and love. With the same majesty as before, the body is taken away from the cathedral. The choir sings "The Mansions of the Lord." He is once again placed into the hearse. Reagan is ready to make his last journey into the west.

No one should be surprised that Reagan's funeral is a well-orchestrated public event rich in imagery and symbolism. Throughout Reagan's presidency, his thoughts on government, public policy, and America and its people appealed not only to the reason of his audience but also to the imagination, to their *intuitive* sense of the truth of his vision. The funeral is no different. It is designed to appeal to the mind, but also to stir the imagination. Whatever else may be said about him as a man or president, the funeral service makes one thing very clear. The shadow of Ronald Reagan looms large over America. But what kind of shadow does he cast? What is the vision that he imparted? That is the question to be explored and answered throughout this work.

In each of the eulogies at the national funeral service, Ronald Reagan was celebrated not only for his policy achievements but also for his success in reorienting the way numerous people, especially Americans, understood themselves and the world around them. His eulogizers attributed his success in reinvigorating America and embuing its people with hope and confidence to his deep sense of optimism and his fervent beliefs in freedom, progress, democracy, and the goodness of America and its people. He shared these sentiments often with the American people, and they responded very favorably. Claro Merced of Orlando, Florida, standing along the funeral procession route, said, "We came to tell him goodbye. We recognize how big he was, how big the things he did were."[8] A teenage boy waiting in the U.S. Capitol building to view Reagan's casket remarked, "I wasn't alive when he was in office, but they call him the great communicator and I can see what they mean from his speeches on TV."[9] Donna Glassman, a mourner who paid her respects to Reagan in California, explained her feelings about the former president: "When I think of him, I think of America. . . . What's that saying—American like Mom and apple pie? He should be in that, too. Because he represented what this country is all about."[10]

The source of Reagan's enduring popularity in the United States transcends his concrete domestic and foreign policy achievements, as important as such accomplishments might be to understanding him. More than most American presidents, Reagan consciously appealed to the *imagination* of his listeners, speaking in pictures and images. His vision, his intuitive sense of the whole of reality and of America, proved both highly appealing and convincing to most Americans.

A preliminary encounter with Reagan's imagination can be had by examining briefly his First Inaugural Address. On a cold January morning in 1981, Ronald Reagan was sworn in as the fortieth president of the United States. His first inauguration, like his national funeral service over twenty years later, was rich in imagery and symbolism. It was the first to be held on the western front of the U.S. Capitol building—a fact of which he reminded his audience. This location has been used by every president since. The stage was decorated with banners and bunting of red, white, and blue, and it looked out upon the vast expanse of monuments and memorials that define the National Mall. Behind the stage on which he stood, Reagan was flanked by two gigantic and awe-inspiring American flags. On his left was an American flag with the original thirteen stars. On his right was the current flag with fifty stars. Together, these flags symbolized Reagan's sense of the continuity between the American past and present. They also signified his inclination to view the present through the lens of the past, as he understood it. With these powerful symbols at his sides, he began to speak to the American people.

Reagan immediately addressed the concern that was at the forefront of most American minds—the economy. Throughout the speech, he established a stark contrast between the good American people and their wayward government. On the economy, he indicated that the United States was experiencing a host of problems including high inflation, high taxes, high unemployment, and excessive government spending. He claimed that various bureaucrats and other elites were to blame for the crisis because they had accumulated vast amounts of power, centralized in the national government, thereby stifling America's economic potential. With a brevity and simplicity that made many of his speeches appealing and effective, Reagan summarized his view of the economic situation with the following statement: "In this present crisis, government is not the solution to our problem; government is the problem."[11] In his mind, the cause of America's economic problems was a government that had lost faith in its citizens and had betrayed the American people.

And yet the seriousness of this situation did not lead Reagan to despair. He stated, "We're not, as some would have us believe, doomed to an inevitable decline. I do not believe in a fate that will fall on us no matter what we do. I do believe in a fate that will fall on us if we do nothing."[12] Reagan had faith in the American people and their capacity to overcome these problems if given the opportunity. He told his audience that heroes were all around them, in American factories, on the farm, and at the lunch counter, the library, and the volunteer association. He knew they were simply waiting for the chance to be the good people they were destined to be. As far as domestic policy was concerned, Reagan understood the mission of his presidency as removing the various impediments to individual liberty and economic prosperity erected by previous administrations. In so doing, he would liberate Americans from the restraints of an omnipresent government. With this task accomplished, the United States would reclaim its position as "the exemplar of freedom and a beacon of hope for those who do not now have freedom."[13] Once the power and goodness of the American people was unleashed, America would again be a strong nation, faithful to its allies, feared by its adversaries.

In Reagan's vision, the United States was poised to fulfill its destiny and to resume its mission as a herald of freedom and democracy for the world. But what must Americans do to bring about this restoration? At the conclusion of this address, Reagan told the American people that the tasks before them required nothing more than "our best effort and our willingness to believe in ourselves and to believe in our capacity to perform great deeds, to believe that together with God's help we can and will resolve the problems which now confront us. And after all, why shouldn't we believe that? We are Americans."[14] Thoughts such as these about the United States, its people, its history, its present, its future, and its place in the world have contributed most to the widespread belief that Reagan personified the best of America and its people.

As president, Reagan was somewhat reluctant to embrace the label "Great Communicator." He felt it was often a backhanded compliment praising the style rather than the substance of his message. And yet Reagan understood the importance of his speeches to his political success and to his rapport with Americans. In his Farewell Address to the Nation, Reagan explained:

> And in all of that time I won a nickname, "The Great Communicator." But I never thought it was my style or the words I used that made a difference: it was the content. I wasn't a great communicator, but I communicated great things, and they didn't spring full bloom from my brow, they came from the heart of a great nation—from our experience, our wisdom, and our belief in the principles that have guided us for two centuries. They called it the Reagan revolution. Well, I'll accept that, but for me it always seemed more like the great rediscovery, a rediscovery of our values and our common sense.[15]

Reagan's belief in the existence of a special relationship between himself and the American people preceded his election to the presidency. During his 1980 presidential campaign, a reporter asked him what he thought was the source of his broad appeal to the American people. Reagan responded, "Would you laugh if I told you that I think, maybe, they see themselves, and that I'm one of them? I've never been able to detach myself or think that I, somehow, am apart from them."[16] Since the late 1940s, Reagan had crafted and perfected a way of seeing the world that he directed toward "the guy on the street," the average American. He believed, after all, that it was such people who elected him president.[17]

A comprehensive account of the motivations and origins of Reagan's imagination is beyond the scope of this study, but a few general remarks on the topic may be helpful. During Reagan's presidency, it was fashionable, particularly among his detractors, to suggest that Reagan had little personal connection to the imagery and ideas conveyed in his speeches. On this view, Reagan was an "amiable dunce" enjoying his latest acting role as president of the United States and the script with which it came. Scholarship over the last decade has refuted this claim. Whatever one may think about Reagan's vision, it was not manufactured out of whole cloth by clever speechwriters.

Others find Reagan's vision to be a genuine expression of his views, at least up to a point. Especially among his admirers, it is not uncommon to hear praise for some elements of Reagan's imagination, while other parts of his vision—especially its dreamy, or chimeric, aspects—are attributed to political necessity or convenience. Given the context of the Cold War and the conventions in American political rhetoric, some argue, Reagan might have felt compelled to use sentimental or utopian imagery in order to inspire the public and to be able to pursue foreign and domestic policy goals that were actually more realistic. He may not have cared much for this part of his own rhetoric, but rather thought that only this kind of imagery would really appeal to Americans.

Still others believe Reagan came to the relevant ideas rather early and on his own and that he genuinely and deeply believed in them. This explanation is the most plausible because it is so strongly supported by the existing scholarship and the evidence to be presented in this study. Reagan spent most of his adult life developing and refining the vision he shared with Americans in his numerous presidential speeches. During his presidency, it was when Reagan shared his very own outlook in his speeches that so many people felt as if he embodied the American spirit. This does not have to mean that each of his formulations perfectly expressed his innermost beliefs. Does any human being fully know his own mind? And who can fully articulate what he does believe? Nevertheless, a great deal can be learned about where Reagan really stood from the pervasive and salient themes and frequently repeated ideas and images in his spoken and written statements. Whatever its ultimate origins and motivations, his vision has an enduring appeal, and it urgently needs to be better understood. It is time to listen to Reagan's words with a more attentive and also more critical ear.

Scholars, politicians, and journalists have observed that Reagan was a highly imaginative president and that his vision was a fundamental source of his popularity and political success. A number of general books have been written about Reagan, his presidency, and his rhetoric.[18] Other works have focused on specific speeches, such as the one Reagan delivered to the British Parliament in 1982, or on specific parts of Reagan's prepresidential life, such as his tenure at General Electric, or on specific events during his presidency, such as his response to the air traffic controllers' strike in 1981.[19] A number of scholars have explored Reagan's foreign and domestic policy ambitions and achievements as well as some aspects of his vision within the broader historical and cultural contexts of the United States in the 1980s.[20]

Scholars and journalists have also examined parts of Reagan's imagination to determine his status as a conservative. Some have argued that Reagan is an exemplary conservative. To support this claim, such writers typically draw attention to Reagan's anticommunism, claiming in a number of cases that he won the Cold War or at least contributed mightily to the downfall of the Soviet Union. They also cite as evidence of Reagan's conservatism his love of and advocacy for liberty, free markets, and democracy around the world; his abhorrence of big government and bureaucracies; and his admiration for the Declaration of Independence, the Constitution, Thomas Jefferson, and other documents and figures commonly associated with the American Founding. Other writers have examined Reagan's understanding of liberty, democracy, human nature, limited government, and the American Founding and concluded that Reagan is actually much more of a progressive—expressing ideas similar to those of Thomas Paine, Ralph Waldo Emerson, and Woodrow Wilson—than a conservative committed to the ideas of George Washington, John Adams, Edmund Burke, and *The Federalist*. Parts of Reagan's vision have also been investigated to discover the influence of religion and religious ideas upon his general worldview and his presidency. Some argue that Reagan was a deeply pious man whose religious beliefs had a positive influence on his broader vision of politics and his policy goals. Others claim that his religious ideas contributed to a rather problematic understanding of politics in the United States.[21] The meaning and legacy of Reagan and his vision is a topic of growing interest. Although writers from the political left and right disagree about the nature and accuracy of Reagan's legacy, many of them agree that Reagan has shaped American political thinking and practice to such an extent that he and his legacy must be acknowledged and taken very seriously.[22]

With varying degrees of success, many studies have helped call attention to the primacy of imagination in Reagan's presidential speeches and to the importance of the intuition in shaping and motivating his political thought and action. A number of works have also suggested that profound paradoxes and peculiarities exist within Reagan's vision of reality and America. Such studies have nevertheless neglected a number of important questions or answered them only in a tentative manner. Despite their popularity, many of the journalistic works on Reagan are driven primarily by narrow ideological concerns. Such works are more interested in effusively celebrating or demonizing Reagan than in providing rigorous and impartial scholarly analysis. The author is fully aware of the serious limitations of such texts, and this study draws upon them only insofar as they illustrate prominent views of Reagan and his vision. The essays and books written by scholars are sometimes of a higher quality than their journalistic counterparts, but even these works tend only to skim the surface of a topic that is widely recognized as important. Existing studies do not provide a systematic examination of Reagan's vision and its major components. A number of works make connections between Reagan and various figures from the American and Western past, but this is usually done in passing or without careful development of and reflection upon how such relationships shed light on the former president's imagination. No existing studies offer a definition of the imagination, nor do they indicate just how the imagination shapes political thought and action. In general, the scholarship on Reagan's vision is incomplete. At times, it even lacks intellectual seriousness. A study of Reagan's imagination is needed that defines imagination or intuition—terms here used synonymously—more carefully and rigorously and explains its role in politics more fully.

It is clear that there is a pressing need to examine and assess the fundamental quality and significance of Reagan's imagination, including its historical resonance in American and Western political thought. This work meets this need by studying Reagan's imagination as it was expressed chiefly in his presidential speeches. Though these are important elements to understanding Reagan and his presidency, this study will not attempt an exhaustive account of his life, public persona, policies, political ideas, or even a comprehensive inventory of every dimension of his imagination. It is understood, and will be explicitly recognized, that his imagination contains more than one strain. This study will concentrate on the general character and components of what is the strongest, most pervasive constituent of his imagination: what will be called its "chimeric" dimension. The meaning of the word "chimeric" will be more fully explained in this chapter and throughout this work. Drawing out Reagan's chimeric imagination will require a systematic presentation and analysis of its most important symbols. In his presidential speeches, Reagan spoke often about religion, democracy, freedom, technology, conservatism, progress, the American people, the American Founding, and peace. These are the fundamental ideas and images that together express his vision of the whole of reality and of America's place in it.

This work draws upon a number of primary and secondary sources. The primary source material is Reagan's presidential speeches as supplemented by his published presidential papers, personal correspondence, prepresidential speeches, diary entries, and autobiographical writings. The secondary source material includes works on Reagan's life, presidency, ideas, and imagination as well as relevant works of American and Western political and religious thought. For reasons that will become clear later, particular attention is paid to the political writings of Thomas Jefferson, Thomas Paine, John Adams, John Locke, Jean-Jacques Rousseau, and Edmund Burke. Attention is also paid to documents and texts such as the Declaration of Independence, the U.S. Constitution, and *The Federalist*.

In chapter one, a biographical sketch of Reagan is provided, paying particular attention to events important for the formation of his imagination up until the mid-1960s when "The Speech" for which he became famous took final shape. Chapter two offers a philosophical discussion of the concept of imagination and how intuition contributes to the formation of knowledge about reality and politics. It is expected that the preceding survey of Reagan's way of imagining the world will assist this elucidation by offering concrete illustrations of what is philosophically defined and clarified in the chapter. Chapters three through ten address and analyze Reagan's optimism and his visions of the American people, the American Founding, contemporary American government, America's role in the world, peace among nations, technology and progress, and Christianity and religion. The conclusion to the study offers a final assessment of the chimeric strain of Reagan's vision. By defining the latter, identifying and analyzing its important symbols, and locating its resonance with the American past and contemporary politics, this work provides a key to understanding the fortieth president and the implications of his kind of imagination for how political problems in America and the world are approached.

A work such as this presents a number of difficulties and challenges for both author and reader. One such difficulty is structural. Insofar as this study is a systematic account of Reagan's imagination, there is a sense in which all the chapters presuppose all the others. Approaching the subject as if it were comprised of so many discrete blocks of thought to be addressed once and then filed away would be counterproductive. This work can be seen rather as exploring and analyzing the distinct but tightly woven threads of the tapestry that is Reagan's imagination. Thus, although each chapter deals with a specific dimension of Reagan's vision, it should be kept in mind that Reagan's understanding of various important ideas and images will come into clearer view as the study progresses.

Another structural challenge is related to the nature of Reagan's speeches. About his approach to public speaking, Reagan writes:

> In fact, that's one of my theories about political speechmaking. You have to keep pounding away with your message, year after year, because that's the only way it will sink into the collective consciousness. I'm a big believer in stump speeches—speeches you can give over and over again with slight variations. Because if you have something you believe in deeply, it's worth repeating time and again until you achieve it.[23]

For this reason, this study will not be able to avoid repetition. In order to elucidate both the general shape and the nuances of Reagan's vision, it will be necessary to refer on more than one occasion to particular aspects of important speeches and to look at them in different contexts.

Other challenges facing this work are methodological. Simply stated, a study similar to *"An Empire of Ideals"* has not previously been done. It is truly an original work of scholarship and thus might be misunderstood on a few fronts. The following comments are offered at the outset to eliminate as much potential confusion as possible. First, although this work addresses the imagination of an American president, it should not be interpreted as belonging to the specialized subfield of American presidential studies as currently conceived. While this study may breathe new life into treatments of American presidents, its methodology is at home in the humanities tradition and draws upon aesthetic and philosophical concepts as well as historical comparisons to conduct its analysis. Second, the need to delve deeply into the American and Western past may raise questions about the discussion of certain political, philosophical, and religious thinkers and texts. The invocation of certain political theorists or American political figures, including those mentioned in this introduction, is not an attempt to praise or condemn Reagan by association. Neither is it intended to suggest that Reagan was deeply familiar with each theorist's or political figure's ideas. Indeed, some of these figures may have been only vaguely familiar to him. This study is not suggesting that Reagan was a political theorist, that he should be treated as a political theorist, or that his ideas are problematic simply because he did not express them with theoretical sophistication. In some instances, reference to thinkers with whom Reagan was not familiar will provide greater clarity about his vision by increasing the awareness of what it is and what it is not. Political theorists and texts from the Western and American traditions will be considered insofar as they can help shed light upon the quality of Reagan's imagination. Some of them will be used to determine the meaning(s) of the word "conservative" and the extent to which this word accurately describes Reagan and his vision.

The greatest challenge is philosophical. The study characterizes Reagan's imagination as predominantly "chimeric"—that is, as having prominent elements of optimism, naiveté, and, some would say, illusion. Too often, the word "imagination" has been used casually in scholarly writing about Reagan or other topics in political theory. Even scholars with a special interest in the imagination and with substantive intellectual reputations have not gone very far explaining just what they mean by this word. Russell Kirk, a prominent twentieth-century conservative intellectual, greatly admired both Burke and Reagan. He celebrated the powerful imaginations of these statesmen. In various works, Kirk stressed the importance of the imagination and its role in constituting ordered politics, but he never gave a precise, in-depth definition of imagination and its relationship to politics. Still, Kirk went further in this regard than those who have written extensively on Reagan. This study tries to remedy this problem. At this time, only a few comments about the imagination and its relationship to politics are necessary to provide the reader with a preliminary understanding of this difficult philosophical concept and this relationship and of how they will be viewed throughout this study.

For centuries the imagination was thought of in the Western world as a passive mental faculty absorbing and rearranging external wholes and images received through the senses. From the romantic period to the present, however, its role has been reconsidered. Aestheticians and poets, in particular, have accentuated the creative role of the imagination. In many articles and books, Claes G. Ryn has stressed this revised conception of the power of intuition and its importance for understanding politics, while denying any necessary connection between it and romantic emotionalism and dreaming. The imagination constitutes preintellectual, purely intuitive wholes, Ryn argues. Most basically it gives us a general but concrete sense of the nature of existence. Intellectual reflection on reality is oriented by that intuition. Ryn writes, the imagination "is an active, visionary power, giving a fundamental, if non-ideational, coherence to life. Most generally, the imagination constitutes an overall sense, concrete and experiential, of what life is like. Such intuition precedes thought in the sense of systematic reflection, ideas and definitions."[24] People of strong, captivating imagination in the arts and elsewhere pull many others into their view of existence, but their vision can be illusory, even fly in the face of everything hitherto known about human nature, Ryn contends. Whether there is a strong bond between a person's intuition of life and the "real world" depends on the type of imagination.[25] Often, highly appealing imagination flagrantly distorts the terms of actual human existence and can have disastrous consequences. This preliminary definition of the imagination will be expanded later.

Whether Reagan's imagination was adequately grounded in reality, or contained an appealing but ultimately dangerous conceit, remains to be seen. Whatever the case, it is clear that his vision has left an enduring mark on American politics. It has been described as providing the ideological foundation of the Republican Party's Contract with America in 1994, the year in which they became the majority party in the House for the first time in a generation. Comparisons between Reagan and George W. Bush began during the 2000 presidential campaign and were made repeatedly during the latter's presidency. Countless Republicans have run for political office claiming to be Reagan Republicans or even to *be* the next Ronald Reagan. Many of the 2008 and 2012 Republican presidential candidates praised Reagan for his optimism and his commitments to strong national defense, to an assertive foreign policy, and to lower taxes and lower spending. They praised him for what they saw as his conservatism.

Reagan's vision certainly has been a source of inspiration and unity among ostensible conservatives in American politics, but it would be a mistake to think that the influence and appeal of Reagan's formidable imaginative legacy are confined to a particular political movement or moment in time. President Barack Obama, a Democrat, certainly has some political ideas very different from those of Reagan, but he has expressed a view of America that appears surprisingly similar to Reagan's in its underlying imaginative quality. Furthermore, like Reagan, Obama has referred to the United States as a "shining beacon on a hill" and as "the last, best hope of Earth."[26] In the 2008 presidential campaign, then candidate Obama earned the scorn of some Democrats when he appeared to compliment Reagan during an interview. Obama said, "I think Ronald Reagan changed the trajectory of America in a way that Richard Nixon did not and in a way that Bill Clinton did not. . . . I think people, he just tapped into what people were already feeling, which was we want clarity we want optimism, we want a return to that sense of dynamism and entrepreneurship that had been missing."[27] Comparisons between Obama and Reagan, on both the political right and left, continue to be made. As president, Obama himself seems to have taken a deeper interest in understanding Reagan and his presidency.

Whether Reagan's vision of and for America is embraced or ridiculed by politicians, journalists, and scholars, it is clear that his particular imagination, which celebrates freedom, democracy, individualism, average Americans, natural human goodness, and unlimited material progress, still resonates with many Americans, political figures, and intellectual activists of seemingly different ideological backgrounds. His vision continues to influence the making of American domestic and foreign policy. Deepening and sharpening the awareness of the nature of Reagan's imagination will help explain how millions of Americans envision the possibilities of politics, not merely clarify who Reagan was. The first step in moving toward a better understanding of Reagan's vision and what it says about America will be to explore important moments in Reagan's life that contributed to the development of his imagination.

1 Ronald Reagan
A Biographical Sketch

Ronald Reagan recognized reality not as a thing to bow to but a thing that could be changed and shaped. . . . He thought he could change reality in part because he had imagination—a rather robust imagination.[1]

—Peggy Noonan

"DUTCH" REAGAN IN THE MIDWEST

Ronald Wilson Reagan was born in Tampico, Illinois, on February 6, 1911. As a child, Reagan did the same things as most other children his age. He fished, hunted, explored the woods, and got into his share of trouble. On one occasion, he and a friend blew a hole through the ceiling after pulling the trigger of what they thought was an unloaded shotgun. When his and his friend's parents ran into the room, the two boys were found sitting upon a couch reading a magazine as if nothing had happened.[2] Reagan also played sports, his favorite of which was football, and as a teenager he became a renowned lifeguard on the Rock River in Dixon, Illinois. Overall, he described his childhood as "one of those rare Huck Finn-Tom Sawyer idylls."[3] Though his family moved frequently within its borders, Reagan lived in Illinois until after graduating college, when he became a radio announcer in Iowa.

The personalities of Reagan's father and mother could not have been more different. Yet Reagan's character, ideas, and imagination were shaped by the best qualities in both of them. The ways in which each parent influenced him were observable throughout Reagan's entire life. John Edward "Jack" Reagan was a shoe salesman, a nominal Roman Catholic, and an alcoholic. In *Governor Reagan: His Rise to Power*, Lou Cannon describes Jack Reagan as "at once a drinker and a dreamer who, much like Willy Loman in *Death of a Salesman*, pursued the big sale or the unlikely deal with a shoeshine and a smile."[4] Reagan attributed his storytelling talents and sense of humor to having observed his father's ability to win over crowds of friends with these skills. Beyond acquiring his father's ability to tell amusing anecdotes, Reagan credited Jack for instilling in him beliefs in the natural equality of all human beings and in the evils of racism and other forms of bigotry. In his first autobiography, *Where's the Rest of Me?*, Reagan proudly recalls how his father forbade the family from seeing D. W. Griffith's *The Birth of a Nation* because it portrayed the Ku Klux Klan in an admirable light.[5] In his second autobiography, *An American Life*, Reagan describes an incident that happened on one of his father's business trips. While making arrangements for a hotel room, the clerk bragged to Jack that the hotel was a fine establishment because it did not rent out rooms to Jews. Jack, disgusted by this open display of anti-Semitism, and conscious of the discrimination he might encounter as a Roman Catholic, refused to take a room at the hotel.[6] From his father, Reagan also claims to have inherited an allegiance to the Democratic Party, a belief in individual liberty, a desire to defend the rights of workers, and a belief that talent and a willingness to work hard are the only limits to what an individual can accomplish.[7]

Jack Reagan also gave his son a valuable lesson in taking care of other people, though not in the way one might think. Jack's alcoholism was of a peculiar variety. He did not drink alcohol constantly, nor did he drink when situations with family or work were stressful. On the contrary, his alcohol binges were often prompted by good news. In other words, Jack got drunk when he was winning. His drunkenness contributed to the family's need to move frequently from one home to another during Reagan's childhood. One winter evening, young Reagan was making his way to what he thought would be an empty house. As he approached the back porch, he saw his father passed out in the snow. In his own accounts of the event, Reagan admits that even though he was only eleven years old, he knew why his father lay motionless on the ground. A part of Reagan simply wanted to go into the house and ignore what he had seen. But he did not abandon his father. About the incident Reagan writes, "I felt myself fill with grief for my father at the same time I was feeling sorry for myself. Seeing his arms spread out as if he were crucified—as indeed he was—his hair soaked with melting snow, snoring as he breathed, I could feel no resentment against him."[8] Reagan bent down, grabbed Jack's coat, dragged him into the house, and put his father to bed. In meeting his father's alcoholism with patience and love as opposed to anger or avoidance, Reagan was also showing one of the many ways in which his mother helped shape his character and imagination.

Nelle Reagan wore many hats in her life. She was a mother, a wife, and a Christian. Although she and Jack were married in the Roman Catholic Church, Nelle joined the Disciples of Christ, or Christian Church, shortly before Ronald was born. Her conversion filled her with an unfailing religious zeal. She bore the trials of marriage to an alcoholic with patience and grace, and she refused to pass judgment upon Jack's character. Nelle took seriously the Christian commandment to love one's neighbor as one's self. She delivered food to the hungry, visited prisoners, and offered prayer and spiritual comfort to people in need.[9] When Reagan was a young boy, a flu epidemic erupted in the Midwest that almost claimed his mother's life. This close encounter with death never led Nelle to despair or to question God. She believed that everything in a person's life happens for a reason and that all events are part of God's plan for each individual. In her mind, even the most difficult trials and tragedies that befell human beings ultimately worked toward a happy result. In *An American Life*, Reagan acknowledges how strongly these views shaped his own understanding of the world. The optimism and religious faith that were so important to Reagan and the vision he communicated in his presidential speeches were some of the many gifts he received from his mother.[10]

Nelle was also a poet and an actress, and her public recitations were well received in the region.[11] Reagan's first experiences with public speaking and acting occurred during performances arranged by his mother. At the age of nine, he recited "About Mother." A month later he recited "The Sad Dollar and the Glad Dollar."[12] Nelle's recitations were often devoted to spiritual topics, but she did not avoid offering her thoughts on politics to the public. In *God and Ronald Reagan*, Paul Kengor provides an excellent description of Nelle's formative influence upon young Reagan. In explaining the breadth of her religious and political interests during the 1920s, Kengor cites a poem she published eight years after the end of World War I. In "Armistice Day Poem," Nelle lauded the American soldiers who "have won for the world democracy, and doomed forever and always the cruel autocracy."[13] She was not alone in her views of the broader significance of World War I.

A few years after publishing "Armistice Day Poem," Nelle hosted a local meeting of the Woman's Missionary Society. As Kengor explains, the topic of the meeting was "The Large World—My Neighborhood." The discussion expressed a concern held by many Americans, especially progressive Christians, that the rest of the world was too slow in applying the commandments of Christ to international relations. At the meeting, many of the women agreed that each nation was capable of undertaking this task and that the successful global adoption of applied Christianity would provide a "cure for war, crime, and sin of every kind."[14] The proposed remedy for seemingly permanent social and political problems was a synthesis of religion and politics. Christianity and democracy, working together, were perceived as the keys to raising the moral standards of nations and changing the world for the better. Reagan's understandings of both Christianity and democracy owe much to the influence of his mother.[15]

REAGAN AND DICK FAULKNER

A little-known, or perhaps deliberately ignored, fact about Reagan is that he liked to read. Though he never read deeply in philosophy or literature, he read widely in newspapers, political magazines, American history, and light fiction. In his autobiographies, he indicates that as a child he frequently checked out books from the Dixon public library. He enjoyed reading *Tarzan, Frank Merriwell at Yale*, and Mark Twain's *The Adventures of Tom Sawyer*.[16] As a young boy, he also read a novel that can be said, without hyperbole, to have changed his life. *That Printer of Udell's*, written in 1903 by former Christian preacher Harold Bell Wright, is a work of progressive Christian fiction. It devotes a great deal of attention to the ways in which "applied Christianity" could improve the morals and prosperity of society. A brief summary of the novel's main plot and characters will help explain some of the ways in which it made a substantial contribution to the development of Reagan's imagination.

"O God, take ker o' Dick!"[17] As Dick Faulkner's mother is dying, she prays for God's forgiveness and asks him not to punish her son for his parents' transgressions. Shortly after she dies, Dick leaves the dirty one-room cabin in which he grew up. There is nothing left for him there—except his abusive alcoholic father—and he becomes a tramp traveling from town to town by rail and on foot.

Sixteen years later, Dick arrives in Boyd City. He previously received training as a printer in Kansas City but was fired as the result of a strike. He makes his way around town looking for decent work, but he finds no one in Boyd City is willing to employ him. Starving, with no job prospects, Dick happens upon a church where a service is about to start. He feels his worries melt away and says, " 'Christians won't let me starve—they'll help me earn something to eat. I'm not a beggar—not me' . . . 'All I want is a chance.' "[18] But Dick's deliverance does not come. At the end of the service, he asks various parishioners for help, but many of them ignore him. Even the clergy are uncomfortable with his beggarly presence. They are unsympathetic to his plight. If Dick is going to find a way to survive, it is clear that these Christians will not be the ones to help him.

However, all hope is not lost. Overwhelmed at his printing shop, George Udell, a decent man, though not a member of a Christian church, desperately needs an additional employee to get all his orders ready for the morning. Into his store walks Dick. Initially suspicious of the tramp, Udell quickly learns that Dick is a hard-working, talented, efficient printer who simply needs a chance to get himself out of poverty. Through his work at Udell's, Dick is able to make money, to sleep at night in a safe and warm place, and, most important, to earn the dignity that has been denied him so long by indifferent and hypocritical individuals.

At this point in the novel, another important character, the Reverend James Cameron, is introduced. Reverend Cameron is working on a sermon that will be delivered at the Sunday service of the same church that refused to help Dick. In "The Church of the Future," Cameron argues that the church has become Christian in name only and is more concerned with form and ceremony than with applying the teachings of Christ to problems such as poverty, immorality, and the suffering of mankind. The narrator explains that Cameron was prompted to write the sermon because he "simply desired to see a more practical working of Christianity. In other words, he wished to see Christians doing the things that Christ did, and using in matters of the church, the same business sense which they brought to bear upon their own affairs."[19] It is not surprising that the sermon, with its bold vision of business Christianity and its call to social service, falls flat with the same audience that refused to help Dick. Cameron's sermon is nothing short of a scandal in Boyd City.

The older members of the church are completely uninterested in, and often actively opposed to, any organized efforts to alleviate the suffering of Boyd City's poor. Many of the older members of the clergy prefer to engage in unending and superfluous doctrinal disputes rather than help those in need; the older laity tends to view the church as a social club rather than an institution of service and salvation. The older generation consists mainly of counterfeit Christians. Cameron's message did find strong support among many of the younger members of the parish and even among some of Boyd City's non-Christians such as Dick and George. The younger generation embraces Cameron's view of Christianity with its emphasis on social justice and practical action rather than dogmatic purity. This dichotomy between the older and younger members of the church and citizens of Boyd City runs throughout the novel.

For the youth of Boyd City, a belief in a difference between Christianity, which is good, and the church, which, while not evil, tends to corrupt and desensitize its members to the real message of Christ, begins to emerge. Energy and enthusiasm for real Christianity grows in their hearts, but they have no clear plan to realize the world Reverend Cameron held before them in his sermon. They need a leader to capture their imaginations and show them the way to translate into action their desires to improve society with business-like, practical Christianity. Boyd City needs Dick Faulkner.

Dick's stature in the community has grown since his arrival, and his plain-spoken, commonsense approach to reforming Boyd City further raises his standing. He comes up with a plan that will provide the truly deserving poor—i.e., people who through no fault of their own have fallen on hard times—with the opportunity to work for food and lodging while excluding idlers seeking merely to abuse the charity of others. Though he does not belong to any church, Dick is doing what he believes a real Christian ought to do. Both he and his plan encounter a number of challenges, but he is eventually victorious. The city's various criminals find respectable jobs, bars are replaced by wholesome businesses, and churches and schools grow in their memberships. Boyd City becomes a symbol of everything that is possible when applied Christianity is given a chance to change society.[20]

After this success, Dick becomes a member of the church that turned away from him at the beginning, but he retains his practical Christianity. At the end of the novel, the citizens of Boyd City send Dick to work in "a field of wider usefulness" as an elected member of the United States Congress. With his new wife at his side, Dick returns to the cabin of his youth, bows his head in prayer before the graves of his parents, and then embarks upon his journey to Washington. He is ready to change the nation, just as he did Boyd City, with the power of practical Christianity.[21]

High art *That Printer of Udell's* is not. In it, one-dimensional characters populate a disjointed plot replete with unbelievable coincidences. Wright's narrative voice is highly didactic and distracting—especially when expounding his views on religion and society. Reagan overlooked the novel's numerous artistic failings, and he was candid about the impression it made upon him. As president, he wrote a letter to Harold Bell Wright's daughter in which he claimed, "That book—*That Printer of Udell's*—had an impact I shall always remember. After reading it and thinking about it for a few days I went to my mother and told her I wanted to declare my faith and be baptized. We attended the Christian Church in Dixon and I was baptized several days after finishing the book."[22] When looking at the essential message of Wright's novel, one can see how it could unify into a more complete and captivating whole many of the ideas about life with which the young Reagan was already comfortable. One can also see a number of ideas and images similar to those that were later expressed in his presidential vision.

Essentially, *Udell's* is a story about a man who raises himself out of poverty and hardship to become a respected citizen, a leader of a town, and perhaps, one day, a nation. It celebrates hard work, individualism, the cause of social reform, and Christianity. It sees the present as mostly decadent, and it looks to a future in which both church and society are redeemed by practical Christianity. Boyd City is a place where poverty, immorality, and other social ills are eliminated as soon as its citizens gather their courage, use their common sense, and adopt Dick Faulkner's plan to create what can be called a merit-based welfare system. Wright suggests that resolving the various problems with which real towns and nations are confronted is as simple as finding the right plan and a man of action capable of implementing it. At the end of the novel, Wright tells the reader that his story's conclusion is believable because "God has but one law for the corporation and the individual, and the teaching that will transform the life of a citizen will change the life of a city if only it be applied."[23] With the right plan and a humble, charismatic leader, average citizens can be relied upon to take up the cause of reform and to redeem the local community, the nation, and perhaps the world.

In the novel, the citizens of Boyd City praised Dick for his common sense, humility, leadership, and ability to attract others to his bold and noble vision. The American people paid many such compliments to Reagan. Many ideas and images in *Udell's* are similar to those expressed in Reagan's vision. His presidential speeches are filled with stories about individuals and communities just like Dick Faulkner and Boyd City. Like Dick, Reagan celebrates individualism, hard work, entrepreneurialism, a practical approach to religion, and the human capacity for unlimited accomplishment. They both believe that human beings are mostly good creatures and that people are simply waiting for the right person, with the right ideas—one who will believe in their goodness, trust in their virtue, and lead them to a new era of peace and prosperity. Dick Faulkner and Ronald Reagan were two such leaders. Both men look back to a golden past and find the present fraught with perils as well as opportunities for systematic reform. Blame for existing disorder rests not with any particular individual but with abstractions called "government" or "society." More than the past or the present, these men think about progress and the future. They dream of a time in which great plans for reform promoted by even greater leaders will defeat the dangers of the day.

These comments are not intended to suggest that all of Reagan's political thinking was consciously or unconsciously appropriated from this novel. These remarks should not be taken to imply that *That Printer of Udell's* is a talisman for understanding Reagan's imagination. Nevertheless, a number of beliefs to which Reagan had grown somewhat accustomed as a child were intensified by the novel's concrete imagery and unified vision of what life is and can be. Wright's novel held an imaginary world before the young Reagan and asked him to claim it for himself. He did. But the growth and development of Reagan's sense of the world did not stop when he was a child.

REAGAN AND EUREKA COLLEGE

In 1932, Reagan graduated from a small school in Illinois named Eureka College. Fifty years later, he gave the commencement address at his alma mater. He explained, "Yes, this place is deep in my heart. Everything that has been good in my life began here."[24] In 1850, the Disciples of Christ established Eureka as a place of higher education with a foundation in Christian values. Reagan's childhood church regularly raised money for Eureka's endowment. Many members of the Dixon church had connections to the school.[25] Getting into college, and then staying there, was a great financial struggle for Reagan. He obtained a partial scholarship from the college, but he had to cover the remainder of his expenses by washing dishes at campus dining facilities. The financial situation at the school was no better. Tuition and donations from churches did not cover expenses. Faculty went without full pay, sometimes without any pay, for long periods of time.[26] Things became worse during the early stages of the Great Depression. In order to keep the school open, the administration sought to reduce costs. In *Governor Reagan*, Lou Cannon writes, "Eureka's financial instability plunged Reagan into the first political activity of his life."[27] As a freshman, Reagan participated in his first strike.

The details of the strike have been covered well by other scholars, especially Garry Wills, and here require only a summary.[28] During Reagan's freshman year, Eureka College president Bert Wilson proposed to restore the school's financial stability by consolidating various departments and eliminating courses and faculty on the periphery of its traditional curriculum.

Reagan claims that Wilson persuaded the board of trustees to accept his restructuring plan without having first consulted with either the faculty or students. The students were concerned that some of them would be unable to finish their degrees as a result of the cutbacks, and they decided to offer the board their own proposal for saving Eureka.[29] When that was rejected, the students called for Wilson's resignation. The board refused to meet this demand as well.

The students had contemplated a strike for some time, but they were waiting for the trustees' final decision on Wilson's plan before deciding to act. At midnight on the night in which the board officially accepted Wilson's plan, the students met in the campus chapel to discuss and pass a strike motion. Reagan claims that he was chosen to present the actual motion to strike because, as a freshman, he had an appearance of disinterestedness unavailable to the upperclassmen affected directly by the consolidation plan. He gave a speech describing the students' grievances and the justice of their cause. Reagan writes, "When I came to actually presenting the motion there was no need for parliamentary procedure: they came to their feet with a roar. . . . It was heady wine. Hell, with two more lines, I could have had them 'riding through every Middlesex village and farm'—without horses yet."[30]

The strike was of short duration. Wilson eventually resigned in order to disassociate his personal unpopularity from the reforms. After his resignation, the board of trustees enacted an even more drastic reorganization of the college's departments, courses, and faculty than the one proposed by Wilson. Reagan's remaining time at Eureka was much more tranquil. In his recollection of the strike decades later, Reagan played a crucial role in the student resistance and eventually won the day. In *Reagan's America*, Garry Wills has argued that the actual sequence of events during the strike, and Reagan's importance in them, tells a different story than the one remembered by Reagan. For the purposes of understanding Reagan's *imagination*, the factual accuracy of his recollections is of secondary importance.

The imagination constructs and continually refines a person's preconceptual awareness of reality by interpreting life experiences through the institution of likenesses and analogies. In *Where's the Rest of Me?* Reagan compares the actions he and other students took during the strike to those of the American colonists and Paul Revere. He even quotes a line from Henry Wadsworth Longfellow's poem "Paul Revere's Ride." In the poem, Revere kept a lonely watch, waiting for a signal as to whether or not the British would invade. If the signal appeared, then his task was to raise the alarm and rouse the colonists to resist. Revere succeeded, and the Americans were eventually victorious in their rebellion. The stakes of the student strike were obviously much lower than those of the American Revolution. Yet it is not difficult to see how Reagan could compare these two situations. The students at Eureka were waiting for a signal—in their case, a church bell tolling, which would tell them to convene at the chapel to discuss a strike. Though Reagan was certainly not alone in the strike, he remembered his role in it as trying to inspire his peers to resist what he perceived as the improper use of power by an external authority.

That Reagan could construct such an elaborate and enthralling image that, nevertheless, bore a tenuous connection to the actual events also points to an important truth about the imagination and its activity. Intuition gives unity, but it does not always give reality. Wills suggests that Reagan's memory of the strike also reveals something not often mentioned when describing his character. Wills shows that while years later Reagan was willing to admit that Wilson was sincere if still inept in his desire to help Eureka, he was much less kind in his characterizations of the former college president during the actual events. Wills writes, "The unattractive side to rectitude, so rarely shown by [Reagan's] mother, or by Reagan himself, is the presumption of vice in those disagreeing with one's consciously righteous position."[31]

Less than a year after graduating college, Reagan moved to Iowa to take a job as a radio announcer. His radio career was a success. His primary responsibility was broadcasting various regional sports events, including college football and Chicago Cubs and Chicago White Sox baseball. While he was able to travel to regional college football games, Reagan's radio station did not send reporters and broadcasters to cover the Cubs or White Sox live. He relied on real-time game information via telegraph in order to *recreate* the experience of hearing the live broadcast for the local audience. During one of his baseball broadcasts, the telegraph was broken for several minutes. Rather than admit this to his listeners and risk losing his audience, Reagan decided to fabricate the game's events until the line was repaired. To those listening at home, it appeared as if nothing unusual had happened.[32] Reagan's work in radio made him a celebrity in the Midwest. His success was such that in the late 1930s he was sent to Catalina Island, California, to cover the Cubs at spring training. This trip afforded Reagan an opportunity for which he had been waiting a long time. Through some of his Midwestern connections, Reagan secured a screen test with Warner Bros. movie studio. Reagan wanted to see if he could break into the movies.

REAGAN IN HOLLYWOOD

Reagan's professional film and television career spanned three decades from the late 1930s to the early 1960s. Most of his film work was confined to the second tier, or B-list, but he was hovering around the rank of A-list movie star shortly before the United States entered World War II. Although Reagan starred in many movies, he viewed *Knute Rockne—All American* (1940) and *Kings Row* (1942) as his greatest films. In *Knute Rockne*, Reagan played the role of George Gipp. Gipp is one of the most famous and most heavily romanticized football players ever to come out of the University of Notre Dame. Reagan *loved* this role. For the rest of his life, he referred to himself as "The Gipper." Countless admirers called him by this name as well. A number of scholars have drawn attention to "The Gipper" symbol as an important part of Reagan's mind. It is part of his presidential character. On occasion, it even emerges in his presidential speeches.

That the nickname "The Gipper" was applied to Ronald Reagan is a strange fact. When looking at each man's character, it is difficult to find two people more different than Reagan and Gipp. In real life, as opposed to Rockne's descriptions, Gipp was a lazy individual who came to football practice infrequently, skipped class regularly, and even disappeared for days at a time from the university. He liked to gamble, drink, smoke, and play pool, and, as a result of his carousing, he contracted viral pneumonia and died at the age of twenty-five. At one point, Gipp was expelled from Notre Dame due to his poor attendance and academic performance. Later, he was readmitted because the university football team and its supporters valued his services more than they disliked his profligacy.[33] No one familiar with Reagan's life could describe him in similar terms. In reality, Reagan bore a much closer resemblance to Rockne than Gipp.

Knute Rockne, the son of Norwegian immigrants, moved to Chicago as a young child. He earned a college degree from Notre Dame and later became one of its fabled football coaches. His success as a coach is extraordinary, and his reputation for using any means to motivate his team to victory is legend. On one occasion, he told his team that he had just received a telegram informing him that his son was critically ill and in the hospital. In the note, young Billy Rockne indicated that he would feel much better if his father's team won the game. The players were motivated to win for their coach's sick son, and they did. After the game, they came home to find none other than Billy Rockne among the crowd waiting to congratulate Notre Dame. He had apparently recovered his full health. Garry Wills writes, "When caught in his tricks, Rockne just admitted them, certain that they were justified if they worked for the team."[34] The most famous of Rockne's pep talks was the one he gave about George Gipp during the 1928 Army versus Notre Dame game. Here, too, Rockne employed mendacity in the service of victory.

Though Rockne was generally a successful football coach, there was one season in which he lost four games. This totaled one-third of his career losses over more than a dozen seasons. Worse than this, the players had little respect for one another and failed to achieve that level of unity necessary to win in sports. The first half of the Army versus Notre Dame game ended in a 0–0 tie. At halftime, Rockne, seeking to motivate his team, told his players the dying words Gipp had spoken to him over eight years earlier. Gipp allegedly said the following: "Some time, Rock, when the team's up against it, when things are wrong and the breaks are beating the boys—tell them to go in there with all they've got and win just one more for the Gipper. I don't know where I'll be then, Rock. But I'll know about it and I'll be happy."[35] The speech was a success. Notre Dame won the game 7–6. Although Rockne's words on that day were very powerful, Gipp never uttered that dying request. Much like the story of Billy Rockne's illness, Rockne excused his use of fiction as a convenient means of accomplishing the important end of motivating his team to win.

The similarities between Rockne and Reagan are much more apparent than are those between Reagan and Gipp. Rockne and Reagan were both men of good character who loved to tell stories aimed at inspiring others to sacrifice for common goals and to undertake heroic acts. That both men knowingly and unknowingly referred to stories and events with little basis in reality does not mean that either one was a cynical manipulator of other people. Like Rockne, Reagan did not mind indulging in fiction to make a moral point he considered to be true. Unlike Rockne, Reagan was not as conscious of his inclination to believe stories of questionable validity. Perhaps the frequent use of the noble lie may be overlooked in a football coach concerned with winning sports games. Whether such an indulgence can be granted to a leader of the United States seeking to encourage, mobilize, and unify an entire nation remains to be determined. In politics, unlike athletics, the grounding of a vision of reality in reality is of the utmost importance.

Though Reagan was one of the most popular actors in Hollywood during the early 1940s, World War II put his film career on hold. As a radio announcer back in Des Moines, Reagan had enlisted in the 14th Cavalry Regiment of the United States Army.[36] Thanks in small part to his cheating during a vision examination, Reagan was commissioned as a second lieutenant. His incredibly poor eyesight was discovered during a physical exam in the months prior to Pearl Harbor, but, when the war came, Reagan was put on active duty in a noncombat role. His service during the war consisted primarily of making motion pictures for the military related to specific missions and general recruitment needs. By the time the war ended, Reagan achieved the rank of Army captain.

Reagan expected great things to happen after the Allied victory. About his hopes for life after the war he writes:

> Like most soldiers who came back, I expected a world suddenly reformed. I hoped and believed that the blood and death and confusion of World War II would result in a regeneration of mankind, that the whole struggle was simply the immolation of the phoenix of human liberties and that the bird of happiness would rise out of the ashes and fly everywhere at once. It seemed impossible that anyone would be blind to the possibilities of the future, or that business could go on as usual. If men could cooperate in war, how much better they could work together in peace![37]

A registered Democrat from the time he was able to vote, Reagan was an ardent supporter of Franklin Roosevelt. At this time in his life, Reagan believed that social injustices could be reduced, if not eliminated, through efficient government management at the national level. He did not trust businesses and markets, he believed that government should own public utilities, and he thought social problems such as housing shortages and the availability of health care should be solved by the national government.[38]

After the war, the transformation of reality Reagan had dreamed of did not occur. About this time in his life he writes: "I discovered that the world was almost the same and perhaps a little worse."[39] And yet he believed the changes he desired were still possible. Thus Reagan embarked upon a much more active role in politics and began "blindly and busily joining every organization I could find that would guarantee to save the world."[40] His more explicit turn to politics after the war coincided with the beginnings of an ideological journey that would conclude with him embracing an approach to politics he called conservatism.

FORCES OF LIGHT AND DARKNESS IN HOLLYWOOD

After World War II, Reagan began to take on speaking engagements devoted primarily to denouncing the dangers of fascism in the world and America. He admitted that the frequent and vigorous applause with which his comments were met "fed my ego, since I had been so long away from the screen."[41] On one occasion, an audience member approached Reagan after a speech and told him that while his comments about fascism were welcomed and accurate, he wondered why Reagan made no mention of the evils of communism. Reagan took this suggestion to heart, and he wrote a new paragraph at the end of his speech denouncing communism. When Reagan delivered his revised remarks, the audience warmly received his criticisms of fascism, but the applause ceased when he got to his anticommunism material.[42] With this experience, a larger realization about the world slowly began to dawn upon Reagan.[43]

In *An American Life*, Reagan refers to the late 1940s as the time in which he learned that communists were much more than misguided or confused liberals.[44] Reagan's growing distrust of communism and communists played an important role in his turn to conservatism. His most intense personal experience with communism occurred in the fall of 1946. The Conference of Studio Unions (CSU), led by Herb Sorrell, launched a strike that brought movie production in Hollywood to a grinding halt. The details of the labor dispute that triggered the strike are complex and have been covered by a number of sources in greater detail than is required here. Essentially, the CSU wanted to represent the Set Erectors, who had theretofore been represented by the International Alliance of Theatrical Stage Employees (IATSE). According to Reagan, the CSU initiated a strike when the movie studios refused to recognize their claim. Upon Reagan's recommendation, the Screen Actors Guild (SAG) positioned itself as a neutral arbitrator between CSU and IATSE.[45] The SAG constructed an independent history of the two unions and a set of facts relating to the dispute. It quickly became clear to Reagan that CSU was pursuing something much larger than a resolution to the conflict. Their seemingly incoherent and unpredictable negotiating strategy appeared to him to be deliberate, and their alleged grievances seemed not to be genuine. Thus he recommended to the SAG that it should cross the CSU picket lines.[46]

Violence broke out along the CSU pickets in late 1946. By February 1947, the strike collapsed and the CSU dissolved.[47] After the strike, Reagan was elected to several terms as president of the SAG. During testimony before the House Un-American Activities Committee (HUAC), the World War II veteran and former American communist Sterling Hayden commented upon communist goals during the 1946 strike. When asked what stopped the communists from gaining control over the labor unions in Hollywood, Hayden answered, "We ran into a one-man battalion named Ronnie Reagan."[48] This experience with the CSU strike strengthened Reagan's view that communism was a highly organized international movement posing a serious threat to the movie industry in particular and the United States in general.

Reagan's personal experience with communist infiltration into Hollywood prepared his imagination to receive a book that sought to explain the appeal and nature of communism. In 1952, an ex-communist named Whittaker Chambers published a book called *Witness*. In *God and Ronald Reagan*, Paul Kengor writes that *Witness* had a profound impact on Reagan. Kengor explains that the book and its author are cited in many of Reagan's presidential speeches and that the former president was able to recite long passages from *Witness* by memory.[49] A few words about *Witness* and its author are required.

REAGAN, CHAMBERS, AND *WITNESS*

Whittaker Chambers joined the Communist Party in the early 1920s and engaged in espionage on behalf of the KGB until he abandoned the party in the late 1930s. Later, he exposed a State Department employee named Alger Hiss as a member of the Communist Party. Hiss denied this allegation and was subsequently convicted of perjury. Hiss served nearly five years in prison. Though the events of the Hiss case were the initial motivation to write *Witness*, Chambers allowed the book to expand into a meditation on communism, tyranny, history, freedom, and God. The book is Chambers's attempt to awaken all who were unaware of the dire threat communism presented not only to the West, but also to human existence itself. *Witness* begins with the well-known "Forward in the Form of a Letter to My Children." Chambers writes:

> For in this century, within the next decades, will be decided for generations whether all mankind is to become Communist, whether the whole world is to become free, or whether, in the struggle, civilization as we know it is to be completely destroyed or completely changed. It is our fate to live upon that turning point in history.[50]

Chambers viewed the Hiss case as one battle in a broader apocalyptic struggle between the forces of freedom and those of communism. In his mind, the victory for freedom was far from assured.

Chambers claims to have grown up with the feeling that the world was on the brink of destruction. Older notions of politics and religion held no interest for him, but he continued to search for something to fill his life with a larger meaning. He found his answer in communism. He writes, "In 1925, I voluntarily withdrew [from Columbia University] for the express purpose of joining the Communist Party. For I had come to believe that the world we live in was dying, that only surgery could now save the wreckage of mankind, and that the Communist Party was history's surgeon."[51] This intuitive sense of saving the world, rather than official Marxist doctrine, is the reason he and most other people became communists, according to Chambers. He explains, "Only in Communism had I found any practical answer at all to the crisis [of history], and the will to make that answer work."[52] Chambers's vague sense that the world was "dying" and in need of "surgery" was intensified and unified to a higher degree by communism's powerful vision of a better world.

Chambers eventually became aware of the ways in which communism distorted or denied morality and tyrannized over the human spirit. He was confronted with the knowledge of the systematic murder of millions of Russians during Stalin's Great Purge in the mid-1930s and with his own complicity in these crimes as an active communist. In Chambers's mind, the reality of Soviet inhumanity in the name of historical necessity outstripped the beautiful image of a world on the verge of establishing a communist paradise. About this moment in his life Chambers explains, "I did not know what had happened to me. I denied the very existence of a soul. But I said: '[Communism] is evil, absolute evil. Of this evil I am a part.' "[53]

According to Chambers, communism was evil because it denied the existence of God and the human soul. This inexorably led to the acts of violence continuously committed by the Soviets and other communists. Despite a deepening awareness of the evils of communism, Chambers struggled with the prospect of leaving the Communist Party. In a fit of panic, he almost convinced himself that he was not strong enough to break away. In the midst of this despair, he felt—perhaps even heard—the following: "If you will fight for freedom, all will be well with you."[54] These words gave him the strength he needed to leave the Communist Party. He left communism in order to be free. From this point in his life, Chambers also considered himself to be a Christian.

Chambers connected the prospects of a victory for Western civilization and freedom over communism with the willingness of others to do what he had done—return to God. He believed that those like himself who abandoned communism ultimately did so because they "wanted to be free."[55] But according to Chambers, freedom means more than civil liberty. Most importantly, freedom is a need of the soul in its search for God. Spiritual freedom makes genuine political liberty possible. He considered attempts to locate freedom outside of the human search for the divine as contributing factors in the emergence of ideologies such as communism. He writes, "There has never been a society or a nation without God. But history is cluttered with the wreckage of nations that became indifferent to God, and died."[56] For freedom to triumph, the West needed a revival of religion.

In Chambers's mind, a dichotomy exists between evil, godless communism on the one hand, and God and freedom on the other. In an allusion to the Fall of Man as it is told in Genesis, he argues that communism is simply the latest incarnation of "man's second oldest faith," insofar as it is a vision of life without God.[57] He holds that freedom's only chance for victory is acknowledging its dependence on the divine. And yet this insight did not bring him a great sense of peace. Though he believed he had chosen the side of righteousness, he also felt that he was now on the losing side. At the time of his break with communism, he informed his wife that one of the long-term consequences of his decision was that they were "leaving the winning world for the losing world."[58] Nevertheless, he felt it was his moral duty to resist the seemingly inevitable victory of communism. It should be recalled that the word "witness" has its etymological origins in the Greek word "martyr."

This brief description of *Witness* has drawn attention to the parts of the book that resonated with Reagan and were incorporated into his imagination. Reagan had concrete experience with the disruptive, deceitful, and violent tactics used by communists during the CSU strike in 1946. Chambers explained that communists took such actions, not because they were confused liberals, but because they were pursuing the realization of their vision of a world redeemed through their efforts. Chambers argues, "This vision *is* the Communist revolution, which, like all great revolutions, occurs in man's mind before it takes form in man's acts. Insurrection and conspiracy are merely methods of realizing the vision; they are merely part of the politics of Communism."[59] This insight never left Reagan's mind. At his first presidential press conference, ABC News's Sam Donaldson asked Reagan about his understanding of the long-term goals of the Soviet Union. Reagan said:

> I don't have to think of an answer as to what I think their intentions are; they have repeated it. I know of no leader of the Soviet Union since the revolution, and including the present leadership, that has not more than once repeated in the various Communist congresses they hold their determination that their goal must be the promotion of world revolution and a one-world Socialist or Communist state, whichever word you want to use.
>
> Now, as long as they do that and as long as they, at the same time, have openly and publicly declared that the only morality they recognize is what will further their cause, meaning they reserve unto themselves the right to commit any crime, to lie, to cheat, in order to attain that,

and that is moral, not immoral, and we operate on a different set of standards, I think when you do business with them, even at a détente, you keep that in mind.[60]

The press excoriated Reagan for these remarks, but he did not think he was saying anything untrue. He was speaking from personal experience informed and strengthened by his encounters with writings such as Chambers's *Witness*.

Reagan also accepted Chambers's arguments that communism was evil and that freedom could defeat it only if it acted in concert with God. In his remarks at the 1981 Conservative Political Action Conference (CPAC) meeting, Reagan paraphrased Chambers's claim that communism was merely the latest form of "man's second oldest faith" and cited Chambers by name when he called upon his listeners to "reassert our commitment as a nation to a law higher than our own, to renew our spiritual strength. Only by building a wall of such spiritual resolve can we, as a free people, hope to protect our own heritage and make it someday the birthright of all men."[61] Like Chambers, Reagan believed that a nation deliberately ignoring God would sooner or later slide into some form of totalitarianism.

In *Where's the Rest of Me?* Reagan recalls another of Chambers's insights into the present, one that resonates with a different part of his imagination. He quotes Chambers as writing, "When I took up my little sling and aimed at Communism, I also hit at something else. What I hit was the force of that great Socialist revolution which in the name of *liberalism*, spasmodically, incompletely, somewhat formlessly, but always in the same direction, has been inching its ice-cap over the nation for two decades."[62] The notion that liberalism is a weigh station on the road to communism rang true with Reagan's experiences during and after World War II. His wartime interaction with federal bureaucracies caused him to reconsider the appropriate role of government in America. After the war, Reagan's trust in government and its ability to manage an entire nation declined. He began to argue that the national government had rejected its constitutional limits and embraced socialism. Reagan's growing distrust of the national government is another major dimension of his movement toward conservatism. This development in Reagan's broader vision can be explored by providing a brief account of his employment at the General Electric Corporation.

REAGAN AND THE GENERAL ELECTRIC CORPORATION

In 1954, Reagan became the host of the new television show *General Electric Theater*. His job at GE included making trips to each of its North American plants as spokesman for the company's headquarters. He often gave short speeches and answered questions throughout the day as he walked the plant floor. In the evenings, he spoke at local meetings of organizations such as the Chamber of Commerce. Initially, his speeches consisted mostly of amusing stories about Hollywood and filmmaking. Later, his speeches became more serious and expressed his views on a variety of political and social topics. According to Reagan, the change in the substance of his speeches had much to do with his encounters with GE employees.[63]

Interacting with the employees was the most politically illuminating part of his time at GE. Reagan claims, "Sometimes I had an awesome, shivering feeling that America was making a personal appearance for me, and it made me the biggest fan in the world."[64] Reagan took seriously the thoughts and concerns of GE employees about the growing interference of the national government in their lives, especially in the areas of taxation and regulation. He shared with them the view that excessive federal taxation and regulatory constraints upon business were stifling American creativity and freedom.[65] Reagan believed that these facts were only symptoms of a larger problem on the horizon. They were indicative of a more sinister effort on the part of liberal Democrats to abandon the United States' fundamental commitments to individual liberty and free markets.[66] Whereas earlier in his life Reagan considered big business to be destructive of individual freedom, after World War II he became convinced that one of the greatest threats to American liberty was big government.

Reagan used his speeches at GE and elsewhere to warn Americans about the slow erosion of their freedom at the hands of the national government. He hoped that raising the alarm would rouse the people to resist the federal government's expansion into areas of American life over which it had no legitimate authority. In his view, if Americans chose to do nothing about the growing socialism in the United States, then they had no one to blame but themselves. Nevertheless, Reagan's confidence in the patriotism and common sense of the American people allowed him to remain optimistic about the future. Drawing upon the inexhaustible reservoir of hope that he began building as a child, he had faith that, once he informed people of the dangers posed to them by the national government, they would act to rescue and restore their country.

Many aspects of the vision of America and its people that Reagan communicated as president took shape during his time at GE. Ideologically, he emerged from this experience as a champion of the free market, a foe of big government, an ardent defender of individual freedom, and a proponent of placing great trust in the people. Reagan understood the present as a mixture of both danger and hope, and he believed in a glorious future made possible by a rebirth of the spirit of the past. It was at this time that he began to consider himself as a conservative. In the 1950s and early 1960s, although he was still registered as a Democrat, he campaigned for Dwight Eisenhower and Richard Nixon in their respective bids for the presidency. During Nixon's unsuccessful 1962 California gubernatorial campaign, Reagan finally registered as a Republican.

Much scholarship has been devoted to Reagan's experiences from the time of his becoming involved in the labor disputes in Hollywood to his official registration with the Republican Party. Some accounts suggest that his political thinking underwent a significant change during this time. In *Ronald Reagan*, Dinesh D'Souza writes that Reagan "became a convert" to the average American's way of thought and eventually "a champion for their interests."[67] In *When Character Was King: A Story of Ronald Reagan*, Peggy Noonan refers to this time in Reagan's life as a "political transformation."[68] These claims have some truth. An individual's imagination is never fixed, but it constantly integrates new experiences into an existing vision creating new unities as a result.

Reagan, perhaps erring in the opposite direction, did not seem to think he changed at all. In *Governor Reagan*, Lou Cannon sides with Reagan and claims:

> [Reagan] was also, for the most part, consistent as he moved during his long lifetime from left to right across the political spectrum. The essence of Reagan's politics in both its Democratic and Republican formulations was a sentimental populism in which he expressed himself as an ordinary man who shared the values of his constituents. Reagan's heroes were, like any good populist, "the people" or the "forgotten Americans." He stood up to the power elites—first in business, then in government and the media.[69]

Reagan and Cannon seem to understand something that is not quite grasped by D'Souza and Noonan. That Reagan was a Democrat and then later a Republican need not imply a radical change in his political ideas. If one turns political parties and ideological inclinations into synonyms, the underlying continuity of Reagan's vision over a long period of time is easy to overlook. Contrary to the claims from D'Souza and Noonan, during the 1940s and 1950s, Reagan seems to have absorbed into his *existing* sense of reality and of America a number of images and ideas about politics, freedom, government, God, religion, communism, free markets, the United States, and the American spirit.

With increasing frequency after World War II, Reagan shared his vision with audiences around the United States by using powerful imagery and persuasive rhetoric. He devoted countless hours to refining the content and presentation of his sense of the world. In 1952, he delivered the commencement address at William Woods College. In his remarks Reagan explained, "America is less of a place than an idea."[70] He also argued, "I believe that God in shedding his grace on this country has always in this divine scheme of things kept an eye on our land and guided it as a promised land for these people."[71] Five years later, Reagan delivered his first commencement address at Eureka College. He spoke to the class of 1957 about their inheritance of the United States. He described America as a country founded by people who possessed "rare qualities of courage and imagination."[72] He argued, "Such courage is part of our inheritance, all of us spring from these special people and these qualities have contributed to the make-up of the American personality."[73] Reagan explained, "This is a land of destiny and our forefathers found their way here by some Divine system of selective service gathered here to fulfill a mission to advance man a further step in his climb from the swamps."[74] This mission had been undertaken by the Founding Fathers, and it was enshrined in the Declaration of Independence. This mission had been the point of focus for the United States in two World Wars, and it needed to remain the focus of the class of 1957 as America sought to defend freedom against communism during the Cold War.

Reagan's remarks at Eureka College also touched upon issues of domestic policy. He said, "Remember that every government service, every offer of government financed security, is paid for in the loss of personal freedom."[75] He stated he was not opposed to government having a role in private life and private enterprise. Nevertheless, he implored his audience to analyze independently and objectively each proposed government curtailment of liberty. Without vigilance, Reagan suggested that they might find that the price they paid for certain conveniences was too high. Reagan closed his remarks with an exhortation to the audience to carry forward the American spirit into the future.

In *God and Ronald Reagan*, Paul Kengor draws attention to both of these speeches and writes, "By the 1950s, Ronald Reagan was publicly speaking of America as a nation chosen by God."[76] During this time Reagan also became increasingly concerned about high rates of taxation and limitations upon individual liberty being imposed upon Americans by their own government. Kengor explains that these sentiments about America and its divine destiny stayed with Reagan throughout his adult life. He contends that a straight line can be drawn from such remarks to many of those made by Reagan during his presidency.[77]

THE FINISHED PRODUCT: RONALD REAGAN AND "THE SPEECH"

After eight years of service, Reagan and GE amicably dissolved their official relationship. In the late summer of 1964, Reagan gave a speech to a gathering of Republicans at the Coconut Grove nightclub in Los Angeles. After he finished his speech, a small group from the audience approached Reagan and asked him if he would be willing to repeat his remarks during a nationally televised speech on behalf of presidential candidate Barry Goldwater. On October 27, 1964, Ronald Reagan gave a speech, later titled "A Time for Choosing," that was described by *Washington Post* reporter David Broder as "the most successful national political debut since William Jennings Bryan electrified the 1896 Democratic Convention with his 'Cross of Gold' speech."[78] Reagan understood and acknowledged the pivotal role this speech played in the subsequent development of his political career.[79] The speech was America's first national introduction to Reagan's vision. Considering his remarks as a whole and identifying important images and ideas expressed in them will make even more clear the connections and continuities of Reagan's prepresidential life and imagination with his presidential vision.

If one phrase can describe the general tone of this speech, then it is apocalyptic optimism. Reagan began by stating that the thoughts and ideas he was about to share on the choice facing the United States in the 1964 presidential election were entirely his own. He admitted that he was once a Democrat, but that the ideas for which that party now stood had forced him to consider taking a different course. He provided the audience with a picture of the present as he saw it. He started by listing a number of facts and examples of the unconstitutional growth of the national government. He explained that the income taxes levied against the average American were excessive, that inflation was eroding individual savings, that bureaucracies were harming American businesses, and that agencies devoted to eliminating social injustice actually made existing problems worse—even as they enlarged their budgets and added regulations.

Reagan did not see all this as coincidental. He explained that these problems were mere symptoms of a larger disease confronting America. In his mind, the dangers facing the United States were such that they transcended any partisan political interests. Reagan said:

> You and I are told increasingly that we have to choose between a left or right, but I would like to suggest that there is no such thing as a left or right. There is only an up or down—up to man's age-old dream—the ultimate in individual freedom consistent with law and order—or down to the ant heap of totalitarianism. . . . Our natural, inalienable rights are now considered to be a dispensation from government, and freedom has never been so fragile, so close to slipping from our grasp as it is at this moment.[80]

Reagan believed Americans were presented with a historic choice between reclaiming the rights and dignities intended for them by the Founding Fathers on the one hand, and continuing on a course that would result in the total destruction of their country on the other. For Reagan, it was truly a time for choosing in the United States.

According to Reagan, this momentous choice had profound implications for international politics. He argued that those who desired the continued growth of the national government were also set upon appeasing global communism. He considered as hypocrites those who condemned American allies that retained colonies abroad while remaining silent about the much more serious plight of countless victims of communist tyranny in the satellite nations of the Soviet Union. He suggested that such people believed indifference or indulgence would eventually persuade America's enemies to abandon their tyrannical ways and to embrace some variant of peaceful, democratic socialism. Reagan argued that pursuing this type of peace would only guarantee the enslavement of the West and America. He claimed that Americans had a special duty to protect freedom at home and to protect people abroad who also wished to live in liberty. Abdicating this responsibility, Reagan continued, would be tantamount to Moses refusing to lead the Israelites out of Egypt, to Christ refusing to take up his cross, and to the American colonists refusing to resist British tyranny. Reagan reminded his audience that they must rouse themselves to resistance because there was nowhere else to run. America was "the last stand on earth."[81]

Reagan's sober description of the present did not diminish his optimism. The general tone of the speech was comforting and devoid of fanaticism. Its delivery was conversational, and its content was occasionally humorous. The tone of the speech suggested that while the speaker considered the situation serious, he also knew that once informed of these dangers, Americans would defend themselves and reestablish the fullness of their rights and liberties. In this speech, it was implied that the redemptive process would begin with electing Barry Goldwater as president. Of course, this did not happen. Goldwater went down to an historic defeat. Nevertheless, the speech concluded on a note that, in hindsight, was rather prescient. Borrowing a phrase from Franklin Roosevelt, Reagan said, "You and I have a rendezvous with destiny."[82] Sixteen years later, he and the American people finally made this meeting.

"The Speech," as it is often called, contains further refinements of a number of ideas and images to which Reagan had already formed strong attachments. Reagan's categorization of the present as a time to choose between going "up or down" is similar to Chambers's view of the choice confronting the West. Like Dick Faulkner in *That Printer of Udell's* and Paul Revere in Longfellow's poem, Reagan presented himself as an average citizen who, concerned with the well-being of his fellow citizens, was sounding the alarm and presenting a commonsense plan for action. His mother, Nelle, instilled in Reagan an abiding optimism, among other things. This contributed mightily to his great faith and trust in the American people. As his time at GE had taught him, once Americans were informed, they would work to reclaim their liberties, avoid disaster and destruction, and build a future reinvigorated with the best of the spirit of the past. Parts of Reagan's biography have been explored with a view to understanding the development of his imagination. In so doing, a preliminary understanding of how life experiences, ideas, and images all contribute to the formation and refinement of any person's imagination has also been imparted.

2 The Imagination
A Philosophical Elucidation

This world is but canvas to our imaginations.[1]

—Henry David Thoreau

The term "imagination" is subject to a variety of definitions containing varying degrees of accuracy and intellectual seriousness. In order to elucidate more fully the general nature and components of Reagan's chimeric imagination, this analysis must move beyond a casual understanding of the imagination. A more sophisticated account of the imagination needs to be provided, and the relationship between imagination and politics needs to be explained. The philosophical concept of imagination being used in this work draws upon and refines elements of existing definitions, and the main components of these existing concepts must therefore be described. Gaining an understanding of the imagination also requires some forays into rather difficult areas of epistemology. While developing a comprehensive epistemology is beyond the scope of this study, acquiring an adequate sense of how human beings come to know about themselves and the world in which they live will enhance the understanding of the term "imagination" as it is being used in this work. Hence the general relationship among imagination and other constituents of knowledge, such as will and reason, must be described.

A BRIEF HISTORY OF AESTHETICS

An initial understanding of how the imagination works can best be provided by examining it in its primary medium of expression, which is art. In *The Mirror and the Lamp*, M. H. Abrams explains prevalent aesthetic ideas that define the romantic movement. He also draws attention to the ways in which the main currents in romanticism depart from older aesthetic ideas and theories. Abrams acknowledges that there are a number of differences between the aesthetics of the ancient Greeks and the neoclassicists of the eighteenth century. These differences notwithstanding, he claims various preromantic aesthetic theories can be treated as parts of one general tradition. According to Abrams, the typical preromantic understands the imagination specifically and the mind more generally as passive faculties. In this older tradition, art is thus seen as an imitation (mimesis) of reality, and the mind is seen as a tabula rasa working mechanically upon external data received from "out there." Abrams uses the image of a mirror as a metaphor for this way of thinking about the artistic process and human cognition.

In this older view, the artist allegedly holds up a mirror (his mind) to the external world of nature and ideas. Preexisting wholes, comprised of various objects and ideas, penetrate the senses from outside and imprint or replicate themselves upon the mind. These various sense imprints are then available either to the imagination for artistic creation, or to the reason for philosophical reflection. About this older understanding of artistic creation, Abrams writes, "The concept that the inventive process, in its boldest flights, consists in the severance of sensible wholes into parts and the aggregation of parts into new wholes, united even antagonistic schools of eighteenth-century philosophy."[2]

One might point out that art prior to the romantic period was much more (or much less) than a direct transcription of the existing world. Most proponents of art as imitation supplemented this theory with norms of artistic creation such as depicting the statistical average or typical beauty of a thing, depicting the familiar, depicting a composite of beautiful things into one beautiful thing, and depicting human nature in general rather than in the particular.[3] It is these aesthetic theories and conventions that lead Abrams to conclude that prior to the emergence of romanticism in the late eighteenth and early nineteenth centuries, the imagination was generally understood as a *passive* faculty of the mind. In most varieties of the imitative theory of art, the artist was held to reveal nothing about his own thoughts and emotions through his depiction of the outside world.

To talk about the romantic movement as a single entity is to pass over many of the theoretical and artistic differences that existed among various poets, painters, musicians, and critics during the late eighteenth and nineteenth centuries. Many parts of the movement inclined toward aesthetic, emotional, and ethical excess. Others varieties of romanticism have yielded valuable insights into the nature of art and the construction of human knowledge. With these qualifications in mind, romanticism still can be described in the most general sense as a movement that revised or rejected many of the analogies and metaphors for art, human knowledge, and creativity that had generally prevailed until the late eighteenth century. The romantics understood art as a process of illumination, rather than one of transcription or imitation. Abrams uses the image of a lamp as a metaphor for the romantic view that the artist expresses his inner thoughts and emotions—that is, his light—in the work of art. The romantics redefined imagination as an active power *creating* intuitive wholes by synthesizing the internal and the external, the spiritual and the formal.[4]

Abrams argues, "The change from imitation to expression, and from the mirror to the fountain, the lamp, and related analogues, was not an isolated phenomenon."[5] The discovery of the creative imagination also affected the manner in which many philosophers, critics, and aestheticians understood the human thought process. The Lockean notion that the mind was analogous to a passive machine, cataloguing various sense impressions, was abandoned in favor of various organic analogies. On this new view, knowledge was believed to be created by a combination of outer and inner forces, much the same way that a plant incorporates sunlight and soil nutrients into its organism in an indistinguishable unity.[6] In general, the romantics understood art and thought as creative, synthetic acts in which the lines between internal and external, between subject and object, became blurred to varying degrees. They also argued that works of art, which is another way of saying works of the imagination, bore the ideational or emotional imprint of the artist. Thus, art tells others not only about beauty, but also about the artist.

This brief summary of the history of aesthetics has been provided because the discovery of the creative imagination is one of the most important contributions of romanticism to aesthetics and philosophy. This aesthetic breakthrough is at the very heart of this study. Along the lines of the older aesthetic described here, Reagan's presidential speeches would indicate very little, if anything, about his actual thoughts on politics and life. In that older view, it would be almost impossible even to conceive of talking about something such as "Reagan's imagination," even though many people have intuited something distinctly "Reagan" about the vision of reality and America that he expressed in his presidential speeches. The discovery of the creative imagination makes it possible for human beings to understand more clearly the relationship between the artist and art and between a thinker and his thoughts. Without this development, no serious and illuminating description of an individual's imagination, whether he be William Shakespeare or Ronald Reagan, would be possible.

Though it is now apparent that the romantics discovered something that can be called the "creative imagination," it is still not clear *what* that term actually means. Neither is it clear how the imagination fits into a broader epistemology in which the intuition works with reason and will in the creation of knowledge. Therefore, additional discussion of the epistemological foundation of this study is necessary. On the imagination and its relationship with politics, specific references have already been made to the ideas of Claes G. Ryn. He is indebted to two early-twentieth-century scholars, Benedetto Croce and Irving Babbitt, both of whom devoted much thought to explaining the nature of imagination and its relationship with philosophy and politics. Examining key ideas that they expressed will provide a better understanding of the role of the imagination in the construction of human knowledge.

CROCE, BABBITT, AND THE IMAGINATION

To some, it may seem strange to refer to both Croce and Babbitt when attempting to describe the imagination. There are a number of differences between the two men on the meaning of imagination as well as other topics.

Croce was perhaps the most famous aesthetician in the first half of the twentieth century, but he was a systematic philosopher who also developed a theory of logic and a theory of volition as parts of his larger philosophy of the spirit. Babbitt, in contrast, was a professor of comparative literature whose scholarship was devoted both to discovering the roots of aesthetic, political, and ethical disorder in Western civilization and to working toward its moral, imaginative, and political rehabilitation. What is distinctive about Babbitt's concerns with imagination in art appears didactic when it is compared to Croce's early aesthetical writings. Croce's philosophical monism and his original refusal to look for the moral dimensions of art has led many of Babbitt's admirers to ignore the more fruitful potentialities of Croce and his work—as Babbitt himself did. Their differences notwithstanding, these scholars shared the sentiment that the imaginative/intuitive dimension of life is an important, basic constituent of knowledge that is often neglected or poorly understood. In uniting their distinct, though partially compatible understandings of the imagination, the concept itself will receive further elucidation.

As a systematic philosopher, Croce was concerned with providing a conceptual account of the categories of human spiritual activity. He divided the activities of the spirit into two major parts called theoretical and practical. The practical category of the spirit was divided further between an ethical will, which aimed at the Good, and an "economic" will, which merely sought efficiency in any action, whether it was moral or immoral. On the theoretical side, he established a division between intuition and conceptual, "logical" knowledge. Here Croce's understanding of the intuition is most relevant to the concept of imagination that informs this work.

In *Æsthetic*, Croce explains that intuition is a synthesis of matter and form in the creation of individual images. His understanding of intuition is similar to the previously described romantic notion of imagination. An illustration of the intuition at work will shed light upon Croce's understanding of the imagination. Imagine a person feeling the first stirrings of hunger. As he becomes conscious of his desire to eat, the imagination immediately constructs images expressing the inchoate desire. Perhaps he envisions the smell, appearance, and taste of a delicious steak, a baked potato, sautéed asparagus, and a glass of red wine. He might construct other images anticipating the joy of the eating experience. Perhaps he imagines eating such a meal with his family sitting at a table discussing the events of the day. He might imagine eating dinner by candlelight at an elegant restaurant with a new love. Through the activity of the intuition, the initial impulse of hunger becomes ever more clearly known as it swells into a whole image of the eating experience replete with anticipated tastes, smells, sounds, human interactions, and other phenomena.

Croce claims that all human beings possess imagination. Most people, such as the individual in the previous example, create relatively simple images connected to the desire to satisfy a pressing need. Yet some human beings are capable of allowing their imagination to express rather intricate and powerful intuitions. Such people are called artists. On the one hand, Croce argues that the difference between the artist and the nonartist is one of degree and not of kind. If this were not true, how could anyone appreciate a work of art apart from its creator? On the other hand, he rejects arguments that claim the difference between an artist, such as Johannes Vermeer, and a nonartist, such as a fishmonger, is merely in the superior technical ability of the former to render onto canvas that which everyone else sees in the same manner. According to Croce, artists are truly such precisely because they have "a more frequent inclination fully to express certain complex states of the soul."[7] The products of these artistic expressions are those rare treasures of civilization called works of art. According to Croce, true works of art disclose something about which others already have an intuition, but cannot express with the same degree of completeness and clarity.

That the artist is one who can express complex intuitions in a compelling manner does not mean that he has seen or expressed knowledge of historical fact. In Croce's view, the correlation of an intuition to the "real" world is not considered during the imaginative production of concrete images. He writes, "Intuition is the undifferentiated unity of the perception of the real and of the simple image of the possible. In our intuitions we do not oppose ourselves as empirical beings to external reality, but we simply objectify our impressions, whatever they be."[8] Thus, the aforementioned person having an intuition about dinner may or may not have intuited something "real." He may have intuited his family as it usually is, or he may actually have a much more vulgar family than the one he imagined. He may have no family at all. The intuition itself is nonetheless real in the sense that it is an image expressed. For Croce, reality may be perceived in an intuition, but questioning after the reality status of an image expressed by the imagination is a subsequent and theoretical, not merely intuitive, activity. The relationship of an imaginative expression to reality is an issue to be determined by the intellect (reason).

This brief explanation of some of Croce's ideas has drawn attention to creative intuition as a source of images, though not necessarily images of historical reality. It has also suggested that the difference between the intuitive expressions of the artist and the nonartist, however important, is a matter of degrees. For all the benefits to be derived from Croce's early aesthetic theory, it suffers from significant philosophical problems. One of the weaknesses in Croce's early philosophy is the sharp contrast he establishes between the intuitive and logical forms of knowledge. He claims that the difference between the intuitive and the logical is the difference between knowledge of the individual (image) and the universal (concept). Croce writes, "Intuitions are: this river, this lake, this brook, this rain, this glass of water; the concept is: water, not this or that appearance and particular example of water, but water in general, in whatever time or place it be realized; the material of infinite intuitions, but of one single constant concept."[9] This distinction between image and concept appears somewhat contrived.

Croce argues that philosophical concepts and insights may be transformed and integrated into intuitive expressions in poetry, fiction, or pictorial art. He goes on to claim that the degree to which they are fused into an imaginative expression is the degree to which they cease to exist as concepts. This seems to be a rather sensible argument insofar as great art is not synonymous with systematic philosophy. Nevertheless, it is especially curious that Croce seems to deny the possibility that the imagination could convey an *intuitive* sense of the universal/conceptual. Claes G. Ryn has commented upon this peculiarity in Croce's early philosophy. In *Will, Imagination, and Reason*, he writes, "Croce's approach to the universal was at first purely conceptual and philosophical: We can know the universal only through concepts. Not until 1917, and then conceivably under Babbitt's influence, did he admit that there can be an 'imaginative perception of the universal.' "[10] That the particular can communicate a preconceptual awareness of the universal is a possibility about which the early Croce is mute or at most ambivalent.

The early Croce also argues that the criterion of judgment for an imaginative expression is expressive coherence or unity. Building upon his own understanding of *l'art pour l'art*, he considers questions about the suitability of certain artistic themes, or assessments of the moral value of imaginative images, to be an invitation to didacticism. He writes:

> The theme or content [of a work of art] cannot, therefore, be practically or morally charged with epithets of praise or blame. When critics of art remark that a theme is *badly selected*, in cases where that observation has a just foundation, it is a question of blaming, not the selection of the theme (which would be absurd), but the manner in which the artist has treated it, the failure of the expression due to the contradictions which it contains. . . . Art is independent both of science and of the useful and the moral.[11]

Croce's comment seems true in at least one way. It would be inappropriate and even dangerous for institutions such as governments to prescribe acceptable artistic themes, or to proscribe their opposites. Preventing such a possibility seems to have been much on his mind. His desire to protect artistic expression from censorship and repression may have stood in the way of his developing adequate critical standards for assessing inadequacies in works of art that are coherently expressed. Later in life, Croce seemed to acknowledge, with Babbitt, that the imagination can communicate universality. But unlike Babbitt, he did not acknowledge the possibility that art can present a warped view of life and its possibilities. His strong intuitions about the deeper failure of much modern art were left in a nascent state of development.[12]

Like Croce, Babbitt believes that all humans possess an imagination that is basic to man's apprehension of the world and that the differences between an artist and a nonartist are of degrees of depth in intuitive vision. Unlike Croce, Babbitt had from the beginning a deep awareness of how the imagination can perceive the universal in the concrete. He believed that the imagination could give concrete artistic expression of ethical universality in a nondidactic manner. Importantly, he also believed that it could present broad, coherent, and appealing images that are nevertheless deformations of life and its possibilities.

To understand Babbitt's view of the role of the imagination, it is necessary to explain his understanding of the human condition in general, especially his view of the relationship between will and imagination. About the close relationship between the two, Claes G. Ryn writes, "To get to the heart of Babbitt's ethico-aesthetical doctrine, it is important to recognize that, in one sense, will and imagination are the same."[13] In various writings, Babbitt used the term "will" in a general sense to describe the numerous impulses within human beings that seek expression.[14] He argued that the human will is dualistic, or, differently put, is comprised of higher and lower inclinations demanding to be translated into action. He also claimed that the demands of each type of volitive inclination become known through the imagination. Will expresses itself in imagery. Babbitt considered the imagination to be capable of creating not only concrete images of this, that, and the other particular impulse, but also visions of life as a whole, the world, human nature, and the possibilities of politics. It does this, in part, by synthesizing past experiences with those of the present by instituting likenesses and analogies. As he did with his conception of will, Babbitt saw the imagination as having two general varieties, which he called moral and romantic (or idyllic).

The moral imagination cooperates with the higher will and creates concrete images of opportunities for moral activity or of dangers to which it is exposed. Moral-imaginative images can suggest ways in which action can avoid moral danger, further the moral life, and contribute to a person's happiness. The moral imagination intuits new possibilities and how to overcome obstacles to the goal and which obstacles are insurmountable. The lower inclinations make themselves known to human beings in the same imaginative way but are defined precisely by neglect of the demands of the higher life. A person who lives merely to indulge sensual desire will make his imagination his accomplice, constructing a vision of life in which such activities seem fulfilling and perhaps even the key to human happiness. The imagination will suggest ways in which such desires can become realized in the future, thus enticing the person to travel farther down the same road. The imagination will conceal or explain away whatever stands in the way of making pleasure the overall goal. In both cases, the imagination gives texture and immediacy to the possibilities of life confronting the will. Will and imagination, whether of the higher or lower varieties, support and reinforce each other.

The interactions between the higher will and the moral imagination, or between the lower will and the romantic imagination, give each individual a more or less unified vision of reality, but such a vision can be more or less consonant with the "real world." Babbitt believes that while the imagination gives unity, it does not necessarily give reality. How can human beings tell the difference? An important part of Babbitt's answer to this question is that reason can discern what is what. In *Democracy and Leadership*, he writes, "To determine the quality of our imaginings, we need to supplement the power in man that perceives and the power that conceives [imagination] with a third power—that which discriminates. . . . In emphasizing the importance of the power in man that discriminates, I mean this power, working not abstractly, but on the actual material of experience."[15] For Babbitt it is reason, disciplined to the actual facts of human experience, that tells an individual whether or not the imaginative unity held in his mind is real or chimerical—that is, rooted in the historical world or in the dream world.

Explaining Babbitt's understanding of reason is difficult because, unlike his concepts of imagination and will, he never established a dichotomy for the concept of reason. Yet such a dichotomy is implicit in the prior comment. Babbitt rejected the type of ahistorical abstract reason that separates itself from the lived experience of human beings and, in particular, does not look there for anything universal. That kind of rationality does not belong in philosophical and humane studies. Babbitt actually favored a type of historical-philosophical reason that takes actual human experience very seriously and encompasses universality experienced in history. Such a notion of historical rationality is never systematically developed in Babbitt's writings, but this is the rationality that he calls "the power in man that discriminates." It is capable of distinguishing between dream and reality.[16]

That individuals use reason to formulate both simple and complex ideas, to say nothing of systematic philosophies and ideologies, is well known and requires little explanation. What is not so well understood is the relationship between reason and imagination. According to Babbitt, the imagination, to paraphrase the previously quoted Thoreau, is the canvas upon which human reason works. Think for a moment about any popular American political figure past or present. When examining a politician's views on topics such as justice, liberty, or equality, one often wonders why he or she came to *those* particular formulations and not others. In brief, the answer is that their ideas are conceptual expressions of their deeper intuitions about life.

Without a more or less unified vision of life and its possibilities, there is no coherent material for reason to work upon and conceptually articulate. Thus, although reason plays a vital role in human knowledge insofar as it creates concepts out of intuitions and arranges them into larger intellectual wholes, a prior imaginative vision is the basis or condition for the rational development of ideas in philosophy and general knowledge. Among other things, this view of the relationship between imagination and reason helps explain why individuals possessing intellectual brilliance often fail miserably in their attempts to provide reliable accounts of human existence. Babbitt's perhaps most important insight is that the imagination, steered by a certain quality of will, can easily lead the mind astray. With a will and an imagination habituated to evade or distort aspects of life, even highly intelligent persons are often unable to see the world realistically or clearly.[17]

IMAGINATION AND POLITICS

This summary of the role of imagination will help explain how the dialectical workings of will, imagination, and reason affect the ways in which political life is conceived and enacted. First, a few words on Babbitt's understanding of the moral and romantic varieties of imagination are needed. Though never moralistic or didactic, the moral imagination is centered in the awareness that human nature is inherently and chronically divided between higher and lower impulses and that a better life requires much moral effort. Human beings are capable of creating decent personal and social circumstances, but, because of their divided nature and weaknesses, they need to have modest expectations. Politics at its best can achieve some nobility—a measure of order, justice, and civilization—but it has to be a limited enterprise. The kind of imagination that can contribute to this admirable but realistic goal is aware of the dangers and limits of life as well as its higher opportunities. It is what Babbitt called "an imagination disciplined to the facts" of existence.[18] In Babbitt's view, Edmund Burke was one of the most powerful exponents of the moral imagination in the modern era. Leading early Americans, such as Alexander Hamilton, George Washington, and John Adams, had a similar kind of imagination.

The romantic imagination, in contrast, is not held back by any allegations of human perversity or weakness, but rather invests life and politics with very different and marvelous possibilities. This kind of imagination is pervaded by emotional excess and puts forth extravagant dreams unaffected by what is actually known about human beings in history. As Babbitt described it, this is an imagination "free to wander wild in its own realm of chimeras."[19] For example, as in the case of Jean-Jacques Rousseau and his numerous followers, it envisions human beings as naturally good; it is concerned with the mass of humanity more than the individual; it longs for the diffusion of brotherhood, freedom, and equality; and it blames social and political disorder on inefficient or malevolent institutions. Admitting no enduring depravity in the human heart, this imagination pictures an idyllic future world. The latter is to be brought into being by radically reorganizing society in accordance with the cherished dream. Remove bad institutions, and freedom and general happiness will flourish. Babbitt regarded Rousseau as the great pioneer for this type of dreamy imagination. Many of the political ideas of Thomas Jefferson, Thomas Paine, and Woodrow Wilson are expressions of this variety of imagination.

For Babbitt, understanding the impact of imagination upon politics was of the highest importance. He was interested in the imagination partly because he had detected a marked change in the imaginative patterns of Americans that explained what he perceived to be an exceedingly important yet poorly understood change in American political thinking. Babbitt believed that during his lifetime the intuitive vision of politics and human nature that had prevailed among the Framers was being rapidly replaced by a new, romantic imagination, which he called sentimental humanitarianism.

During the early twentieth century, it was not uncommon to hear leading Americans from a wide range of political and religious backgrounds articulate intuitive visions proclaiming human natural goodness and the ability of politics to transform society and even the world. Interpretations of social and political disorder as products of the inefficient management of institutions or of the incomplete realization of progress, equality, or democracy became more frequent in the United States. Increasingly, the person perceived as deserving of society's attention and praise was the one who had great plans to serve and save mankind. In politics and social life, this type of person often presented himself as an unselfish leader proposing to eliminate problems such as war, inequality, poverty, crime, and depravity, which had theretofore been considered permanent features of human existence. Key to such a vision of regenerating politics and society was the spread of progress, freedom, and democracy, which would herald in a new age of prosperity, peace, and brotherhood for all of mankind. Such a program also required that a substantial amount of power be given to the saviors of humanity. Babbitt grouped together proponents of these notions during this period in American history as sentimental humanitarians. For many, their ideas appeared—and still appear—to be expressions of the highest morality. To Babbitt, they were not.

Babbitt considered sentimental humanitarianism to be fraught with dangers for political order in America and the larger Western world. He argued that for all of the apparent idealism and benevolence of many of his contemporaries, the ethico-imaginative disposition of the time was emotionally and otherwise expansive and lacking that vital element important in any historical time or place—that is, individuals willing to practice ethical self-control. To his mind, an individual's ethical maturity was not discerned from the emotional intensity with which he communicated his thoughts and desires. On the contrary, Babbitt considered the effusive expression of solidarity with amorphous groups such as the downtrodden, or of an unyielding desire for freedom, often to be excuses for avoiding the more important and difficult inner work of willing morality in personal life. Unlike the sentimental humanitarians, Babbitt was not sanguine about the ability of politics to transform the human condition and dissolve the tension between the higher and lower wills. He believed that the expansive tendencies of sentimental humanitarianism were actually dangerous signs of hubris. On his view, expressions of such ideas often masked the sentimental humanitarian's will to power.

In contrast to the sentimental humanitarians, Babbitt did not conceive of politics as an enterprise devoted to accomplishing some sort of political apocalypse. Like the ancient Greeks and early Christians, Babbitt viewed politics as a much more limited undertaking. In his mind, government existed primarily to restrain the most heinous effects on society that could be wrought by the lower will. Politics was the art of creating some order out of a chronically disordered world. As has already been stated, Babbitt considered the human condition as grounded in a permanent tension between the higher and lower will inclinations. In Babbitt's view, an individual's primary moral responsibility was not to mankind, but to what was best in himself. Drawing upon ideas deeply rooted in Western and Eastern civilization, Babbitt believed ethical self-mastery was required before an individual could discern and seize genuine opportunities to help others in his family, community, country, and world. Babbitt distinguished between the man of character and the ethical huckster not on the basis of emotional utterance, but on the basis of real fruits brought forth by the exercise of the ethical will. That his view of politics and human nature is vastly different from that held by the typical sentimental humanitarian is obvious. The typical sentimental humanitarian would have described Babbitt's view as lacking in sympathy and as "selfish." In *Democracy and Leadership*, Babbitt acknowledged that the difference between these positions was one of first principles and not peripheral.[20]

In concluding this section on Babbitt and politics, it is worth noting that the great difference between his view of morality and politics and the one he describes as sentimental humanitarianism does not have as much to do with the functioning of reason as one might think. Both sides are clearly capable of providing coherent arguments for their political and ethical ideas. The difference between the two must be sought at a deeper level—namely, where the will and the imagination interact. As an expression of an active, ethical will, the moral imagination actually raises the moral quality of political life. Babbitt believed that the imaginative vision of sentimental humanitarianism was merely one of many and diverse historical manifestations of the lower will and its idyllic imagination. It had the practical fruits one would expect. The horror and carnage of World War I and the crass economic materialism of the late nineteenth and early twentieth centuries were only two of many concrete examples of what Babbitt saw as evidence of his broader claims about the dangers of the typical sentimental humanitarian's imagination. The "idealism" masked moral corruption.

RONALD REAGAN AND THE CHIMERIC IMAGINATION

Babbitt's insights into the ethical qualities of varieties of imagination are of high value. So too are his explanations of the ways in which different types of imagination conceive of and become manifest in politics. Drawing in part upon these strains of Babbitt's broader thought, the concept of chimeric imagination can be defined as intuition containing strong elements of optimism, dreaminess, and illusion. The previous examination of Reagan's religious upbringing, his childhood experiences and literary encounters, and his life as an actor and political activist already suggest that he was often and strongly prone to optimistic and idyllic imaginings about the world, human nature, and the possibilities of politics. It will become more evident as this work progresses that Reagan's chimeric imagination has a great deal in common with the romantic/idyllic varieties of imagination described by Babbitt. Now that a philosophical understanding of imagination and its relationship to politics has been provided, a broader and deeper exploration of the prominent chimeric elements in Reagan's imagination and presidential speeches can continue.

3 "A Talent for Happiness"[1]
Ronald Reagan, Optimism, and Politics

Twilight? Twilight? Not in America. Here, it's a sunrise ever day—fresh new opportunities, dreams to build.[2]

—Ronald Reagan

One might have the impression that the term "imagination" and all of the terminological equivalents used in this study are merely other words for "ideology." Obviously, ideas are vital parts of an intuitive sense of reality. After all, it is through the process of forming ideas that individuals gain conceptual awareness of the various components of their own visions. But the imagination is not an aggregate of ideas. Ideology ultimately rests on and expresses a general intuition about what life is like. Beneath all the ideational explications of a person's ideology, one finds a deeper sense of the general unity of life—its "feel" or "flavor." The intuition underlying Reagan's expressed ideas and other remarks about politics can be more clearly observed by examining one of the central components of his chimeric imagination—optimism. Reagan's optimistic outlook was shaped by a number of people, including Nelle Reagan, Knute Rockne, and Franklin Roosevelt, but his hopefulness was not artificial. The confidence he had in the future of America and its people was deeply appealing to many Americans, and it was also believable because Reagan seemed genuinely to *embody* optimism. Reagan's efforts to inspire hope and optimism in the American people are present in many of the other elements of his vision that will be described in subsequent chapters. At this point it is enough to identify some of the major ways in which optimism was an explicit or implicit component of his images and ideas.

REAGAN, OPTIMISM, STORYTELLING, AND THE AMERICAN PRESIDENCY

During his presidency, Reagan held that the American people needed more from him than explanations of his various ideas and policy goals. They needed hope. Reagan believed that one of his important presidential duties was to inspire Americans with confidence, and he took seriously this role as a national motivator and comforter. In *The Reagan Rhetoric*, Toby Bates explains that even an accomplished speechwriter such as Peggy Noonan struggled at times to maintain the consistent use of positive language that reflected Reagan's genuine and relentless optimism.[3] Especially in the early years of Reagan's presidency, a central concern of his was invigorating the United States with hope. A representative example of the ways in which Reagan attempted to instill optimism in others can be observed in remarks he made to members of his administration after completing his first year in office.

Reagan started by commending the hard work of his administration, telling them that through their efforts the United States was beginning to overcome the economic and political challenges of the previous year. At the same time, he did not want them to become complacent. He explained, "But any coach worth his salt knows that it's not the season that just ended that counts; it's the season that's just beginning. As a team we're about to launch our second season, and it's going to be a tough one. To keep our recovery program working, to get an ailing America back on its feet and running again will take a massive team effort."[4] To encourage his administration for the coming year, Reagan told them a story.

Reagan began by describing a father who had two sons, one of whom was "a pessimist beyond recall," and the other "an optimist beyond reason."[5] The father happened to meet a child psychiatrist, and the father explained to the doctor the unusual character traits of his two boys. Intrigued, the psychiatrist suggested a scheme to cure the children. He explained that he would place the pessimist in a room filled with the best toys a boy could imagine. In the face of such wonderful things, the psychiatrist reasoned that the boy would be cured of his pessimism. About the optimist, the psychiatrist told the father that he would place his son in an unclean horse stable—i.e., a stall full of manure. With such an unpleasant sight before his eyes, the second son undoubtedly would be cured of his immoderate optimism.

The father agreed to the experiment, and the boys were placed in their respective rooms. After about five minutes, the psychiatrist and the father checked on the pessimistic son. When the two adults entered the room, the boy looked up at them and said, "I know somebody's going to come in and take these away from me."[6] The crowd laughed. Reagan explained that the father and the psychiatrist next went into the horse stable and found the other boy covered in manure. In fact, the young boy was throwing manure all over the place. They asked him why he was doing this. The boy replied, "There's got to be a pony in here somewhere."[7] The audience laughed even harder this time. Against the best hopes of the father and the psychiatrist, the children's natural characteristics were unchanged.

Although Reagan got the audience to laugh at his story, he did not tell it merely for amusement. He applied it to his more immediate task of strengthening the resolve of his administration for the tasks ahead. He admitted that America was facing an array of serious political and social problems and said, "But I'm confident that if we all do our best today and in the months ahead, we can turn things around. There is a pony in here."[8] With faith, commitment, and confidence, he told his audience they could "make today's government and today's America a model for generations to come."[9]

This story sheds great light upon Reagan's brand of optimism. He often acknowledged a number of foreign and domestic problems confronting America and its people, but his stress was always on the possibilities for a better future, for renewal, and for progress. In his life and as president, Reagan was almost always the boy convinced that there was a pony to find in the muck no matter how hard or how long he had to look.

REAGAN, OPTIMISM, PESSIMISM, AND THE AMERICAN SPIRIT

In *Governor Reagan*, Lou Cannon claims that Reagan's optimism was such that Pangloss looked like a pessimist by comparison.[10] Reagan did not believe that his sense of hope was a personal idiosyncrasy. There was something distinctly *American* about his view. In his imagination, America was a special land of hopes and dreams; Americans were natural dreamers and optimists. In *An American Life*, Reagan writes, "The dreams of people may differ, but everyone wants their dreams to come true. . . . And America, above all places, gives us the freedom to do that, the freedom to reach out and make our dreams come true."[11] These beliefs made the dwindling self-confidence of Americans during the 1970s and early 1980s all the more distressing for Reagan.

Reagan claimed that his decision to run for the presidency in 1980 was based upon a number of factors. He thought that President Carter desired too much control over the nation's economy, that the Carter administration was weak on national security, and that Carter's lack of strong leadership contributed mightily to America's high inflation, unemployment, and interest rates.[12] Although these were all serious problems, they were of secondary importance when compared to the true crisis confronting the American people. Reagan believed that Carter had started to succeed in persuading Americans that the United States was in a self-inflicted and irrevocable decline.[13] Reagan believed this crisis of confidence was the product not only of the Carter presidency but also of the inept leadership and excessive growth of government about which he had been warning Americans since the early 1960s.

Without a high degree of confidence in themselves, Reagan felt that the American people might find his vision appealing, but ultimately a momentary escape from the actual problems with which they were confronted. Without optimism, they would not be able to see or feel the real hope that he saw and felt. About his mission in 1980 Reagan writes, "We had to recapture our dreams, our pride in ourselves and our country, and regain that unique sense of destiny and optimism that had always made America different from any other country in the world."[14] In order to make his vision appealing and appear as a real possibility for shaping the future, Reagan believed he needed to reorient the imaginations of the American people.

Reagan's efforts to refocus the American imagination consisted of two major components. One was to downplay the gravity of the various problems facing the United States and to dismiss those who dwelled upon such problems as irrelevant and even somewhat irritating. In remarks he gave at Kansas State University, Reagan explained, "I do not dismiss the dangers of big deficits, nuclear conflict, or international terrorism. Each could destroy us if we fail to deal with them decisively. But we can and will prevail if we have the faith and the courage to believe in ourselves and in our ability to perform great deeds, as we have throughout our history."[15] Reagan often told his audiences to ignore people who talked too much or too seriously about these problems. In this same speech he argued, "Let's reject the nonsense that America is doomed to decline, the world sliding toward disaster no matter what we do. Like death and taxes, the doomcriers will always be with us. And they'll always be wrong about America."[16] These people, whom he variously called "doomcriers," "naysayers," "doubting Thomases," and "false prophets of decline," were the real source of America's crisis of confidence.

Reagan was not mean-spirited when making such comments. When he dismissed the "doomcriers," Reagan did so with a mild exasperation and benignity that sprang from his confidence that he knew better than they did. But how could he get the American people to see the golden future that he saw? He needed to do more than politely discredit the arguments of his opponents. He needed to remind the American people of that which he knew to be true about them and their nation. He needed to get them to start dreaming again. This was the second part of his plan to reshape the imaginations of the American people.

In remarks at the 1981 CPAC, Reagan said, "There is, in America, a greatness and a tremendous heritage of idealism which is a reservoir of strength and goodness. It is ours if we will but tap it. And, because of this—because that greatness is there—there is need in America today for a reaffirmation of that goodness and a reformation of our greatness."[17] A few months after his first inauguration, Reagan delivered an Address to a Joint Session of Congress on his economic recovery plan. At the end of his speech, he mentioned that the space shuttle *Columbia* had just successfully completed the first human space flight in six years. He extolled the technological genius of the space shuttle engineers and explained, "The space shuttle did more than prove our technological abilities. It raised our expectations once more. It started us dreaming again."[18] Reagan allowed this dream of returning human beings to space flight to expand into a general meditation upon the character of Americans.

Reagan quoted from Carl Sandburg's poem "Washington Monument by Night" and said, " 'The republic is a dream. Nothing happens unless first a dream.' And that's what makes us, as Americans, different. We've always reached for a new spirit and aimed at a higher goal. . . . all we need to begin with is a dream that we can do better than before. All we need to have is faith, and that dream will come true. All we need to do is act, and the time for action is now."[19] About what should Americans dream? What beliefs and hopes should they expect to come true? In a different speech Reagan argued, "If we can imagine America once again strong and vibrant and alive with jobs for all our people, security for our elderly, wealth enough for our poor, and new opportunities for every new generation, then I believe we, too, can find the strength to make our dreams come true."[20]

At an event commemorating the 250th anniversary of the birth of George Washington, Reagan told the young children listening to his remarks, "You can take us to new frontiers in space, find medical cures for deadly diseases, discover technological breakthroughs, develop better ways to grow food, provide shelter, and produce energy. The world's hope is still America's future. America's future is in your dreams. Make them come true. The only limits are your imagination and your determination."[21] In another speech, he told a different group of American schoolchildren to imagine and hope for an America "without poverty, without unemployment, free of class struggles, and in a world at peace."[22] These comments represent some of the possibilities for the future about which Reagan asked Americans to dream. He told Americans of all ages to expect more than a nation and a world merely improved. He asked them to envision and work toward a transformation of America and the world.

Reagan believed his message of hope succeeded during the first term of his presidency. In a 1983 speech, he drew attention to the recovering U.S. economy and explained, "It's taken time, but I'm proud to tell you that together we've turned around a desperate situation, and we're never going back to the policies of tax, spend, and inflate that brought our country to the edge of disaster."[23] He attributed the economic recovery and other elements of America's rejuvenation to a resurgent spirit of optimism. In his 1984 State of the Union Address, he said, "There is renewed energy and optimism throughout the land. America is back, standing tall, looking to the eighties with courage, confidence, and hope."[24] In accepting the 1984 Republican presidential nomination, Reagan declared, "We can all be proud that pessimism is ended. America is coming back and is more confident than ever about the future."[25] In Reagan's mind, the optimism he promoted and embodied was reviving the American spirit and leading the United States to new heights of progress and glory.

VIEWS ON REAGAN'S OPTIMISM

The importance of optimism to Reagan's popularity among Americans has been recognized by a number of scholars and journalists. In *Morning in America*, Gil Troy argues, "[Reagan's] Hollywood-slick, small-town faith in America as a shining 'city upon a hill' restored many Americans' confidence in themselves and their country."[26] In *Ronald Reagan*, Dinesh D'Souza claims that Reagan's optimism explains much of his political success as a conservative. D'Souza states that unlike Barry Goldwater, Reagan "looked to the past, but only to discover the foundation on which to build the future."[27] In *Reagan's America*, Garry Wills comes to a similar conclusion and writes, "Modern conservatism in America is, for all reasonable purposes, Reaganism. . . . He gave conservatism the elements it had signally lacked—humanity, optimism, hope."[28] In *President Reagan*, Lou Cannon identifies optimism as an enduring source of Reagan's appeal. Cannon writes that when Reagan talked about the dreams and hopes of the American people, "he transcended partisan barriers."[29]

Other writers have reflected on the positive and negative effects of Reagan's brand of optimism upon the United States and its people. As Reagan's presidency came to an end, George Will wrote an article for *Newsweek* in which he explored the ways Reagan had changed America. About Reagan's optimism Will claims, "The cheerfulness that has defined Reagan's era of good feelings has been, on balance, salutary. But it also has been a narcotic, numbing the nation's senses about hazards just over the horizon."[30] In *Reagan Speaks*, Paul Erikson argues that Reagan could have tried to alleviate the despair of the American people in 1980 by reorienting them toward a realistic view of politics. But, Erikson continues, "Reagan sought just the opposite effect . . . as he told his countrymen to believe in even more splendid visions. Rather than force people to face the constraints of life in our world, Reagan stressed their capabilities. And like many good storytellers, he promised that it could all come true if Americans could only find it in their hearts to believe."[31] According to Erikson, Reagan encouraged Americans to depart from an extreme of despair to an extreme of hope. These comments raise the possibility that Reagan's optimistic vision, with its calls to dream and to hope for a better future, may be just as dangerous as the pessimism he was trying to dispel.

Some insights into the potential merits of these reservations about Reagan's type of hopefulness can be obtained by examining briefly his personal reservoir of optimism. If society can be considered as the individual written in larger letters, then identifying problems Reagan himself may have experienced with his type of optimism might suggest potential hazards for other individuals and a society that share that same disposition. In *President Reagan*, Lou Cannon writes that Reagan personally relied so heavily upon his cheerful outlook that when it failed him it had an almost paralyzing effect. In such instances, Cannon writes, "Reagan denied reality and withdrew inside himself, leaving the decisions of his life to others until he could construct a rationalization that enabled him to function."[32] Cannon cites a few incidents to support his claim.

One event to which Cannon draws attention is Reagan's divorce. In 1938, Reagan made a movie called *Brother Rat* with actress Jane Wyman.

The two fell in love during the film's production, and they were married in 1940. They had one child, daughter Maureen, and they adopted a son, Michael. During their marriage, Reagan and Wyman were portrayed by various media outlets as the ideal husband and wife. Their family life was described as representing the high morals of most actors in Hollywood. Cannon explains that shortly after Reagan married Wyman, the Warner Bros. publicity department released a story with the title "THE HOPEFUL REAGANS. They Are Looking Forward to More of Everything Good—Including Children."[33] The optimism and hope expressed in this title accurately capture Reagan's image of the marriage. But the postwar years brought a great strain to bear upon their marriage. While Reagan's acting career plateaued and then went into decline, Wyman's star was on the rise. As her career developed, and as Reagan grew increasingly more interested in politics, the two drifted apart. When Wyman told Reagan that she wanted a divorce in 1948, reality shattered Reagan's cherished image of marriage and family life.

Rather than admit that the divorce was a painful experience that he preferred to keep private, Reagan went to great lengths to erase any memory of it. In his two autobiographies, he devoted less than a combined paragraph to his near-decade-long first marriage. Neither he nor Wyman said much about their marriage publicly after the divorce. In an interview over thirty years after the divorce, the best Reagan could do was explain the event in the passive voice. The divorce happened *to* him.[34] On the one hand, the criterion for holding a balanced view of life is obviously not a willingness to share one's most intimate feelings or painful experiences with millions of faceless readers or television viewers. On the other hand, the difference between a desire for personal privacy and an apparent unwillingness or inability to incorporate painful experiences into one's sense of life should not be overlooked.

The second event Cannon mentions is the Iran-Contra affair. The facts surrounding Iran-Contra are complex, and a detailed explanation of them is not necessary in this study. To be brief, in late 1985, the Reagan administration began selling weapons to Iran. This activity was undertaken in the hopes that the Iranians would use their influence to free American hostages being held in Lebanon by terrorist organizations. Such actions violated the arms-embargo against Iran and stood clearly at odds with Reagan's publicly stated and categorical refusal ever to negotiate with terrorists. When the situation became public in the fall of 1986, Reagan categorically denied that he had engaged in any exchange of arms for hostages.[35] Then, in a nationally televised address on March 4, 1987, Reagan explained, "A few months ago I told the American people I did not trade arms for hostages. *My heart and my best intentions still tell me that's true, but the facts and the evidence tell me it is not.*"[36] Cannon writes, "[Reagan] persuaded himself in defiance of all the facts and his own diary entries that he had never traded arms for hostages."[37] He could persuade himself that he had done nothing wrong because his *heart* and his *best intentions* told him he was blameless. Reagan's hopes of freeing American hostages obscured the reality that his actions were undermining the Constitution and encouraging terrorists to take more American hostages. When reality finally came crashing in, Reagan's optimism could not sustain him.

Reagan's responses to these events shed much light upon the nature of the imagination in general, and upon Reagan's imagination in particular. Fundamental reorientations of one's long-standing vision of how the world holds together are not common. Events intuited as destructive of one's cherished sense of life are often explained away, passed over in silence, or simply denied. If they happen to be incorporated into an individual's imagination, it is usually only after great and prolonged effort. In these two instances at least, Reagan chose denial. He could not reconcile the reality of divorce with the idealized notion of his marriage he and the public held at the time. Neither could he reconcile his actions and inactions during the Iran-Contra scandal with his vision of himself as a good president and man always intent upon doing what was right as well as what was best for the United States and its people.

CONCLUSION

Optimism is not a bad thing in life or in politics. When it is grounded in a relatively accurate perception of the world, hope can have a truly salutary effect upon an individual and his outlook on life. In politics, a well-tempered sense of optimism can be a great asset for an individual leader and for the people as a whole. On the other hand, when hope and optimism are based on and inform a vision loosely connected to reality, then they may actually set individuals up for disappointment and blind them to looming dangers. People possessing this type of optimism often have little interest in or even ability to account for the inevitable disappointments life brings. When disillusionment comes, such people tend either to remain in a state of despair or to deny the very occurrence of the unpleasant events, excising them from their memories. This type of hopeful vision often experiences titanic swings between despair and joy.

Reagan's optimism seems to have buoyed the spirits of the American people, giving them hope when they were in the midst of a serious crisis of confidence. Nevertheless, if Reagan's type of optimism is based upon a faulty or incomplete understanding of life and its possibilities, then it may turn out in the longer term to be destructive of the very order Reagan sought to protect and regenerate. Such possibilities cannot be contemplated fully or fairly without developing deeper understandings of the other elements of Reagan's imagination.

4 "I Hear America Singing"[1]
Ronald Reagan and the American People

> May all of you as Americans never forget your heroic origins, never fail to seek Divine guidance, and never lose your natural, God-given optimism.[2]
>
> —Ronald Reagan

In his speech on behalf of Barry Goldwater, Reagan said, "This is the issue of this election. Whether we believe in our capacity for self-government or whether we abandon the American Revolution and confess that a little intellectual elite in a far-distant capital can plan our lives for us better than we can plan them ourselves."[3] This issue was still on his mind during the 1980s. It was still a time for choosing in America. Reagan's faith in the American people led him to believe that the problems confronting the United States were temporary. He knew, after all, that Americans were good and moral beings. Reagan was convinced that once they were made aware of the dangers ahead, they would garner their strength, use their common sense, and act to restore their nation and their freedom. As president, Reagan articulated his vision of the American people with vivid and enthralling imagery. Exploring this part of his mind will shed light upon his understanding of the human condition, and it will further clarify his broader sense of America and the world.

REAGAN'S INTUITIVE VISION OF THE AMERICAN PEOPLE

During his First Inaugural Address, Reagan argued that in previous years many people had talked of various special interest groups in the United States. He let it be known that he represented a forgotten special interest group—the American people. Who were the American people, in his view? They were not politicians, bureaucrats, or lobbyists. Rather, the real American people were the "men and women who raise our food, patrol our streets, man our mines and factories, teach our children, keep our homes, and heal us when we're sick—professionals, industrialists, shopkeepers, clerks, cabbies, and truck drivers."[4] In Reagan's mind, the people belonging to these seemingly ordinary professions had a number of things in common. First, they were all heroes.

According to Reagan, the tradition of American heroism extends all the way back to the Founding of the United States. In various speeches, he argued that the American Revolution began when a group of average Americans, including lawyers, farmers, and businessmen, declared their independence from England. In an address at the University of Notre Dame, Reagan explained about the heroes who signed the Declaration of Independence: "They pledged their lives, their fortunes, and their sacred honor. Sixteen of them gave their lives. Most gave their fortunes. All preserved their sacred honor."[5] Reagan believed that the virtue and heroism of the Founders, their selflessness and sacrifice in defense of liberty and self-government, was alive and well in America. In February of 1986, he explained:

> The truth is, uncommon valor is often a common virtue in this country of ours. America's the land of the free *because* she is the home of the brave. These United States are built on heroism and sustained and protected by it. We see it in the bravery of those defending our nation on the frontiers of freedom; the pilot landing high-performance fighter planes on the heaving deck of an aircraft carrier; the soldier on patrol on the Korean border, in Europe, or on a peacekeeping mission in the Middle East.[6]

The heroism of the American military was matched by that of local law enforcement, firefighters, doctors, nurses, and social workers. Each vocation was simply a different means to express this general American characteristic. All Americans were heroes, actual or potential. All they need to do was believe in themselves and in their capacity for heroic actions.

Reagan held that Americans express their natural heroism in other ways, and he gave special attention to the heroic undertakings of American entrepreneurs, including businessmen, farmers, and technological pioneers. In a 1982 speech, he explained, "I think entrepreneurs are the forgotten heroes of America. Most of them contribute far more to this country than they get back, and they rarely receive the recognition they deserve."[7] Two years later, he told an audience in Georgia: "It's people like you who show us the heart of America is good, the spirit of America is strong, and the future of America is great. You give meaning to words like entrepreneur, self-reliance, personal initiative and, yes, optimism and confidence. And you will lead America to take freedom's next step."[8] To Reagan, entrepreneurialism meant industriousness, self-sacrifice, and self-reliance. These characteristics drove America to declare independence and to settle the West, and they would lead America into a glorious future. All that the government needed to do was get out of the way of these American heroes.

According to Reagan, another characteristic of the American people was that they are free. At the centennial celebration of the Statue of Liberty, he explained, "Call it mysticism if you will, I have always believed there was some divine providence that placed this great land here between the two great oceans, to be found by a special kind of people from every corner of the world, who had a special love for freedom."[9] In his First Inaugural Address, Reagan argued, "Freedom and the dignity of the individual have been more available and assured here than in any other place on Earth," and, "We are a nation under God, and I believe God intended for us to be free."[10] Reagan also found American historical precedents for his views. In his 1983 remarks to the National Association of Evangelicals, Reagan approvingly quoted Thomas Jefferson as once writing, "The God who gave us life, gave us liberty at the same time."[11] Americans were free because they had been given the divine gift of liberty.

For Reagan, the freedom of the American people was closely linked to their religiosity. In his speeches Reagan often referred to the historical origins of the earliest North American colonies and to the experiences and thoughts of the Founders as evidence that religious liberty was as important to Americans as civil liberty. In a speech given during a prayer breakfast, he said, "The truth is, politics and morality are inseparable. And as morality's foundation is religion, religion and politics are necessarily related. We need religion as a guide. We need it because we are imperfect, and our government needs the church, because only those humble enough to admit they're sinners can bring to democracy the tolerance it requires in order to survive."[12] Only by acknowledging Providence could the American people hope to invigorate their civil freedom with new life and to impart that robust liberty to others.

In Reagan's imagination, Americans were also naturally patriotic. In his Farewell Address to the Nation, he claimed that he was especially proud of the "resurgence of national pride that I called the new patriotism" that occurred during his presidency.[13] Reagan considered the increase in military morale one of the many examples of the rebirth of pride in America. In remarks to basic training graduates of the Marine Corps, he explained, "Each day of my Presidency I work to keep our nation strong and secure so that we may always remain free and at peace. And each day you follow one of the most difficult but noble callings: the calling of freedom fighters and peacemakers. . . . The news about our country today is good, and it's getting better. Pride is back. Patriotism is fashionable once again."[14]

Reagan felt that the resurgence of American patriotism was rather vividly displayed during the 1984 Olympic Games in Los Angeles. During his 1984 Republican presidential nomination acceptance speech, he expressed his awe and admiration for the way in which the Olympic torch traveled to its final destination. He said:

> In Richardson, Texas, [the torch] was carried by a 14-year-old boy in a special wheelchair. In West Virginia the runner came across a line of deaf children and let each one pass the torch for a few feet, and at the end

these youngsters' hands talked excitedly in their sign language. Crowds spontaneously began singing "America the Beautiful" or "The Battle Hymn of the Republic."

And then, in San Francisco a Vietnamese immigrant, his little son held on his shoulders, dodged photographers and policemen to cheer a 19-year-old black man pushing an 88-year-old white woman in a wheel-chair as she carried the torch.

My friends, that's America.[15]

These citizens, despite different ethnicities, races, genders, ages, and degrees of physical well-being, were all united in their patriotic love of America.[16]

Reagan also imagined the American people as naturally good. Among other things, this meant they were inclined to act upon their good impulses to help and care for others. At the 1981 Annual Meeting of the National Alliance of Business, he explained, "Over our history, Americans have always extended their hands in gestures of assistance. They helped build a neighbor's barn when it burned down, and then formed a volunteer fire department so it wouldn't burn down again. They harvested the next fel-low's crop when he was injured or ill, and they raised school funds at quilt-ing bees and church socials. They took for granted that neighbor would care for neighbor."[17] For Reagan, this spirit was still alive.

Reagan believed that his sense of the American people as naturally good and compassionate would be met with incredulity by various elites. He explained:

> Now, I know there are cynics who dismiss the notion of Americans help-ing other Americans. They say that I speak of an America that never was and never can be. They believe voluntarism is a mushy idea, the product of mushy thinking. They say that our society today is too complex or that we're trying to repeal the 20th century.
>
> Well, the cynics who say these things have been so busy increasing Washington's power that they've lost sight of America.[18]

Reagan knew he was right and the cynics were wrong about the Ameri-can people.[19] Getting intrusive government out of the way of the American people so they could be their true selves was a primary goal of Reagan's presidency.

Reagan also held that the American people were more trustworthy than most of their representatives in government believed them to be. He felt Americans were imbued with enough common sense to see the obvious solutions to America's problems. In his speeches and personal letters, he liked to quote Thomas Jefferson as once claiming, "The people will not make a mistake—*if* they have *all* the facts."[20] Hence he believed that once he explained the importance of a particular program or policy initiative, the American people would act to make real the possibilities held before their eyes. Reagan's belief in the trustworthiness and common sense of the American people can be observed in his televised address to the nation on the American economy in February of 1981.

Reagan began by explaining that he recently received a detailed, technical report on the state of the American economy. He told his viewers that he would not "subject [them] to the jumble of charts, figures, and economic jargon of that audit, but rather will try to explain where we are, how we got there, and how we can get back."[21] He then conveyed the seriousness of the dangers facing the American economy, especially the danger of inflation, through the effective use of a visual aide. He said, "Here is a dollar such as you earned, spent, or saved in 1960. And here is a quarter, a dime, and a penny—36 cents. That's what this 1960 dollar is worth today."[22] No one watching that speech needed an advanced degree in economics to understand that inflation was robbing the American people of their money, hopes, and dreams. Reagan concluded the speech by telling the American people that there was a solution to these problems. He explained, "All it takes is a little common sense and recognition of our own ability. Together we can forge a new beginning for America."[23] He often made this type of appeal to the common sense of Americans when articulating his policy goals and political ideas.

Reagan also saw in the American people a reverence for the experiences, ideas, and values of the American past and optimism about the future. He thought the American people possessed both conservative and progressive inclinations. He felt the American people shared his personal reverence for the American Founders, the Declaration of Independence, and the U.S. Constitution. He also believed they supported traditional moral values. In a 1985 speech, he claimed, "Perhaps the greatest triumph of modern conservatism has been to stop allowing the left to put the average American on the moral defensive."[24] In Reagan's mind, Americans opposed to and disturbed by the perceived secular and amoral drift of American popular culture had a voice in Washington, DC, and access to political power as long as he was president. He imagined that part of being an American meant embracing the political and moral ideas and practices of the past and working toward their reconstitution in the present.

Reagan also believed Americans were naturally optimistic. Like him, Americans thought that, somehow, their lives would always be better tomorrow than today. Part of this belief was connected to his hope that the American people's love of the ideas and values from the American past would generate a rebirth of the American spirit in the future. Another part of this feeling was tied to the awe he shared with Americans of the technological accomplishments of the twentieth century. His speeches were replete with expressions of pride in achievements in areas such as human space exploration, medicine, and agriculture. A number of his speeches give the impression that technological progress will inevitably generate qualitative improvements in other important areas of life. Much more will be said about Reagan's understanding of conservatism and technology, and of the past, present, and future. At this point, these comments on conservatism and technological progress are sufficient to impart an even more complete sense of how Reagan imagined the American people.

REAGAN'S VISION OF AMERICANS AND HUMAN NATURE IN HISTORICAL AND THEORETICAL CONTEXTS

With this part of Reagan's vision in mind, it is now possible to provide some preliminary insights into his understanding of the human condition. This can be accomplished by placing his notions of Americans as naturally good, reasonable, and free within a wider historical and philosophical context. This will necessitate an exploration of relevant ideas associated with certain historical figures he was often inclined to invoke publicly, such as Thomas Jefferson. It will also require an explanation and analysis of ideas expressed by figures, such as John Locke and Jean-Jacques Rousseau, with whom Reagan may have had only a passing familiarity or even none at all. Often, exploring contrasting ideas can elucidate complex concepts and intuitive images. In other words, one can come to understand something in part by discovering its opposite. Thus, a clearer understanding of Reagan's sense of human nature can be gained by comparing it with notions held by thinkers who were known by Reagan to varying degrees, including John Adams, Publius, and Edmund Burke.

A few words are needed about the spirit in which this historical and philosophical endeavor to illuminate the underlying quality of Reagan's imagination is being undertaken. Reagan's consciousness of and affinity for ideas and figures from the American and Western past varies. The influence upon his mind of certain ideas from Jefferson is more readily apparent than are those from Burke or Rousseau. It is possible that Reagan misunderstood the ideas of many of the figures he invokes in his speeches. Offering exhaustive accounts of the thoughts of various politicians and philosophers, or clarifying completely the degree to which Reagan accurately invoked various historical figures and ideas in his speeches, is beyond the scope of this study. Further, this type of analysis should not be interpreted as a covert attempt to assail or celebrate Reagan by associating him with certain philosophical and political bogeys or icons. A wide array of historical figures and ideas will be invoked and discussed in this work only insofar as they shed greater light upon Reagan's vision than can be had by examining his speeches alone.

One of the most important historical American figures in Reagan's imagination is Thomas Jefferson. Reagan invoked Jefferson often on many topics including the American Revolution, liberty, religion, education, and the relationship between U.S. states and the national government. Jefferson's political thought also shaped to a high degree the way in which Reagan imagined the American people.

Jefferson believed that the American people were defined to a great extent by their status as free people. He held that Americans had a natural right to liberty and possessed liberty to a higher degree than any people in history. In his mind, their liberty was not only a right but also a divine gift. In *A Summary View of the Rights of British America*, he argues, "The god who gave us life, gave us liberty at the same time: the hand of force may destroy, but cannot disjoin them."[25] The Declaration of Independence, written largely, though not exclusively, by Jefferson, claims that "all men are created equal" and that they "are endowed by their Creator with certain inalienable rights; that among these are life, liberty, and the pursuit of happiness."[26] These are phrases repeatedly invoked by Reagan during his presidency. The main purpose of government, in Jefferson's political theory, is to secure these natural, god-given rights for its citizens.

Jefferson also understood the American people to be reasonable as well as naturally good. This was based on his belief that all human beings possess a "moral sense, or conscience," that is "as much a part of man as his leg or arm."[27] He held that while the intellect plays a role in the cultivation of this moral sense, the conscience functions best when its contact with reason is kept to a minimum. In a letter Jefferson explained, "Morals were too essential to the happiness of man to be risked on the incertain [sic] combinations of the head. [Nature] laid their foundation therefore in sentiment, not in science."[28] In another letter, he provided an example of how reason often inhibits the moral sense. He wrote, "State a moral case to a ploughman and a professor. The former will decide it as well, and often better than the latter, because he has not been led astray by artificial rules."[29] In Jefferson's mind, an excessive emphasis upon formal rules of morality ultimately impedes the function of the moral sense, thereby making the people more susceptible to moral corruption. When forced to choose, Jefferson sided with the common sense of the "ploughman" rather than the ideas of the "professor."

Jefferson also imagined the American people to be industrious and independent. In his heart, he held a special place for the American farmer. In a letter to John Jay, he explained, "Cultivators of the earth are the most valuable citizens. They are the most vigorous, the most independant [sic], the most virtuous, and they are tied to their country and wedded to it's [sic] liberty and interests by the most lasting bands."[30] In *Notes on the State of Virginia*, Jefferson argues, "Those who labour in the earth are the chosen people of God, if ever he had a chosen people, whose breasts he has made his peculiar deposit of substantial and genuine virtue. . . . Corruption of morals in the mass of cultivators is a phenomenon of which no age nor nation has furnished an example."[31] Jefferson preferred agriculture to manufacturing because farmers were independent whereas manufacturers were dependent upon the acts of others for their subsistence. Farmers were self-reliant; manufactures *need* consumers.[32] For Jefferson, farmers were also praiseworthy because the virtues imparted by their vocation were vital to the existence of free government. Farmers were Jefferson's American heroes.

Whether or not he was completely aware of the similarities, Reagan shares with Locke a number of thoughts about human nature. Like Reagan, Locke places a strong emphasis upon human freedom, equality, rationality, and natural rights. In the *Second Treatise*, Locke argues that in their natural state, human beings are completely free and equal. In the state of nature, they are totally free to act upon their desires because there is no government or common authority to restrain them. Human beings are also rational creatures. This is an extremely important point for Locke. He writes, "The *state of nature* has a law of nature to govern it, which obliges every one: and reason, which is that law, teaches all mankind, who will but consult it, that being all *equal and independent*, no one ought to harm another in his life, health, property, or possessions."[33] Locke's state of nature is a much more peaceful and tranquil place than, for example, the one imagined by Thomas Hobbes in *Leviathan.* Locke maintains that it is only because of relatively minor inconveniences that human beings leave this state, form a political community, and establish a civil government limited to protecting each citizen's natural rights.

Locke's ideas about labor and property remain highly influential in Western and American political thought and are worth considering. He claims that the world was given equally to all, but that it was never meant to remain in this state. Locke explains:

> God gave the world to men in common; but since he gave it them for their benefit, and the greatest conveniences of life they were capable to draw from it, it cannot be supposed he meant it should always remain common and uncultivated. He gave it to the use of the industrious and rational (and *labour* was to be *his title* to it;) not to the fancy or covetousness of the quarrelsome and contentious.[34]

In the state of nature, human beings acquire property by mixing their labor with the uncultivated world. Without human labor, the world is little more than a wasteland.[35]

Locke places great importance upon the industrious individual. He celebrates the "doer," the person who makes things that enhance the comfort and material well-being of himself and others. The producer, it may be argued, is Locke's economic hero. Locke seems to be more skeptical of the social contributions made by those who inherit, rather than create, wealth and by the educated, the artists, the clergy, and other elites who produce less tangible goods. Reagan also seems to hold many of these assumptions about the value of labor, the social importance of the merchant and producer, and the potential dangers to society posed by those who do not embrace and embody these ideas.

It will be helpful to reflect for a moment upon Locke's use of the word "reason." For Locke, reason does not have the same meaning as the *nous* of Plato and Aristotle or the *ratio* of Thomas Aquinas. For these older thinkers, reason is primarily the faculty through which human beings participate in the search for the universal or the divine. In this older view, the right functioning of reason depends greatly upon individual moral and spiritual maturity. Individuals lacking in ethical self-restraint are not capable of using this type of reason to the same extent as those who possess moral self-discipline. The ethical and spiritual disorder in the lives of the former can be attributed, in part, to a lack of interest in or even a fear of responding to the divine pull felt by reason. These older thinkers acknowledge that this type of disordered individual can obtain some degree of pleasure during life. Nevertheless, as a result of the closure toward reason, such pleasure is superficial and of limited duration. True and lasting happiness, what the ancient Greeks call *eudemonia* and the Christians describe as "the peace that passeth all understanding," is not within reach for the disordered, immodest, and licentious. The lives of such people are incomplete.

In contrast, Locke articulates a more modern understanding of reason in which it is viewed as a practical, even utilitarian, faculty. In Locke's view, reason is not the organ through which human beings search for God, or for the Good, the True, and the Beautiful. Rather, it is that which enables human beings to learn *useful* facts about the world. Its functioning is not conditioned by an individual's ethical wisdom or spiritual development. Discerning the law of nature is open equally to all by the mere fact that they exist and possess this type of reason. When analyzed within the context of his understanding of property, Locke's reason is also similar to the Greek conception of *techne* insofar as it is the means individuals have to think about doing, making, and building things that increase their material comfort, thereby improving certain aspects of their lives. This Lockean notion of reason appears to have been embraced to a greater extent by Jefferson than by Reagan, but both Americans seem to incorporate something similar to it into their understandings of human beings.

Other aspects of Reagan's understanding of the American people and the human condition can be illuminated with reference to Rousseau. In some respects, Rousseau's political theory is similar to those of Hobbes and Locke. Like Locke and Hobbes, Rousseau posits an imaginary state of nature from which he draws conclusions about the human condition. All three of these modern theorists searched for the essence of human nature, not by contemplating an ideal human type, as did the ancient Greeks and early Christians, but by analyzing human beings in their most elemental or primitive state. In the state of nature, Hobbes discovers a violent, calculating individual afraid of violent death. Locke finds the human type described earlier. In contrast to Locke and Hobbes, Rousseau finds human beings who are isolated, peaceful, equal, and free. In his state of nature, Rousseau discovers human beings who are completely good by nature.

Rousseau expresses his thoughts on the natural goodness of human beings in a number of his writings. In *Emile* he declares, "Let us set down as an incontestable maxim that the first movements of nature are always right.

There is no original perversity in the human heart."[36] He also provides a number of vivid descriptions of the lives of these naturally good creatures in the state of nature. In the *Second Discourse*, he explains, "Nothing is so gentle as man in his primitive state," and "savage man breathes only tranquillity [sic] and liberty; he wants simply to live and rest easy."[37] These gentle, noble savages were truly happy because their lives were regulated only by the instinct of self-preservation tempered by the ability to feel pity or compassion for other creatures.

Pity is one of the most important concepts in Rousseau's philosophy. He considered it to be the only genuine natural virtue of human beings. He argues, "Pity is what carries us without reflection to the aid of those we see suffering. Pity is what, in the state of nature, takes the place of laws, mores, and virtue, with the advantage that no one is tempted to disobey its sweet voice."[38] In the *First Discourse*, Rousseau offers a broader insight into his understanding of how human beings come to know virtue. He writes:

> O virtue! Sublime science of simple souls, are there so many difficulties and so much preparation necessary in order to know you? Are your principles not engraved in all hearts, and is it not enough, in order to learn your laws, to commune with oneself and, in the silence of the passions, to listen to the voice of one's conscience?[39]

These notions led Rousseau to claim: "Man did not begin by reasoning but by feeling."[40]

A corollary of Rousseau's understanding of pity and virtue is his low regard for reason. He states, "If nature has destined us to be healthy, I almost dare to affirm that the state of reflection is a state contrary to nature and that the man who meditates is a depraved animal," and "Reason is what engenders egocentrism, and reflection strengthens it. Reason is what turns man in upon himself."[41] As these thoughts on pity, virtue, and reason suggest, Rousseau associates human moral behavior with an unreflective response to the spontaneous, sentimental impulses of the heart. Reason, he believes, actively works against each person's ability to feel pity and know virtue. It corrupts human beings, alienating them from their natural state, and it leads them down a path at the end of which they are miserable. Reason is the enemy of human happiness.

In various works, Irving Babbitt contrasts his belief in the ethical duality of the human condition, which he draws in large part from ancient Greek and Roman as well as older Christian sources, with prevalent modern notions. He believes many Enlightenment rationalists and sentimental romantics rejected the views of human nature held by the ancients and Christians, proclaiming instead various notions of human natural goodness. Babbitt argues that such claims shape the ways in which many modern political theorists conceptualize liberty. In *Democracy and Leadership*, he writes that as modern ideas about human goodness have become accepted, "Liberty has come more and more to be conceived expansively, not as a process of concentration, as a submission or adjustment to a higher will."[42] He identifies these expansive notions of human natural goodness and liberty in the political thoughts of both Locke and Rousseau.

For Rousseau and Locke, liberty is natural and makes few if any ethical demands on human beings. It is neither earned nor conferred upon individuals by other human beings. Whether they attribute it to the presence or functioning of reason or pity, these thinkers also assert variations of human natural goodness. Each theorist implies that natural goodness prevents individuals from abusing liberty on all but the rarest of circumstances. Thus, few if any restrictions need to be placed upon individuals and liberty. It seems as if Locke and Rousseau each imagine the human condition as more or less devoid of any inherent or chronic moral problems. Babbitt believes that each of these thinkers creates serious theoretical and practical problems for politics because they ignore the reality of the lower will. Their ideas might actually create more favorable conditions for the emergence of the lower will than would otherwise be the case precisely because these thinkers downplay or deny the existence of the lower will. This is also a possibility for those who promote similar ideas about human nature and liberty.

A deeper insight into Reagan's understanding of the American people and human nature can be reached by comparing his vision to what appear to be contrasting ideas held by leading American thinkers such as John Adams and Publius and by other important and like-minded figures such as Edmund Burke. Beyond clarifying further this part of Reagan's intuition, introducing some of the ideas of these historical figures will be especially helpful to this study insofar as they are all commonly associated with conservatism, a tradition of political thought Reagan claimed to embody and carry forward.

AN ALTERNATIVE VIEW OF AMERICANS AND HUMAN NATURE

The belief that America and its people were presented a unique, even providential, opportunity to constitute a republic of order and liberty was widespread during the Founding. Even John Adams, who was a much more conservative thinker than his long-time friend Thomas Jefferson, held such views. And yet, Adams's hopes for success in America's political undertaking were tempered by an understanding of human nature that is very different from Jefferson's. Adams did not believe that human beings are naturally good.

In *Discourses on Davila*, Adams argues that history demonstrates that "bad men increase in knowledge as fast as good men; and science, arts, taste, sense, and letters, are employed for the purposes of injustice and tyranny, as well as those of law and liberty; for corruption, as well as for virtue."[43] Thus, an individual's profession or education neither imparted nor indicated the existence of virtue. Adams also believed that human beings of all vocations often choose to abuse their liberty. In a letter to John Taylor of Caroline, Virginia, he wrote that if liberty "can distinguish between moral good and moral evil, and has the power to choose the former and refuse the latter; it can, if it will, choose the evil and reject the good, as we see in experience it very often does."[44] Thus, Adams did not consider liberty to be an unqualified good, leading inexorably to the moral life, only needing protection from government interference in order to thrive. On the contrary, in his mind one of the primary functions of government is to restrain the effects upon society of freely and consciously chosen abuses of freedom.

A similar view of the human condition is expressed repeatedly in *The Federalist*. Like Adams, Publius—the pseudonym under which Alexander Hamilton, John Jay, and James Madison wrote all eighty-five papers—expresses his wonder at the confluence of events that enabled Americans to build an independent republic. But Publius is also deeply aware of the difficulties human nature presents to maintaining a free government and a responsible society. In "Federalist No. 6," he describes human beings as "ambitious, vindictive, and rapacious." In the well-known "Federalist No. 10," he argues, "The latent causes of faction are thus sown into the nature of man," and "So strong is this propensity of mankind, to fall into mutual animosities, that where no substantial occasion presents itself, the most frivolous and fanciful distinctions have been sufficient to kindle their unfriendly passions, and excite their most violent conflicts."[45] These views of the human condition do not mean that Publius, or for that matter, Adams, think human beings are naturally evil or incapable of practicing responsible liberty. In "Federalist No. 55," Publius explains:

> As there is a degree of depravity in mankind, which requires a certain degree of circumspection and distrust: so there are other qualities in human nature, which justify a certain portion of esteem and confidence. Republican government presupposes the existence of these qualities in a higher degree than any other form.[46]

Both Publius and Adams have a stronger awareness of the lower inclinations of human nature than Jefferson, Locke, and Rousseau. Adams and Publius see human liberty as a moral problem, insofar as it can be abused, as much as they see it as a means to realizing the good life. They do not understand freedom as a guarantor of individual virtue or as an unqualified social and political good. On their views, human beings are capable of achieving a high degree of moral order, but only after having made protracted efforts to restrain their lower impulses. Such efforts, they maintain, need to be made both by the individual and society. As John Adams writes, "We must not then depend alone upon the love of liberty in the soul of man for its preservation. Some political institutions must be prepared, to assist this love against its enemies."[47] Both Adams and Publius can be considered proponents, not of natural human goodness, but of human ethical dualism. They represent a vision of human nature more widespread than Jefferson's during the Founding.

These notions about human nature are similar in many respects to ideas held by Edmund Burke. Much of Burke's most important political thought took place within the context of his efforts to understand and critique the French Revolution. Among other things, Burke was apprehensive about the open disregard with which many French revolutionaries held the organically developed social, religious, and political structures that gave France its identity. The Jacobins in particular were not interested in prudential political and social reforms in France consistent with French traditions and history. They celebrated abstract notions of reason, liberty, democracy, and equality, and they invested their ahistorical ideology with normative authority for France and the world. Burke was deeply concerned about the ultimate consequences of the Jacobins' desires to abolish the existing regime, to wipe the slate of France clean, as it were, and to replace it with one built upon their untested vision for politics.

Some insight into Burke's understanding of the human condition can be gained by looking at his thoughts on liberty and his critique of the use of this term by French revolutionaries. Many of the Jacobins lavished praise upon liberty in the abstract, asserting, in the spirit of Rousseau, that liberty is a natural right and an unqualified good for individuals and society. About the inadequacies of such a vision, Burke writes, "Is it because liberty in the abstract may be classed amongst the blessings of mankind, that I am seriously to felicitate a madman, who has escaped from the protecting restraint and wholesome darkness of his cell, on his restoration to the enjoyment of light and liberty? Am I to congratulate a highwayman and murderer who has broke prison upon the recovery of his natural rights?"[48] For Burke, the Jacobin vision of liberty is both naïve and dangerous because it ignores the human tendency to use freedom for immoral purposes. Jacobin notions of freedom actually widen the field for immoral activity.

That Burke rejects the Jacobin notion of liberty does not mean that he discards the concept altogether, or that he believes human beings are incapable of using freedom responsibly. On the contrary, he is acutely aware of the fact that individuals are capable of using liberty to advance civilization through great accomplishments in politics, religion, the arts, and other areas. Unlike the Jacobins, Burke believes that freedom and restraint are intimately related concepts. He argues:

> Men are qualified for civil liberty, in exact proportion to their disposition to put moral chains upon their own appetites. . . . Society cannot exist unless a controlling power upon will and appetite be placed somewhere, and the less of it there is within, the more there must be without. It is ordained in the eternal constitution of things, that men of intemperate minds cannot be free. Their passions forge their fetters.[49]

Learning the habits of responsible liberty is difficult even under the best of circumstances. On Burke's view, if individuals are either unable or unwilling

to restrain their passions, then the liberty of such people needs to be regulated by forces outside of themselves, including government. Such ideas
about human nature and liberty indicate that Burke, like Adams and Publius, is a type of ethical dualist.

The term "ethical dualism" has been used to describe a particular way of
understanding human nature. A few words specifically about this concept
are necessary. In *Democracy and the Ethical Life*, Claes G. Ryn describes
human ethical dualism and the relationship between this concept and constitutional government. He argues, "The human self, then, is a unity of two
opposing wills, one of which tends to predominate."[50] As Ryn describes
it, the lower will is that which draws human beings into "disharmony and
destructivity."[51] Conversely, the higher will "refers to that in our being which
pulls us in the direction of our own true humanity, that is, towards the realization of our highest potential as defined by a universally valid standard."[52]
He also describes the higher will as the ethical conscience. According to Ryn,
all individuals have both these elements. He criticizes monistic visions of the
human condition that proclaim natural human goodness, as in the case of
Rousseau, or total human depravity, as in the case of Hobbes.

In Ryn's view, the ethical life is not a permanent achievement to be gained
at a particular point in time. Rather, it is the perpetual striving of each
person to restrain the lower will while responding to the demands of the
ethical conscience. Ryn argues that this makes the moral life a protracted,
often painful, exercise in self-discipline. It requires each person to scrutinize
every stirring of the will and to restrain each incipient immoral desire. In
describing the duality of the human will in this manner, Ryn consciously
draws inspiration from Babbitt and the older Western tradition of political
and religious thought. These thoughts from Ryn provide philosophical support to the intuitive visions of human nature expressed by Burke, Adams,
and Publius.

CONCLUSION

It appears as if Reagan was inclined to imagine the human condition in
ways that are similar to Jefferson, Locke, and Rousseau. Like these political theorists and figures, Reagan celebrated the natural goodness of human
beings. He envisioned both human nature and liberty in ways that seem to
downplay or ignore the darker, grimmer aspects of life. The human ethical
dualism articulated by Adams, Publius, Burke, and Ryn is mostly absent
from the predominant strain of Reagan's imagination. The concerns raised
by these theorists about liberty freed from restraints are also difficult to find
in Reagan's vision.

5 "The Mystic Chords of Memory"[1]
Ronald Reagan and the American Revolution

Our Revolution was won by and for all who cherish the timeless and universal rights of man. This battle was a vindication of ideas that had been forming for centuries in the Western mind.[2]

—Ronald Reagan

In the late winter of 1982, Reagan addressed a joint session of the Alabama State legislature. During his remarks, he told a brief anecdote about Massachusetts' Senator Edward Kennedy. In a birthday celebration for former New York governor Averell Harriman, who was in his nineties at the time, Kennedy quipped that Harriman was only half as old as Reagan's ideas. Reagan took these remarks as a compliment. He said, "And you know, he's absolutely right. The United States Constitution is almost 200 years old, and that's where I'm proud to get my ideas."[3] Perhaps more than any American president in the twentieth century, Reagan located his vision of politics in the era he referred to as the American Founding or the American Revolution.

Reagan's strong attachment to this era is well known. In *The Essential Ronald Reagan*, Lee Edwards explains that research shows Reagan talked more about the Founding Fathers than any president "in living memory." He writes, "Indeed, Reagan mentioned the 'Framers' or the 'Founding Fathers' more often than all of his nine predecessors combined. His favorite founders were Thomas Jefferson and Thomas Paine."[4] In *God and Ronald Reagan*, Paul Kengor stresses the importance of this period to Reagan. He argues, "There was no group of historical individuals that Reagan held in higher esteem than the Founders, and as president he celebrated their wisdom often. He admired the Declaration of Independence, whose language he had borrowed throughout his public life, and put great stock in the ideals of government the Founders had instilled in the Constitution."[5] Despite the widespread acknowledgement of the importance of these people and documents to Reagan, scholars have drawn rather different conclusions about the light this sheds upon his political ideas and vision.

In *Ronald Reagan: How an Ordinary Man Became an Extraordinary Leader*, Dinesh D'Souza provides a common interpretation when he argues that Reagan's invocations of people and ideas from the American past are indicative of Reagan's political conservatism. He writes, "[Reagan] was forward-looking and optimistic and liked to quote the Revolutionary War pamphleteer Tom Paine, 'We have it in our power to begin the world over again.' Unlike Goldwater, Reagan was a populist whose conservatism was based on widely shared American values and was not afraid to place its trust in the good sense of the American people."[6] John Patrick Diggins identifies Reagan's inclination to quote from figures such as Jefferson and Paine as evidence of a type of radicalism in the fortieth president's political thought, rather than conservatism. In *Ronald Reagan: Fate, Freedom, and the Making of History*, Diggins argues, "Conservative literary intellectuals and legal scholars, following Edmund Burke, believed in history, precedent, and order; Reagan, following Paine, believed in hope, experiment, and freedom."[7]

These interpretations of Reagan are not without merits, but they are incomplete and, in important respects, flawed. Diggins and D'Souza in particular seem to base their political categorizations of Reagan's vision on cursory assumptions and the use of vague terminology. A deeper exploration of Reagan's vision of the Founding will impart greater clarity about his sense of the American past. It will also begin to address directly concerns about the relationship between Reagan and conservatism. Reagan's repeated invocations of the documents, events, and figures associated with the Founding notwithstanding, it seems as if his vision has a more complex relationship with the American past than he and other writers have realized.

REAGAN'S VISION OF THE FOUNDING
AND THE AMERICAN REVOLUTION

In Reagan's mind, the terms "American Founding" and "American Revolution" are more or less synonymous. He used them generally to describe the period of American history between 1776 and 1791, or the time from the drafting of the Declaration of Independence through the adoption of the Bill of Rights. Whichever term he used, it symbolized a watershed moment in human history. At Notre Dame in 1981, Reagan said the following about the legacy of the Founders: "They gave us more than a nation. They brought to all mankind for the first time the concept that man was born free, that each of us has inalienable rights, ours by the grace of God, and that government was created by us for our convenience, having only the powers that we choose to give it."[8] In a speech commemorating the American victory at Yorktown, he explained, "There have been revolutions before and since ours, revolutions that simply exchanged one set of rulers for another. Ours was a philosophical revolution that changed the very concept of government."[9] He gave the American Founding and Revolution this unique status because it is the period in which humanity first discovered and applied the universal principles of politics—that is, liberty and democracy. For Reagan, to celebrate the American Revolution is to celebrate the victory of an idea.[10]

Reagan further elucidated his vision by speaking about various documents, events, and figures from this period. He had a deep reverence for the Declaration of Independence. He believed America was defined by the axioms contained in the second paragraph of the Declaration, in which all human beings are described as "created equal" and possessing "unalienable rights" to "Life, Liberty, and the pursuit of Happiness" that are granted to them by God. In remarks announcing America's Economic Bill of Rights, for example, Reagan praised these passages from the Declaration as "the phrases that captured the essence" of the Founding.[11]

Reagan was fond of telling a story about the signing of the Declaration. In the midst of vigorous debate, he would say, a general feeling of anxiety about the consequences of failing to declare independence began to take hold among the delegates. At this time, an unknown man stood up and began to speak. This man encouraged the Founders by saying, "[The British] may turn every tree into a gallows, every hole into a grave, and yet the words of that parchment can never die. To the mechanic in the workshop, they will speak hope, to the slave in the mines, freedom. Sign that parchment. Sign if the next moment the noose is around your neck, for that parchment will be the textbook of freedom, the bible of the rights of man forever."[12] Reagan argued that this prophecy had come true. In a different speech, he explained, "Our Declaration of Independence has been copied by emerging nations around the globe, its themes adopted in places many of us have never heard of."[13] Thus, the Declaration held great significance not only for Americans, but also for the rest of the world and for human history.

The Declaration was important to Reagan for other reasons. He invoked Benjamin Franklin's well-known pun about the need for colonial solidarity during the Revolution: "We must all hang together . . . or, assuredly, we will all hang separately."[14] Before signing a proclamation for a Bill of Rights Day and Human Rights Day and Week, Reagan argued, "Unlike many other countries which find their cohesion in cultural and social traditions, the citizens of our country find their unity and their heritage in the liberty that is shared by people with diverse cultural backgrounds."[15] In Reagan's mind, the Declaration consists of ahistorical ideas that unite the Founders and all subsequent generations of Americans. It is a creed that enables anyone, and potentially *everyone*, to become an American. 1776 is the year America and its people were born. In his vision, the United States is a nation baptized in the spirit of the Declaration of Independence.

If 1776 is the birth year of America and its people, then the years from 1776 to 1781 are the birth pangs of the Republic. Reagan reflected upon this period because it provided him with the opportunity to describe the people who inherited the philosophy of the Declaration. In his Yorktown speech, Reagan painted a vivid picture of the Continental Army and all the hardships they endured before, during, and after the battle. He said the Continental Army was made up of "farmers, backwoodsmen, tradesmen, clerks, and laborers—common men from all walks of life, anxious to return to their families and the building of a nation."[16] Unlike their British adversaries, the Continentals were "a band of colonists with bandaged feet and muskets that couldn't be counted on to fire."[17] Reagan claimed, "Those rebels may not have had fancy uniforms or even adequate resources, but they had a passion for liberty burning in their hearts."[18]

A love of liberty and a willingness to sacrifice for its survival sustained the Continental Army in its darkest hours. It was the key to the American victory at Yorktown and eventually in the Revolutionary War. But Yorktown meant more than this. Reagan explained, "The commemoration of this battle marks the end of the revolution and the beginning of a new world era. The promise made on July 4th was kept on October 19th. The dream described in that Pennsylvania hall was fulfilled on this Virginia field."[19] Yorktown signified that "a revolution was won, a people were set free, and the world witnessed the most exciting adventure in the history of nations: the beginning of the United States of America."[20] Once again, the uniqueness of the American Revolution and its commitment to realizing certain ideas was explained and celebrated. To these ideas, Reagan added a description of the virtues of the Continental Army and of early Americans in general that is imbued with romantic and sentimental imagery.

According to Reagan, the crafting and ratification of the U.S. Constitution symbolized a further realization of the ideals of the American Revolution. In 1987, Reagan delivered a speech at the "We the People" Bicentennial Celebration at Independence Hall in Philadelphia. He described some of the difficulties faced by Americans during the constitutional framing period. In the midst of the political strife and tension in America during the mid-1780s, how did the delegates at the constitutional convention find the strength to craft what remains the oldest working written constitution in the world? Reagan's answer needs to be quoted at some length. He explained:

> No, it wasn't the absence of problems that won the day in 1787. It wasn't the absence of division and difficulty; it was the presence of something higher—the vision of democratic government founded upon those self-evident truths that still resounded in Independence Hall. It was that ideal, proclaimed so proudly in this hall a decade earlier, that enabled them to rise above politics and self-interest, to transcend their differences and together create this document, this Constitution that would profoundly and forever alter not just these United States but the world. In a very real sense, it was then, in 1787, that the Revolution truly began. For it was with the writing of our Constitution, setting down the architecture of democratic government, that the noble sentiments and brave rhetoric of 1776 took on substance, that the hopes and dreams of the revolutionists could become a living, enduring reality.[21]

The Constitution remained relevant because "it is an oath of allegiance to that in man that is truly universal, that core of being that exists before and beyond distinctions of class, race, or national origin."[22] The ideas of the Founders allowed Americans to transcend cultural differences and individual human characteristics as well as historical circumstances and social divisions.

When talking about the Constitution, Reagan repeatedly invoked the first three words in its preamble, "We the People," as evidence of the popular foundation and historical uniqueness of America and its government. During his 1987 State of the Union Address, Reagan took the opportunity to tell Americans just who "We the People" really are. According to Reagan, "We the People" are "the kids on Christmas Day looking out from a frozen sentry post on the 38th parallel in Korea," and "the warmhearted whose numbers we can't begin to count," and "farmers on tough times, but who never stop feeding a hungry world."[23] They are mothers just like Nelle Reagan, "who never knew a stranger or turned a hungry person away from her kitchen door."[24] They are also "the entrepreneurs, the builders, the pioneers, and a lot of regular folks—the true heroes of our land who make up the most uncommon nation of doers in history."[25] Most importantly, they are the people "starting the third century of a dream and standing up to some cynic who's trying to tell us we're not going to get any better."[26] Here, as in other instances, Reagan imagined the American people as good, hard working, ready to sacrifice for others, and full of common sense and optimism. These are the people fused together by the great experiment called America.

The American flag was also an important symbol in Reagan's imagination. On several occasions he argued, "But with the birth of our nation, the cause of human freedom had become forever tied to that flag and its survival."[27] In other remarks, Reagan called attention to the War of 1812, which he considered a "second war for independence."[28] Like the patriots of the first American Revolution, the patriots fighting in the War of 1812 were able to succeed because they too "were sustained by the ideal of human freedom."[29] He explained that during the Battle of Baltimore, American soldiers defending Fort McHenry withstood a gruesome British bombardment that lasted for more than a day. After the smoke of the battle cleared, the American flag, the one that inspired Francis Scott Key to write the Star Spangled Banner, was "a little tattered and torn and worse for wear, but still flying proudly above the ramparts."[30] At Fort McHenry, Americans saved Baltimore from the fate that had already befallen Washington City. More importantly, Reagan said, "The United States, this great experiment in human freedom," was able to continue.[31] With each new state added to the Union, a star was added to the flag, and "the ideal of freedom grew and prospered."[32] Whether it was planted in the Kentucky, California, or the Moon, the flag remained "a symbol of the indomitable spirit of a free people."[33]

Reagan also spoke often about individual Founding Fathers because he believed they embodied various American ideas and virtues. George Washington is one Founder to whom Reagan frequently referred. In a speech at Mount Vernon, Reagan praised Washington's heroism and virtue as the leader of the Continental Army. Reagan explained that when the war was finally over, "[Washington] wanted to return here to Mount Vernon to be with his family, to farm, to hunt, to engage in commerce. But he loved his country and his country needed him."[34] When the unity of the United States was in doubt, Washington was pressed into public service. He served as the president of the constitutional convention and then as the first president of the United States. Reagan argued that Washington's personal standing with the American people was such that he could have been made king of America had he wanted the title. But, Reagan continued, "[Washington] had no hunger for personal power. His love was liberty, and his trust was in the people. He believed they were dependable and right-minded and he believed that a leader's responsibility is to bring out their best qualities."[35] To Reagan, Washington was both a champion of popular democracy and an American Cincinnatus.

Washington possessed other qualities highly prized by Reagan. Washington did not receive the same degree of formal education as other prominent Founders, such as Hamilton, Madison, Adams, and Jefferson. Nevertheless, Washington achieved great things in life because he worked hard and was determined to succeed. Most important of all, Washington "was a man of deep faith who believed the pillars of society were religion, morality, and bonds of brotherhood between all citizens."[36] Later, Reagan remarked, "It has been written that the most sublime figure in American history was George Washington on his knees in the snow at Valley Forge. He personified a people who knew it was not enough to depend on their own courage and goodness; they must also seek help from God, their Father and Preserver."[37] Reagan drew attention to Washington's belief in a special relationship between God and American freedom because, in Reagan's mind, this was a view held by most Americans at the time.

Washington is not the only member in the Reagan pantheon of Founding Fathers. Thomas Jefferson is also a prominent member of this group. With less frequency, and then generally as a means to make a point about Jefferson, Reagan would refer to John Adams. He would cite the friendship that existed between Adams and Jefferson as a concrete example of how the American commitment to freedom and self-government transcended ideological differences. Reagan also invoked the radical pamphleteer Thomas Paine, whom he considered to be a Founding Father, especially when he sought to explain the historical significance of the American Revolution and its implications for the rest of the world.

The Declaration of Independence, the U.S. Constitution, the Revolutionary War, the American flag, Washington, Jefferson, Adams, and Paine represent the wide range of sources and images from which Reagan drew together his vision of the Founding. In stressing the uniqueness and freshness of the American Revolution, Reagan believed he was carrying forward—conserving—a tradition of thinking about these events and symbols that can be traced all the way back to the Founding. Whether or not Reagan's vision of the American past is as representative as he believed remains to be seen.

REAGAN'S VISION OF THE FOUNDING IN HISTORICAL AND CONTEMPORARY CONTEXTS

Like Reagan, Jefferson was enthralled by the uniqueness of the American Revolution and Founding era. In his First Inaugural Address, Jefferson referred to the United States as "a rising nation," as a country "in the full tide of successful experiment," as "the world's best hope," as having "the strongest government on earth," and as "possessing a chosen country."[38] Writing to Dr. Joseph Priestley a few weeks after this address, he claimed, "We can no longer say there is nothing new under the sun. For this whole chapter in the history of man is new. The great extent of our Republic is new."[39] Jefferson frequently expressed such sentiments in public discourse and private correspondence.

Jefferson did not view the American Revolution as sharing a high degree of continuity with the American past or with the history of Great Britain and Western Europe. In his mind, America was new and different. In an 1824 letter, Jefferson explained, "Our revolution . . . presented us an album on which we were free to write what we pleased. We had no occasion to search into musty records, to hunt up royal parchments, or to investigate the laws and institutions of a semi-barbarous ancestry. We appealed to those of nature, and found them engraved in our hearts."[40] Elsewhere he declared that America was presented with a "clean canvas" upon which it created a government based on the principles of reason and natural rights.[41] In Jefferson's mind, the American Founding did not symbolize a creative conservation of the spirit of the American past, but rather a radical break from it.

In his last piece of correspondence, Jefferson stated the following about the American Revolution:

> May it be to the world, what I believe it will be, (to some parts sooner, to others later, but finally to all,) the signal of arousing men to burst the chains under which monkish ignorance and superstition had persuaded them to bind themselves, and to assume the blessings and security of self-government. . . . All eyes are opened, or opening, to the rights of man. The general spread of the light of science has already laid open to every view the palpable truth, that the mass of mankind has not been born with saddles on their backs, nor a favored few booted and spurred, ready to ride them legitimately, by the grace of God.[42]

With these ideas, words, and images from Jefferson in mind, one can see an even deeper connection between him and Reagan than might be suggested solely by Reagan's frequent invocation of Jefferson. When talking or writing about the Revolution, both men stress the transformative power of the United States. Both men view the Revolution as a liberating event, a political experiment, and a symbol of human progress. Both understand the American people primarily in reference to the revolutionary history of the United

States. In their minds, America accomplished something unprecedented in human history. Someday, they both held, the entire world would embrace America's vision of politics. Millions of people around the world would be forever grateful to the United States.

Thomas Paine had similar ideas about the American Revolution. In Paine's mind, all people were free, equal, rational, and good, and the individual was the primary unit of society. He desired a society in which an individual could succeed only on the basis of personal merit. He believed that human beings were social creatures insofar as they needed to cooperate with one another in order to satisfy basic needs for food, shelter, clothing, and so forth. He viewed government as a necessary inconvenience that provided better security for individual rights to life, liberty, and property than could be obtained otherwise. Nevertheless, Paine thought that government needed to be strictly limited to the few tasks with which it could reasonably be charged because it has a natural inclination to grow into a tyranny. Paine was also deeply skeptical of historical traditions, organized religions, inherited property, wealth, social distinctions of all kinds, landed aristocracy, and monarchy. He felt these conventions prevented the establishment of a society and government based on the principles of reason and natural rights. He characterized those who defended religious, social, and political traditions as either ignorant or evil.

Reagan often quoted the following from Paine's pamphlet *Common Sense*: "We have it in our power to begin the world over again."[43] Reagan invoked this expression to describe what he perceived as the unique opportunity afforded by history to the Founders to create a free, democratic government. He also used this quotation to inspire the Americans of the present to act as boldly as the Founders in confronting their own moment in history.

Paine seems to have intended his thought to be taken literally, for he too viewed the American Revolution as a radical break from the past. In *The Rights of Man*, he argues, "The independence of America, considered merely as a separation from England, would have been a matter but of little importance, had it not been accomplished by a revolution in the principles and practice of governments. She made a stand, not for herself only, but for the world, and looked beyond the advantages herself could receive."[44] The desires of mankind for "universal peace, civilization, and commerce," Paine claims, could only be realized by emulating America and initiating "a revolution in the system of governments."[45]

In a letter to the Abbé Raynal, Paine explained the extent and nature of the changes to the American people wrought by the American Revolution. He wrote:

> Our style and manner of thinking have undergone a revolution more extraordinary than the political revolution of the country. We see with other eyes; we hear with other ears; and think with other thoughts, than those we formerly used. We can look back on our own prejudices, as

if they had been the prejudices of other people. . . . We are now really another people, and cannot again go back to ignorance and prejudice. The mind once enlightened cannot again become dark.[46]

Like Jefferson, Paine was strongly inclined to celebrate the uniqueness of the American Revolution in human history as well as its transformative effects on the character of America and its people.

Reagan's sense of the Founding appears to have drawn strength from other American figures, including Abraham Lincoln. Like Reagan, Lincoln held Jefferson and the Declaration of Independence in high esteem. In an 1859 letter, Lincoln wrote, "The principles of Jefferson are the definitions and axioms of free society."[47] Reagan quoted Lincoln, somewhat incorrectly, as having referred to "the definition and axioms of free society contained in the Declaration of Independence."[48] In an 1861 speech, Lincoln claimed, "I have never had a feeling politically that did not spring from the sentiments embodied in the Declaration of Independence."[49] Lincoln's emphasis on the Declaration in his Gettysburg Address is well known.

In a number of public remarks, Reagan expressed approval of Lincoln's high opinion of the Declaration. Reagan understood that the Declaration's liberty clause was very important to Lincoln. In a speech Reagan argued, "This is Lincoln's greatest lesson, this lesson in liberty. He understood that the idea of human liberty is bound up in the very nature of our nation. He understood that America cannot be America without standing for the cause of freedom."[50] Reagan told the audience that Lincoln also found the source of American unity in the Declaration's liberty principle. He explained, " 'It was not,' [Lincoln] said, 'the mere matter of the separation . . . from the motherland.' It was something more. It was '. . . something in that Declaration of Independence giving liberty, not alone to the people of this country, but hope to the world . . . it was that which gave promise that in due time the weights should be lifted from the shoulders of all men.' "[51] Reagan and Lincoln held similar views about the historical significance of the Declaration and the unifying power of its liberty commitment for the United States and its people.

Reagan and Lincoln also had similar views on the relationship between the Declaration and the Constitution. In a fragment written shortly before he became president, Lincoln argued, "All this is not the result of accident. It has a philosophical cause. Without the *Constitution* and the *Union*, we could not have attained the result; but even these, are not the primary cause of our great prosperity."[52] The cause of union was the American commitment to liberty for all expressed in the Declaration. Lincoln continued, "The assertion of that *principle*, at *that time*, was *the* word, '*fitly spoken*' which has proved an 'apple of gold' to us. The *Union*, and the *Constitution*, are the *picture* of *silver*, subsequently framed around it. The picture was made, not to *conceal*, or *destroy* the apple; but to *adorn*, and *preserve* it. The *picture* was made *for* the apple—*not* the apple for the picture."[53] Like Lincoln,

Reagan believed that the Constitution was the institutionalization of the ideas proclaimed in the Declaration.

This type of vision of the American Revolution has been enthusiastically embraced by a number of contemporary scholars. Although they devote little if any specific attention to Reagan and his ideas, Allan Bloom and Harry Jaffa each express understandings of the Founding similar to Reagan's. In an essay titled "Equality as a Conservative Principle," Harry Jaffa contends that American conservatism ought to be defined as conserving the revolutionary character of the Founding era. He writes, "The Founders understood themselves to be revolutionaries, and to celebrate the American Founding is therefore to celebrate revolution. However mild or moderate the American Revolution may now appear. . . . It remains the most radical attempt to establish a regime of liberty that the world has yet seen."[54] Thomas Paine provides the most complete account of the ideas driving the American Revolution, according to Jaffa. To Jaffa, the spirit of the American Revolution is virtually indistinguishable from that of the French Revolution.[55]

In *The Closing of the American Mind*, a work ostensibly devoted to preserving American traditions against the encroachments of cultural relativism and nihilism, Allan Bloom argues that modern political thought, with its notions of liberty, equality, and self-government, is "a self-conscious philosophical project, the greatest transformation of man's relation with his fellows and with nature ever effected."[56] He lauds the radical nature of modern conceptions of democratic government and writes, "Democracy liberates from tradition. . . . Prejudices of religion, class and family are leveled, not only in principle but also in fact, because none of their representatives has an intellectual authority."[57] In his mind, modern political thought changed forever the foundations of political legitimacy, the ends of politics, and the bonds of political community. The American Revolution yielded the first and most impressive fruits of this radical departure from the past. Bloom explains, "The American Revolution instituted this system of government for Americans, who in general were satisfied with the result and had a pretty clear view of what they had done. The questions of political principle and of right had been solved once and for all."[58]

Bloom claims that most Americans are aware of and embrace this revolutionary heritage. He writes, "Americans . . . have generally believed that the modern democratic project is being fulfilled in their country, can be fulfilled elsewhere, and that that project is good."[59] He argues that America has one of the longest uninterrupted political traditions in the world and that it "tells one story: the unbroken, ineluctable progress of freedom and equality. From its first settlers and its political foundings on, there has been no dispute that freedom and equality are the essence of justice for us."[60] He holds that American identity and community are grounded in the mutual recognition of natural rights, and that as a result, "class, race, religion, national origin or culture disappear or become dim when bathed in the light of natural rights, which give men common interests and make them truly brothers."[61]

Bloom expresses disagreement with those who claim or imply that the American Revolution sought relatively modest ends such as independence from Great Britain. For him, America is the great philosophical project breaking away from the past and blazing a trial toward the ever more complete realization of abstract political ideas. Those ideas are the soul of America and its people. This is the American tradition Bloom tries to defend against the encroachments of moral and cultural relativism. The revolutionary ethos that he sees in the Founding is what he wants to conserve.

At this point it might appear as if Reagan spoke from within a long-established and representative tradition of interpreting the Founding and the American Revolution. To varying degrees, Reagan, Jefferson, Paine, Lincoln, Jaffa, and Bloom stress the unique and transformative character of the American Revolution. They tend to downplay or ignore the historical circumstances that gave rise to this period of American history. Instead, they are inclined toward ahistorical contemplation of the meaning of the American Revolution. They tend to dwell upon what they perceive as the universal authority and timeless relevance of selected ideas, images, and textual passages from the Founding. The passion with which these political figures and scholars express their beliefs does not necessary mean their views are as representative of the American tradition of thinking about the Founding as they claim or imply. Leading Founders and contemporary scholars have interpreted this period in American history rather differently than did Reagan. They have done so from intellectual and political perspectives commonly described as conservative. A sense of this different tradition of interpreting the Founding can be gained by turning first to John Adams.

A DIFFERENT VIEW OF THE AMERICAN FOUNDING AND REVOLUTION

Reagan occasionally invoked Adams when talking to audiences about the American Revolution. In his Remarks Announcing America's Economic Bill of Rights, Reagan explained that both Jefferson and Adams died on July 4, 1826, exactly fifty years after American independence was declared. He quoted Adams's last words as "Thomas Jefferson survives." He argued that although Adams's words were factually false, they were prophetically true. Reagan stated, "But Adams was right. All of us stand in tribute to the truth of those words. We proclaim it again and again with our dedication to keeping this a land of liberty and justice for all, and through our deeds and actions, to ensure that this country remains a bastion of freedom, the last best hope for mankind. As long as a love of liberty is emblazoned on our hearts, Jefferson lives."[62]

It is possible that Reagan simply assumed Adams and Jefferson had similar thoughts about America and the Founding. There is some evidence in Adams's writings, however limited, that might support such an assumption. In *A*

Defence of the Constitutions of the United States, he argues, "The people in America have now the best opportunity and the greatest trust in their hands, that Providence ever committed to so small a number."[63] Here one could interpret Adams as investing the Founding with great expectations and historical importance. But hopes for the success of the American Revolution can be of many varieties. When examined in more detail, the predominant strain of Adams's political thought consists of ideas about the American Revolution very different than those expressed by Jefferson and Paine.

Against abstract political thought, Adams argues, "The principles in nature which relate to government cannot all be known, without a knowledge of the history of mankind."[64] Adams's historically oriented approach to thinking led him to reject the view that the American Revolution was a radical departure from the past. In a letter to John Taylor of Caroline, Virginia, he wrote, "There may be principles in nature, not yet observed, that will improve all these arts; and nothing hinders any man from making experiments and pursuing researches, to investigate such principles and make such improvements. But America has made no discoveries of principles of government that have not been long known."[65] He believed that the ideas of the American Revolution had deep roots in America's colonial experience as well as in Western political thought and practice. Adams observed a strong continuity between the ideas and governments of America and England, and he held many English writers as well as the English constitution in high esteem.[66]

In many writings, Adams expressed genuine hope for the success of the United States and its government. But his thoughts on human nature and his knowledge of history led him to reserve his judgment on whether or not his hopes had been or ever could be realized. He argued, "Unhappily, political experiments cannot be made in a laboratory, nor determined in a few hours."[67] Hence, he cautioned his fellow citizens against proclaiming the historical uniqueness of the American Revolution. In a letter to John Taylor, Adams warned, "We may boast that *we* are the chosen people; we may even thank God that we are not like other men; but, after all, it will be but flattery, and the delusion, the self-deceit of the Pharisee."[68] In his mind, to think about the American Revolution in the manner of Jefferson or Paine is to exhibit hubris. In comparison to the visions of Jefferson and Paine, Adams's sense of this pivotal period in American history is permeated by modesty.

Some contemporary scholars have studied the American Revolution in the same spirit in which Adams interpreted it. In *The Basic Symbols of the American Tradition*, Willmoore Kendall and George W. Carey take a different view of this period of American history and of the Declaration of Independence from Reagan, Paine, Lincoln, Jefferson, Jaffa, and Bloom. About the Declaration they explain, "The document's primary purpose is to announce publicly the severing of those 'bands' that had, until July 4, 1776, tied us morally and legally to Great Britain. *That* is the purpose of the document and *that*, we submit, should be foremost in the minds of those who read and interpret it."[69] They argue that the Declaration cannot "be considered a manual for the construction of new governments."[70] According to these authors, the Declaration claims nothing about a specific, mandatory arrangement of political institutions. The rights declared therein were not abstract rights, recently discovered, but rather concrete rights, existing, retained, and defended against actual British usurpations. In their minds, the Declaration gave voice to the modest political goals of the Framers.

Kendall and Carey claim that the Declaration grew out of and built upon an existing political tradition in America that included the Mayflower Compact (1620), the Fundamental Orders of Connecticut (1639), and the Massachusetts Body of Liberties (1641). This last document claims the right to alter or abolish tyrannical government and to replace it with "one that 'shall seem' to the people '*most likely* to effect their Safety and Happiness.'" These authors claim that the Declaration belongs within the larger American tradition of seeking the means to the end of, as it is put in the Fundamental Orders, "an orderly and decent Gouerment [sic]."[71] The Declaration is neither a symbol of a radical departure from and rejection of the American and Western past nor an announcement to the world of a list of abstract rights and ideas upon which all legitimate governments must be based.

Kendall and Carey are aware of the tendency to interpret the Declaration in a more universalistic and expansive manner, but they argue that the document itself was not invested with such a meaning until many years after 1776. They use Abraham Lincoln's Gettysburg Address as a representative example of this revised interpretation of the Declaration. As Kendall and Carey explain, Lincoln "informs us that the 'new nation' of the United States of America was established with the signing of the Declaration and that it is to this document we must look if we are to understand our origins and thus the meaning of our political experience as a people, organized for action in history and capable of defining its appointed role in history."[72] They argue that such an interpretation contains historical inaccuracies and questionable theoretical assumptions about politics. Their detailed analysis leads them to conclude the following: "To fix upon the Declaration and to extract from it our basic commitment in the manner that Lincoln has done cannot help but create a distorted picture of our tradition."[73] One can assume that these authors would object to any political figure or scholar making what they see as a fundamental error in interpreting the American tradition.

Russell Kirk also dissents from views of the American Revolution such as Reagan's. Kirk thought very highly of Reagan both as a person and a political leader. Reagan was aware of Kirk and thought well of his writings. Both men met on occasion and had some written correspondence. Reagan was certainly very kind to Kirk during his presidency. In the last days of Reagan's time in office, Kirk was awarded the Presidential Citizens Medal.[74] In *The Politics of Prudence*, Kirk devotes attention to explaining Reagan's central role in the American conservative movement. He writes, "As everyone well knows, Mr. Reagan was the catalyst that brought together the disparate elements of American conservatism in 1980, giving them control of the Executive Force."[75] Kirk continues his description of Reagan's place in American conservatism and explains, "If, then, I am asked to declare what the typical American conservative believes in—why, he believes in Ronald Reagan and Mr. Reagan's general principles and prejudices. Mr. Reagan did not create the American conservative character, of course; but he embodies it."[76] In *The Sword of Imagination*, Kirk celebrates what he sees as Reagan's presidential achievements and writes, "Someone should have presented Mr. Reagan with a tremendous medal, studded with emeralds, for having restored the repute and the popularity of the American presidency. . . . He deserves praise from future historians."[77]

Despite Kirk's deep respect for Reagan, Kirk's praise of Reagan is rather difficult to understand. In many writings, Kirk celebrates the wisdom of figures such as Burke, Babbitt, and Adams, and he draws attention to the importance of history and tradition to understanding political and social order. He eschews abstract political thought, and he criticizes Jefferson and Paine for their ahistorical and sentimental notions about politics and human nature. One might speculate that Kirk's favorable view of Reagan consisted of a willingness to overlook the content of Reagan's speeches while praising his concrete presidential achievements, but such a possibility is not easy to reconcile with Kirk's enthusiastic comments about Reagan. Whatever the reasons for Kirk's approval of Reagan, and despite his strong and sincere admiration for Reagan, Kirk holds a view of the American past that is in many ways deeply at odds with Reagan's vision.

In *The Roots of American Order*, Kirk explains the following about the Declaration of Independence: "[It] spoke of instituting 'new Government,' not of overthrowing the state itself, or the social order. That is another aspect of the moderation of the American 'revolutionaries': they argued that *governments* might be altered or abolished, but contemplated no pulling down of fundamental institutions and ways of life."[78] This view emanates from Kirk's broader understanding of the Founding. In *Rights and Duties: Reflections on our Conservative Constitution*, he claims, "The American Revolution did not result promptly in the creation of a new social order, nor did the leaders in that series of movements intend that the new nation should break with the conventions, the moral convictions, and the major institutions (except monarchy) out of which America had arisen."[79] In his view, the American Revolution was a conservative event insofar as it sought practical redress for concrete grievances first within and then outside of the British Empire. Kirk writes, "In their act of separating from Britain, Americans did no more than *reassert* a political autonomy, or independence, rooted in the North American continent ever since the landings at Jamestown and Plymouth."[80]

The difference between Kirk's and Reagan's views of the Founding can be observed more clearly through a brief comparison of their understandings of constitutionalism. For Reagan, the word "constitution" seems to signify a written document establishing general rules for and limits to a government. Reagan frequently referred to phrases, words, and images from various written documents, and he located the source of American unity in a common assent to abstract ideas allegedly expressed in Founding documents. His tendency to focus upon written documents contributed to his vision of the American Revolution as a unique—even radical—event in human history. Kirk, in contrast, saw the Revolution as harmonious with the American past because he apprehended something about constitutionalism that Reagan either overlooked or did not fully understand. Kirk argues, "True constitutions are not invented: they grow."[81] In other words, Kirk was aware of what he called America's *unwritten* constitution.

Kirk writes, "The true constitution of any political state is not merely a piece of parchment, but rather a body of fundamental laws and customs that join together the various regions and classes and interests of a country, in a political pattern that is just."[82] This unwritten constitution gives a fundamental shape and texture to culture, and it is ultimately more important than any written document. Specifically about the United States, Kirk claims, "The American Republic possesses an underlying unwritten constitution— of which the written Constitution of the United States is an expression. The written Constitution has survived and has retained authority because it is in harmony with laws, customs, habits, and popular beliefs that existed before the Constitutional Convention met at Philadelphia—and which still work among Americans today."[83] Unlike Reagan, Kirk finds the source of American unity in centuries of accumulated experience with self-government and liberty extending back to the earliest British colonies in North America and beyond. He writes, "Thus the Constitution was no abstract or utopian document, but a reflection and embodiment of political reality in America."[84] Whereas Reagan's way of thinking about the American Revolution can be considered abstract, Kirk's can be viewed as historical and organic.

In holding such a view of the relationship between the written and unwritten constitutions of America, Kirk draws upon the insights of a number of thinkers, including Edmund Burke. In Burke's mind, historical experience *shapes* the present. In *Reflections on the Revolution in France*, he writes, "We are but too apt to consider things in the state in which we find them, without sufficiently adverting to the causes by which they have been produced and possibly may be upheld."[85] A strong awareness of the historical roots of the present formed Burke's understanding of England's constitution and the nature of the Glorious Revolution in 1688. He referred to "ancient chivalry," to Magna Charta, and to the reigns of various monarchs when he drew attention to the experiences and ideas that together constituted the English way of life.[86] About the Glorious Revolution he claims, "[It] was made to preserve our *ancient*, indisputable laws and liberties and that *ancient* constitution of government which is our only security for law and liberty. . . . We wished at the period of the Revolution, and do now wish, to derive all we possess as *an inheritance from our forefathers*."[87] In contrast to the revolution then sweeping through France, Burke considered the Glorious Revolution to be an act of conservation aimed at preventing arbitrary and unsound changes to the British constitution at odds with England's traditional way of life.

The emphasis Burke placed upon the ancient, the ancestral, the traditional, the historical, and the customary in his political thought is one of the main reasons he is described as a conservative thinker. But his approach to understanding politics did not go uncontested in his lifetime. In *The Rights of Man*, Thomas Paine, one of Burke's contemporaries and most vituperative adversaries, ridiculed Burke precisely for using such notions to describe the English constitution. Paine argues, "A constitution is not a thing in name only, but in fact. It has not an ideal, but a real existence; and wherever it cannot be produced in a visible form, there is none."[88] He then asks rhetorically, "Can then Mr Burke produce the English Constitution? If he cannot, we may fairly conclude, that though it has been so much talked about, no such thing as a constitution exists, or ever did exist, and consequently that the people have yet a constitution to form."[89] If Paine's understanding of constitutionalism is correct, then his claim about the nonexistence of an English constitution must also be true. On the other hand, if the broader and deeper meaning with which Burke and Kirk invest the word "constitution" more accurately accounts for the nature of political and social order, then Paine's argument about the English constitution reveals his rather impoverished and facile understanding of constitutionalism.

CONCLUSION

At this time, an issue raised at the beginning of this chapter can now be briefly explored. In 1988, Reagan spoke to a group of junior high school students. His remarks were permeated by an underlying awareness of the possibility that these young students might not understand the enduring relevance of the American past. He explained:

> Now, the Revolution may seem like something they say happened a long time ago . . . but I think it'll prove to be America's most important guidepost for the future. I believe that the chief moral task for America in your generation—a period destined for great change—will be not so much to chart a new course or launch a new revolution, but to keep faith with the original American Revolution and that remarkable vision of freedom that has brought us two centuries of liberty and is still today transforming the world.
>
> Over these 200 years, country after country has followed our path, and I believe that ultimately all nations will do so. It's no exaggeration to say that the political vision of our Founding Fathers has become the model for the world.[90]

In Reagan's mind, the American Revolution was worth remembering because it was still in progress. Consciousness of the symbols and ideas upon which America was based could not be lost because they are a model for the United States and the world. Like Kirk and others, Reagan was interested in conserving something in the American past. But the desire to conserve does not mean that the object of conservation is always the same. Whereas Kirk appears to be interested in conserving and refining an organic, historically developed American tradition, Reagan seems to be committed to conserving abstract and revolutionary political ideas he associates with the Founding because these ideas hold the hopes for reforming the United States and transforming the world.

Here it is worthwhile to recall some words from Burke. Not everyone in England was as skeptical as Burke of the French Revolution. Leading citizens were encouraging their countrymen to embrace the revolution in France. After all, some argued, it was akin to the aforementioned Glorious Revolution of 1688. Against such sentiments Burke writes:

> Those who cultivate the memory of our Revolution and those who are attached to the constitution of this kingdom will take good care how they are involved with persons who, under the pretext of zeal toward the Revolution and constitution, too frequently wander from their true principles and are ready on every occasion to depart from the firm but cautious and deliberate spirit which produced the one, and which presides in the other.[91]

In other words, Burke was warning his readers that not everyone who spoke reverentially about England's past understood the nature of its genuine constitution. Some even spoke thusly only as an act of expedient political deception. Reagan certainly did not deliberately promote a dubious vision of the American past in order to manipulate the American people. But, if this analysis is correct, he may nevertheless have expressed an incomplete and deeply flawed understanding of the American Revolution and the Founding in his presidential speeches.

6 "Puzzle Palaces on the Potomac"[1]
Ronald Reagan and Contemporary American Government

> In this present crisis, government is not the solution to our problem; government is the problem.[2]
>
> —Ronald Reagan

Reagan imagined the Founding era as a golden age in American history. Although he had some awareness that this period of history had its share of partisan politics, shady characters, and missed opportunities, he still held it in the highest regard because it symbolized for him the very best qualities and ideas of America and its people. By comparison, the present was much more disappointing. To Reagan, the United States of the present was like the statue of Glaucus described by Rousseau in his *Second Discourse*. America's once-glorious image had been ravaged by abuse and neglect; the luster of its past was barely recognizable. Reagan believed the economic, social, and political problems facing the United States existed because the federal government had lost faith in the American people and abandoned the principles of the Founding. Government needed to serve Americans more faithfully. It needed to respond more completely and quickly to the desires of the American people while ceding back to Americans the liberty government had taken away, many through regulation and taxation. In Reagan's mind, American government needed to be reshaped in a way that reflected its historical and noble origins.

REAGAN'S VISION OF THE STRUCTURE AND POWERS OF THE FEDERAL GOVERNMENT

A clearer sense of this part of Reagan's intuition can be gained by examining first his more theoretical understandings of government and American government. For him, an inherent tension exists between individual freedom and government. Like Thomas Paine, Reagan considered government, especially the federal government, at its best to be a necessary evil. In *An American Life*, he describes the national government as "a kind of organism with an insatiable appetite for money, whose natural state is to grow forever unless you do something to starve it."[3] Although Reagan believed that government had an inherent tendency to tyrannize over its citizens, he felt that it did this in an incremental rather than a dramatic fashion.[4] For this reason, government needs to be limited explicitly and strictly in both its ends and means by a written constitution. To minimize the damage government could do to individual liberty, Reagan encouraged constant popular vigilance of government activity.

Reagan generally argued that the national government should provide only those few things the people need but cannot secure through their own efforts. On many occasions, Reagan quoted portions of the following from Thomas Jefferson's First Inaugural Address to explain his own understanding of the limits of national power: "A wise and frugal government, which shall restrain men from injuring one another, which shall leave them otherwise free to regulate their own pursuits of industry and improvement, and shall not take from the mouth of labor the bread it has earned. This is the sum of good government."[5] Reagan held that American political practice during the Founding era conformed to Jefferson's idea. With this image as a guide, Reagan believed the federal government was charged with providing national defense, protecting individual freedoms described in the Bill of Rights, allowing the free market and entrepreneurialism to develop unhindered by excessive government regulation and taxation, and respecting the federal design of the Constitution. Within these limits government was legitimate as well as accountable to the people. Beyond these restrictions, the national government could only encroach upon the rights and freedoms of the American people, eventually degenerating into tyranny.

In Reagan's mind, federalism is an important structural restraint upon national power. He often argued that by design the national government is subordinate to both the national popular will and the U.S. states. This notion is based, in part, on Reagan's understanding of the Tenth Amendment to the Constitution, which he claims "carefully spells out that all powers not specifically given to the federal government in the Constitution shall remain with the States and the people."[6] More generally, Reagan's believed the states were sovereign entities.[7] States were not created by the national government, but they created the national government. Thus, states do not exist simply to make the exercise of federal power more efficient.[8] For Reagan, the Founders made the states more powerful than the national government because they believed government works best when power is kept close to the people.[9] In his mind, state sovereignty is a practical issue, insofar as it allows communities and states to address local issues more effectively. But federalism is also a constitutional and moral issue for Reagan, insofar as it provides the people with better means to govern themselves and prevent the deterioration of their decentralized, limited government into a centralized national despotism.

Reagan's views of federalism and of strict limits upon national power were shaped to a great extent by his understanding of Jefferson. Jefferson was a rigid defender of the rights of local and state governments and of the Tenth Amendment. In the Washington administration, Jefferson warned against chartering a national bank without expressed constitutional authorization for fear that such an action would inevitably leave open the door for the national government to usurp all powers possessed by other levels of government. Jefferson argues:

> I consider the foundation of the Constitution as laid on this ground: That "all powers not delegated to the United States, by the Constitution, nor prohibited by it to the States, are reserved to the States or to the people." To take a single step beyond the boundaries thus specially drawn around the powers of Congress, is to take possession of a boundless field of power, no longer susceptible of any definition.[10]

Nearly a decade later, in "The Kentucky Resolutions," Jefferson declares that the Constitution is a compact among the various states and that only "certain definite powers" have been delegated to the national government. Further, he argues that each state, as a member of the constitutional compact, reserves the right to decide for itself whether or not a particular act of the national government is constitutional.[11] Both Jefferson and Reagan share a deep desire to defend federalism and state sovereignty. They often use similar, though not identical, arguments to express their views.

Perhaps surprisingly, Reagan's suspicion of national power diminished when he reflected upon presidential authority and the relationship between the legislative and executive branches. In *An American Life*, he expresses the following frustration: "I have often wondered about a paradox in American government: Every four years, voters elect a president and in California a governor, the only officeholders elected by *all* the people; then, the same people in their individual districts turn around and elect a legislature and congress that is often controlled by the opposing party, enabling it to prevent the president or governor from carrying out the things they elected him or her to do."[12] Reagan knew that the president was technically elected by votes from the Electoral College, but he *envisioned* the president as a national leader elected more or less directly by something similar to a national plebiscite held every four years. In his mind, this made the president the true representative of the people in the national government. The president promoted the real agenda of Americans. He stood between them and the more questionable inclinations of Congress, and he was charged with a special responsibility to ensure that government responded to and enacted the popular will.

These views strongly influenced Reagan's governing style. He believed that although some members of Congress actually represented the interests of their constituents, most of them—especially those in the majority Democratic Party during his presidency—were beholden to special interests deeply at odds with the will of the American people and the national interest. As president, Reagan encountered frequent congressional resistance to his legislative programs and ideas, and he attributed this opposition to the shortsightedness and deceitfulness of members of the House and Senate. This made him feel compelled to appeal directly to the American people for support in order to accomplish his goals. Reagan claims that he started taking his message directly to the people as governor of California.[13] As governor and later as president, Reagan believed that once he explained his position on a particular topic to the American people, they could then be relied upon to pressure their elected representatives to support his objectives. In Reagan's view, his direct relationship with the American people ultimately enabled him to achieve many of the legislative goals of his presidency.

Reagan's understanding of executive power and the relationship between the president and the American people is similar in important ways to Woodrow Wilson's. About Congress, Wilson explains, "There is no one in Congress to speak for the nation." In his view, "Congress is a conglomeration of inharmonious elements; a collection of men representing each his neighborhood, each his local interest; an alarmingly large proportion of its legislation is 'special'; all of it is at best only a limping compromise between the conflicting interests of the innumerable localities represented."[14] In Wilson's way of thinking, *e pluribus unum* is a phrase of dubious value. Wilson contrasted what he saw as the parochialism and inefficiency of Congress with the national focus and concentrated energy of the president. He believed the president was the true voice of the nation because he was the only official elected by all the people of the United States. About the president, Wilson writes:

> The nation as a whole has chosen him, and is conscious that it has no other political spokesman. His is the only national voice in affairs. . . . His position takes the imagination of the country. . . . When he speaks in his true character, he speaks for no special interest. If he rightly interpret the national thought and boldly insist upon it, he is irresistible.[15]

In Wilson's mind, presidential authority was not defined by the Constitution or by traditional usage. Rather, as Gary L. Gregg explains about Wilson's understanding of executive power, "The *zeitgeist* has replaced the Constitution as the source of institutional position, power, and influence."[16]

REAGAN ON THE DECLINE OF AMERICAN GOVERNMENT

Reagan believed these notions represented the main political ideas and practices upon which a sound American government must rest. And yet he felt that the government under which he had lived for most of his life and had inherited as president operated on a very different theory of politics. According to Reagan, the national government began turning away in earnest from the wisdom of the Founders during the Great Depression. During the 1930s and 1940s, he had encounters with federal bureaucracies that made him rather skeptical about their commitments to limited, constitutional government. In *An American Life*, Reagan describes his encounters with federal welfare workers who discouraged able-bodied men in Dixon, Illinois, from working for the Works Progress Administration (WPA). These bureaucrats convinced many men that with welfare they could make more money and do less work than if the worked for the WPA.[17] Reagan also related his experience with a different group of bureaucrats during World War II. They asked Reagan if the First Motion Picture Unit in which he worked needed civilian employees. When Reagan told them his unit could not accept such a security risk, the bureaucrats simply smiled, ignored his objections, and told him his unit would have civilians anyway.[18]

Reagan synthesized these and other similar experiences into a unified intuition about contemporary American government. He believed that the national government had created a harmful, ever-expanding system of bureaucracies. These bureaucracies were seizing control of the free market and private business through excessive regulation. Individual property and the nation's wealth were being confiscated through excessive taxation. In short, the government and its bureaucracy "began leading America along the path to a silent form of socialism."[19]

Reagan considered this abrupt change in American government to be the result of a fundamental change in the political ideas of many American politicians and bureaucrats. He explained this change, in part, by dichotomizing the word "liberal." To Reagan, true liberals were men such as Jefferson, Lincoln, and himself. True liberals believe in limited government, free enterprise, individual rights, and liberty. False liberals, on the other hand, reject these ideas. They are elites, "manning the barricades in these puzzle palaces on the Potomac," who believe in the supremacy of the state.[20] False liberals crave national control over private business and the economy. They desire higher taxes on working individuals that are redistributed as the government sees fit. False liberals disdain federalism. They want national control over all levels of government—e.g., cities, towns, counties, and states. Most grievously, false liberals ignore the American people, often holding them in contempt. For Reagan, it was these changes that signified a general rejection of the wisdom of the American Founding. It was these ideas that revealed that politicians and bureaucrats had lost faith in the American people.

As president, Reagan blamed the ideas and policies of the recent past for America's high unemployment, decaying industries, high inflation, and high taxation. In his First Inaugural Address, he explained that inflation was eroding each individual's income and that income taxes were not indexed for inflation. Average Americans were thus living in a situation that "distorts our economic decisions, penalizes thrift, and crushes the struggling young and the fixed-income elderly alike."[21] In February of 1981, he delivered an Address to the Nation on the Economy. He explained that American industry was at its lowest level of productivity because the government's "punitive tax policies and excessive and unnecessary regulations" discouraged capital investment and hindered economic growth.[22] He also told Americans, "All of you who are working know that even with cost-of-living pay raises, you can't keep up with inflation. In our progressive tax system, as you increase the number of dollars you earn, you find yourself moved up into higher tax brackets, paying a higher tax rate just for trying to hold your own. The result? Your standard of living is going down."[23] For Reagan, the political ideas and practices of the recent past were destroying the American economy and decreasing every American's incentive to work.

The growth of the national government also abraded federalism and the autonomy of local and state governments. In remarks before the Annual Convention of the National Association of Counties, Reagan argued that state and local governments were precious resources because they promoted diversity, which, among other things, enabled the American people to "reach across a vast continent for ideas and experience"[24] when searching for solutions to various problems. These levels of government were also valuable because their small size and close proximity to the people made them more accountable to their constituents and more qualified to address the daily concerns of citizens, including education, road repairs, fire protection, and law enforcement. Reagan explained, "The more government we can keep at the local levels, in local hands, the better off we are and the more freedom we will have."[25] In his view, this type of relationship between the governed and their government was an embodiment of the true spirit of democracy.

Reagan contrasted this vision of local and state governments with one of the national government, which he referred to as "big brother government" and "swollen government."[26] He argued, "I believe the extent of the problems that we face today is in direct proportion to the extent to which we have allowed the Federal Government to mushroom out of control."[27] He lamented the blurring of distinctions between the various levels of government and said, "Ignoring careful checks and balances, Federal bureaucrats now dictate where a community will build a bridge or lay a sewer system. We've lost the sense of which problems require national solutions and which are best handled at the local level."[28] He also stated that these circumstances were having a homogenizing effect upon the United States. He claimed, "As the Federal Government has pushed each city, county, and State to be more like every other, we've begun to lose one of our greatest strengths—our diversity as a people."[29] Reagan loathed the growth of the national government because it replaced local autonomy and diversity with inefficiency, corruption, and tyranny. It even threatened the existence of genuine democracy in America.[30]

Reagan also believed that the nationalization of American life had a direct impact upon social mores and individual morality. In a speech on welfare reform, he expressed his long-held view that welfare, as it currently existed, was both a financial disaster and a moral danger. He claimed that the economy of the 1950s provided abundant opportunities for all Americans and that the number of them living in poverty was declining. Nevertheless, the Lyndon Johnson administration decided to declare a war on poverty, devoting more financial resources and government attention to the problem than ever before.

Reagan argued that despite these vigorous, well-meaning efforts, poverty in American actually *increased* as a result of the War on Poverty. This happened because the benefits paid to welfare recipients were calculated in ways that reduced the incentive to work and weakened the integrity of the family. He argued, "In States where payments are highest, for instance, public assistance for a single mother can amount to much more than the usable income of a minimum wage job. In other words, it can pay for her to quit work. Many families are eligible for substantially higher benefits when the father is not present. What must it do to a man to know that his own children will be better off if he is never legally recognized as their father?"[31] In his vision, the financial costs associated with welfare were secondary to these types of degrading social and individual consequences. These problems reflected an even more serious danger posed by big government to America and its people.

Like a number of his supporters, Reagan believed the American people were under direct attack from radical, secular values. Groups motivated by this philosophy often used government—especially the courts—to force their unpopular views and desires upon the American people. In various speeches, Reagan cited a number of examples of the ways in which the secularist mind-set corrupted both politics and society. In his 1983 speech to the National Association of Evangelicals, Reagan expressed frustration with a government that enabled young girls to obtain birth control without parental notification. He claimed that in his administration, "The right of parents and the rights of family take precedence over those of Washington-based bureaucrats, and social engineers."[32] He also disputed the constitutional and moral basis used by the Supreme Court to legalize abortion in *Roe v. Wade*. For Reagan, these issues represented some of the gravest dangers contemporary government presented to the rights of families and unborn children; they proved that the secularist movement driving the expansion of government was ultimately dehumanizing.

Reagan was also disturbed by the ways in which public displays of religion were under assault from special interest groups and the courts. He argued, "Freedom prospers when religion is vibrant and the rule of law under God is acknowledged."[33] He explained that God and religion were invoked in many of the major Founding documents, and he reminded his audience that Congress continued to open each session with a prayer. He also reminded them that the First Amendment was only designed to protect individuals and "churches from government interference."[34] But the same amendment was now being used to attack public religious expressions such as prayer in public schools. He argued that this was a total departure from the ideas of the Founders because "they never intended to construct a wall of hostility between government and the concept of religious belief itself."[35]

These social and moral problems, coupled with the existing economic and political problems, convinced Reagan that the ideas and practices of the past fifty years were intellectually indefensible and practically bankrupt. The national government and its bureaucracies were grinding down individual freedom. They were prohibiting the goodness, creativity, and common sense of the American people from flowing forth. Like a cancer, government and bureaucracy were eating away at the American body politic, consuming its soul. Reagan, the "one-man battalion," was the surgeon called forth by the people to excise the tumor of "big government" and to restore health to the American republic. In Reagan's mind, the most effective medicine was getting the national government out of the way of the American people. Reduce the size of the national government, restore the balances among local, state, and national authorities, and return to the ideas of the Founding, Reagan frequently argued, and the power of the American people would be unleashed and individual liberty would thrive. America and its people would again be great.

REAGAN ON REJUVENATING THE AMERICAN SPIRIT BY GETTING GOVERNMENT OUT OF THE WAY

As is the case with all American presidents, the distances between Reagan's various policy desires and his actual achievements are of varying lengths. Many of the goals he set regarding domestic social issues, such as abortion and school prayer, and constitutional issues, such as federalism, largely went unmet. He did have a higher degree of success bringing the American economy into line with his vision for restoring the true spirit of American government, and he was proud of his achievements.[36] Examining Reagan's understanding of his success in restoring the economy provides an excellent opportunity to observe his "get government out of the way" approach to politics in action.[37]

During a nationally televised address on the state of the American economy shortly after his first inauguration, Reagan said, "We're threatened with an economic calamity of tremendous proportions, and the old business-as-usual treatment can't save us. Together, we must chart a different course."[38] He then offered a brief explanation of the steps he would take as president to bring about an economic recovery in the United States. He encouraged Americans to take his vision to heart and said, "We must not be timid. We will restore the freedom of all men and women to excel and to create. We will unleash the energy and genius of the American people, traits which have never failed us."[39] He concluded his remarks by stating that the choice America faced was one between a shattered economy or a land of freedom and opportunity. With their common sense and natural abilities, Reagan told the American people they could accomplish anything they desired.[40] He knew they would make the right choice.[41]

Two weeks later, he unveiled his economic recovery program. He and Congress spent the next several months debating and reshaping its details.[42] One of the most important pieces of his program, a 25 percent across-the-board income tax cut over three years, was scheduled for a congressional vote in the last week of July. Two days before the actual vote, Reagan again appeared before the nation and made a direct appeal for support of his bill. He explained that his bill would reduce the taxes of all Americans while the competing bill offered by the Democrats was essentially a tax increase. After stating his case to the American people, he asked them to contact their members of Congress and tell them which bill they supported. The White House also received a number of calls about his remarks, and Reagan claimed they were overwhelming in support of his plan.[43] On July 29, 1981, Congress passed Reagan's tax bill by a large margin. Reagan's end run around Congress worked.

Reagan never took personal credit for his legislative successes, and the passage of his tax bill was no exception. The day after the bill passed, he explained that although he invested much of his personal time and political capital in negotiating with Congress over the details of the legislation, he attributed its passage to a different source. He stated, "You know, there was much in the news about lobbying and arm-twisting and every kind of pressure, but what really sold this bill was the lobbying of the American people. . . . My gratitude to the American people is as deep as my respect for what they can do when they put their minds to it."[44] Reagan's faith in the American people, and in their capacity to accomplish great things when government stopped undermining their liberty, was vindicated. In subsequent years he would attribute decreases in inflation, interest rates, and personal income tax rates; reductions in unemployment; and the general growth of the American economy to the actions and common sense of American people. In getting government out of their way, he merely liberated their natural genius.

REAGAN'S VISION OF GOVERNMENT AND THE PEOPLE: HISTORICAL AND PHILOSOPHICAL PERSPECTIVES

Further insights into this part of Reagan's imagination can be obtained by placing it within a wider historical and philosophical context. This will require an exploration of ideas held by thinkers such as Jefferson, Rousseau, Adams, and Burke. This analysis can be conducted most efficiently by drawing out from Reagan and these thinkers some of their thoughts on the necessity of government, their criteria for judging a government to be good, and their understandings of the typical reasons for the emergence of a bad government.

In American politics, expressions of antipathy toward the national government along with a deep love for and ardent faith in the American people and their capacity for self-government extend all the way back to the Founding era. Jefferson's sketch of "a wise and frugal government" in his First Inaugural Address restricted government to fulfilling a few clearly delineated constitutional responsibilities. He harbored a strong distrust of the national government and its tendencies to transcend these limits and move toward despotism. In the "Kentucky Resolutions," Jefferson argued that it would be a "dangerous delusion" if Americans believed that confidence in the characters of their elected representatives was a sufficient protection against tyranny. He explained, "Free government is founded in jealousy, and not in confidence; it is jealousy and not confidence which prescribes limited constitutions, to bind down those whom we are obliged to trust with power."[45] Within the iron manacles of the Constitution, Jefferson reluctantly accepted the existence of the national government. Nevertheless, he was not sanguine about the government's desire or even ability to stay tethered to its constitutional moorings.

Jefferson's assessment of the nature and limits of the national government was combined, somewhat paradoxically, with sentimental beliefs in the goodness of the American people and their capacity for self-government and in the superiority and justice of a republic governed by majority rule. About the ability of the American people to practice self-government, Jefferson held "the good sense of the people will always be found to be the best army. They may be led astray for a moment, but will soon correct themselves. The people are the only censors of their governors: and even their errors will tend to keep these to the true principles of their institution."[46] Such views shaped his belief that the will of the majority, which he called "the Natural law of every society," was the only true guardian of the rights of every American citizen.[47] He argued "absolute acquiescence in the decisions of the majority" is "the vital principle of republics."[48]

Jefferson believed that a well-informed, educated citizenry was a sufficient defense against despotism. Once the people knew the facts about a particular situation, they could be trusted to draw sound conclusions and formulate their will. The role of government was to translate the will of the majority into action consistent with the limits of the Constitution. A respect for strictly limited powers and a willingness to respond quickly and completely to the popular will were the essence of good government, according to Jefferson. Since the people were both good and reasonable, the likelihood of Americans oppressing themselves under these circumstances was all but a theoretical impossibility. In Jefferson's mind, if tyranny emerged, then its source had to be something outside of the American people.

Reagan held a number of similar ideas about limited government, the American people, and popular rule. In the minds of Jefferson and Reagan, it seems as if a dichotomy exists between the good people, seemingly incapable of doing wrong, and the government, which often fails the people and even seeks to undermine and tyrannize them. This dichotomy is one of the most important images in Reagan's imagination. In order to understand its meaning and significance more clearly, it will be necessary to return for a moment to the political philosophy of Rousseau.

In the *Second Discourse*, Rousseau suggests that human beings, free and alone, lived happily and peacefully in the state of nature for ages. At some point, the most unfortunate of accidents occurred. Individuals came into increasing contact with one another. They started living together in communities and relying upon one another for food, shelter, and defense. These developments were the early stages of a historical process in which human beings became increasingly alienated from their nature, or "civilized." About the life of this "civilized man" Rousseau laments, "It was necessary, for his own advantage, to show himself to be something other than what he in fact was. Being something and appearing to be something became two completely different things; and from this distinction there arose grand ostentation, deceptive cunning, and all the vices that follow in their wake."[49] In his day, Rousseau felt that the distance between human beings and their natural goodness was so great that he began the *Social Contract* with the following sentence: "Man is born free, and everywhere he is in chains."[50]

Rousseau held human beings to be naturally good. That he did not find them to be so in his own time was the result of the accidental and ultimately tragic decline of humanity into civilization. It was not a state of affairs for which human beings were responsible. "Society" was to blame. Society, not people, perpetuated the existence of an artificial and immoral environment. It alone continued to corrupt human nature. Hence, Rousseau drew a strong contrast, created a rigid dichotomy, between good people and evil society.

Rousseau never suggested that human beings could return to the state of nature. He believed a literal return to the state of nature was impossible. As he explained in the *Social Contract*, he did not want to abolish the chains that bound humanity. He wanted to make them legitimate. If only society could be transformed in a way that captured the spirit of the Arcadian state of nature in his imagination, then human beings would be able to live together in true brotherhood, freedom, and equality. Their natural goodness would once again gush forth unimpeded.

Irving Babbitt devotes much attention to exploring the impact of Rousseau's ideas about the relationship between the people and society on Western political thought and imagination. Babbitt believes that Rousseau's philosophy is highly appealing precisely because it uses powerful romantic images to suggest that human beings are not responsible for the disorder in their lives. In *Rousseau & Romanticism*, he explains, "Evil, says Rousseau, foreign to man's constitution, is introduced into it from without. The burden of guilt is thus conveniently shifted upon society. Instead of the old dualism between good and evil in the breast of the individual, a new dualism is thus set up between an artificial and corrupt society and 'nature.' "[51] Babbitt also sees this new dualism at work in the political thought of Jefferson.

About Jefferson's understanding of the relationship between the people and government, Babbitt writes, "[Jefferson] was for diminishing to the utmost the role of government, but not for increasing the inner control that must, according to Burke, be in strict ratio to the relaxation of outer control. When evil actually appears, the Jeffersonian cannot appeal to the principle of inner control."[52]

For Babbitt, idyllic reveries or romantic imaginings are not inherently dangerous. On occasion, they provide a necessary reprieve from the difficulties with which all human being are confronted on a daily basis. Where Babbitt finds fault with Rousseau and the type of political thought and imagination he represents is in his tendency to mistake the dream world for the real world. According to Babbitt, the prevalence of this type of romantic vision, when combined with an attachment to Rousseau's new dualism, often has dangerous social and political consequences. He states, "Unfortunately when the real refuses to vanish in favor of the ideal, it is easy to persuade the simpleminded that the failure is due not to the ideal itself, but to some conspiracy."[53] For many who, like Rousseau, feel that they are victims of a conspiracy and that a clandestine cabal stands between them and genuine happiness, nothing short of a destructive, revolutionary transformation of society is imagined as capable of making the dream world real.

To be clear, Rousseau and Reagan diverge on a number of specific points. Reagan believed deeply in the sanctity of private property. Rousseau thought it was a problematic convention at best. Reagan was a proponent of decentralized political power that protected individual rights. Rousseau championed an irresistible general will for the whole of society and considered any divisions to be threats to the social contract. And yet, underneath these particular differences, some common ground exists between their visions.

Both Rousseau and Reagan fashioned versions of a dichotomy between good people and disordered or evil government or society. In a manner similar to Rousseau, Reagan believed that human beings, especially Americans, were naturally good. Both men developed visions of the past that included strong elements of romanticism. Like Rousseau, Reagan was dissatisfied with his political environment. In Reagan's case, he felt as if the national government had forgotten, perhaps even conspired against, the true will and happiness of the American people. Reagan believed that the situation could be vastly improved mainly through political reform. In a more radical way, Rousseau believed that society could be completely transformed through politics alone. For Rousseau and Reagan, and for that matter Jefferson, political and social disorder seemed to have very little if anything to do with the moral character and maturity of citizens. And why should it have? All that prevents citizens from being good are disorganized or malevolent institutions in need of restructuring or transformation.

John Adams and Publius represent a view of human nature, common during the Framing period, which is at odds with the notions of Reagan, Jefferson, and Rousseau. Adams and Publius reject natural human goodness in favor of human ethical dualism. With this in mind, it should not be surprising that Adams and Publius understand the relationship between the people and their government differently from Jefferson, Rousseau, and Reagan.

The touchstone of Adams's political thought is his understanding of human nature. In *A Defence of the Constitutions of the United States*, he argues, "The passions and appetites are parts of human nature, as well as reason and the moral sense. In the institution of government, it must be remembered that, although reason ought always to govern individuals, it certainly never did since the Fall, and never will, till the Millennium; and human nature must be taken as it is, as it has been, and will be."[54] Adams rejected as absurd schemes of government promising to remove the constant threat posed to political order by human moral failing.

In Adams's view, politics based on faith in the goodness of the people is imprudent and dangerous. He explains, "We may appeal to every page of history we have hitherto turned over, for proofs irrefutable, that the people, when they have been unchecked, have been just as unjust, tyrannical, brutal, barbarous, and cruel, as any king or senate possessed of uncontrollable power. The majority has eternally, and without one exception, usurped over the rights of the minority."[55] For Adams, political and social disorders are caused by permanent defects in human nature, not by abstractions called "government" or "society." To those who ignore the pervasiveness of human wickedness when thinking about politics, Adams writes, "It would be as reasonable to say, that all government is altogether unnecessary, because it is the duty of all men to deny themselves, and obey the laws of nature and the laws of God. However clear the duty, we know it will not be performed; and, therefore, it is our duty to enter into associations, and compel one another to do some of it."[56] In Adams's mind, diminishing the impact on society of the sordid impulses of human beings is one of the primary obligations of any government aspiring to wisdom and justice. This is difficult but necessary work. On these points, the visions of Adams and Reagan diverge significantly.

Publius expresses similar ideas about government and the people in *The Federalist*. Like Adams, Publius is a proponent of a type of republican government. But his view of human nature leads him to conclude that a just political order must consist of a number of different constraints upon government and the people. In "Federalist No. 51," he argues that a separation of powers is vital to preventing the emergence of a tyranny in the national government. Publius allows his argument briefly to expand into a broader philosophical comment about politics and the human condition. He states, "It may be a reflection on human nature, that such devices should be necessary to control the abuses of government. But what is government itself, but the greatest of all reflections on human nature? If men were angels, no government would be necessary. If angels were to govern men, neither external nor internal controls on government would be necessary."[57] For Publius, restraints upon the powers of the national government, such as the separation of powers, address only one of the ways in which political disorder can emerge. The people are in need of as much restraint as is their government.

In "Federalist No. 10," Publius prescribes an extended representative republic for the United States because he feels it will go far in preventing a majority faction from gaining political power. By a majority faction, Publius means "a number of citizens . . . who are united and actuated by some common impulse of passion, or of interest, adverse to the rights of other citizens, or to the permanent and aggregate interests of the community."[58] Here Publius indicates that not all majorities are good. Majority tyranny is a notion of which Reagan does not seem to have a strong awareness.

According to Publius, an extended republic can thwart majority faction in part because it will "refine and enlarge the public views, by passing them through the medium of a chosen body of citizens, whose wisdom may best discern the true interest of their country, and whose patriotism and love of justice, will be least likely to sacrifice it to temporary or partial considerations."[59] He even claims that under these circumstances the popular will might receive a more genuine expression than if it were announced "by the people themselves, convened for the purpose."[60] This scheme of representation is designed mainly to minimize the opportunities of the people to act upon the impulses of the moment and tyrannize themselves in the process. Specifically about the role of the U.S. Senate in "Federalist No. 63," Publius argues, "such an institution may be sometimes necessary, as a defence to the people against their own temporary errors and delusions."[61]

Along these lines, Publius also offers a vision of the presidency rather different from the one provided by Reagan. In "Federalist No. 71," he writes, "The republican principle demands, that the deliberate sense of the community should govern the conduct of those to whom they intrust the management of their affairs; but it does not require an unqualified complaisance to every sudden breeze of passion, or to every transient impulse which the people may receive from the arts of men, who flatter their prejudices to betray their interests."[62] Publius does not envision the president as a national tribune of the people elected to represent the spontaneous will of Americans against the parochialism and dithering of Congress. For him, and for most of the leading figures of the Framing period, the president is supposed to act as a restraint upon the hasty desires of Congress and the people. Publius explains, "When occasions present themselves, in which the interests of the people are at variance with their inclinations, it is the duty of the persons whom they have appointed, to be guardians of those interests; to withstand the temporary delusion, in order to give them time and opportunity for more cool and sedate reflection."[63]

Publius has a reasonable estimation of and respect for Americans and their capacity to govern themselves justly. At the same time, he does not pander to Americans about their moral and intellectual virtues. That human beings often choose to oppress themselves is a truth about politics that

Publius confronts. For Publius, government is not a necessarily evil. Insofar as it restrains the lower will of the people and allows the common good to be realized, government is a positive good for human beings.

Publius interprets the republican design of the constitution as a type of filter for human action in politics. Federalism, various methods of election, and separation of powers all work together and create conditions in which members of government can discern and embrace the true, enduring will of the people while thwarting the strictly partisan passions that might grip the public and its representatives at any given moment. In this sense, the Constitution reflects a deep awareness of human ethical dualism. In general, Publius argues that the Constitution protects the life, liberty, and property of Americans while providing as effective a remedy against disorder and tyranny as is realistically possible, given the intractable problems of the human condition. With these sentiments, Adams generally agrees. It is difficult to find substantive common ground between these notions and those expressed by Reagan.

The issues raised by Adams and Publius about the restraining effects of representative government are related to other theoretical concerns, including those about the qualifications for political leadership. Here it is worthwhile to return for a moment to the political thought of Edmund Burke. Unlike Reagan, Burke refrains from effusive celebration of the ostensible wisdom, virtue, and heroism of businessmen, mechanics, farmers, and merchants. In *Reflections on the Revolution in France*, he criticizes the French Jacobins precisely for such tendencies. Burke writes:

> The occupation of a hairdresser or of a working tallow-chandler cannot be a matter of honor to any person—to say nothing of a number of other more servile employments. Such descriptions of men ought not to suffer oppression from the state; but the state suffers oppression if such as they, either individually or collectively, are permitted to rule. In this you think you are combating prejudice, but you are at war with nature.[64]

Today, such words most likely sound snobbish, aristocratic, and cruel. But that may not be the fault of Burke as much as it is of the present age. In *Democracy and Leadership*, Babbitt argues, "The democratic idealist is prone to make light of the whole question of standards and leadership because of his unbounded faith in the plain people."[65] Indeed, much modern theorizing about democracy simply avoids questions about the leadership qualifications individuals need in order to be trusted with political power.

For Burke, as for many of the Framers, questions about what type of person is deserving of political power and responsibility are of the utmost importance. At the same time, Burke flatly denies that he is an advocate for a permanent ruling class determined solely by hereditary relations or titles of nobility. He argues, "You do not imagine that I wish to confine power, authority, and distinction to blood and names and titles. No, Sir.

There is no qualification for government but virtue and wisdom, actual or presumptive."[66] Burke believes finding people qualified for political leadership is difficult because individuals possessing the necessary qualities are rare. Developing these characteristics often comes at the price of great individual moral struggle, and too few people are willing to undertake such work. Burke defends a type of political leadership, one based on ethical character and prudence, against another type dedicated to extolling the virtues of the divine average in society. Especially when Reagan's vision of the presidency is taken into consideration, it seems as if he has little in common with Burke and Publius on the topic of political leadership.

CONCLUSION

A great deal has been revealed about Reagan's intuitive vision of contemporary American government, and an important dichotomy in Reagan's imagination between good people and bad government has emerged. This dichotomy has much in common with the ideas of Jefferson and Rousseau, but it stands in contrast to relevant ideas from Adams, Publius, and Burke. This dichotomy, along with Reagan's understandings of human nature, the American people, and the American past, shapes other important areas of his broader chimeric imagination, including his understanding of America's role in the world.

7 "A Crusade for Freedom"[1]

Ronald Reagan and America's Role in the World

In a world wracked by hatred, economic crisis, and political tension, America remains mankind's best hope. The eyes of mankind are on us, counting on us to protect the peace, promote new prosperity, and provide for them a better world.[2]

—Ronald Reagan

Reagan's vision of U.S. foreign policy consisted of a complex mixture of ideas that was not without paradoxes and internal tensions. In some of his presidential speeches, he invoked important U.S. strategic, economic, and national security concerns in support of specific goals in Asia, the Middle East, Latin America, and elsewhere. Despite the existence of serious disagreements with other nations, he sometimes stressed that a successful U.S. policy would need to include restraint, flexibility, realism, and openness to dialogue—especially with the Soviet Union. Thoughts like these suggested that he viewed politics and foreign policy as the art of the possible, not as an attempt to realize some great ideal.

But there was another and more prominent aspect of Reagan's foreign policy thinking that pointed in a much different, far more "idealistic" and ambitious direction. This part of his vision of America's role stemmed from his belief that human beings were basically good and entitled to individual liberty and democratic government. He felt that the United States had a unique, moral responsibility to bestow these rights on people around the world, thereby advancing the global growth of democracy and freedom. Although Reagan's foreign policy imagination contained a rich assortment of images, not all of which pointed in the same direction, it is this latter, more optimistic and "idealistic" vision that clearly predominated. It suffused virtually all of his major comments on America's role in the world.

When explicating his vision, Reagan gave the impression that he was drawing on deeply held ideas from the American past, extending all the way back to the Founding. Whether or not they are writing specifically about Reagan, a number of scholars support Reagan's claims that visions like his represent a long-standing and widespread tradition of American foreign policy thought. The works of other scholars suggest that Reagan's primary way of understanding America and its role has much more in common with the foreign policy ideas of American progressives, especially Woodrow Wilson, than with the views expressed by leading figures in the early American republic. Thus it may be the case that Reagan's perception of America's past was flawed in fundamental ways. This dimension of Reagan's imagination may also contain dubious elements and perhaps even serious dangers of which he seemed unaware and which his devotees have not questioned. Before all such possibilities can be contemplated, a deeper awareness of Reagan's foreign policy vision must be obtained.

REAGAN'S FOREIGN POLICY VISION: AMERICA AS CRUSADER FOR LIBERTY AND DEMOCRACY

In January of 1984, Reagan gave an address to the nation on the relationship between the United States and the Soviet Union. He claimed that underneath the various differences between the two countries was a stronger bond of common humanity. He said, "Just suppose with me for a moment that an Ivan and an Anya could find themselves, oh, say, in a waiting room, or sharing a shelter from the rain or a storm with a Jim and Sally, and there was no language barrier to keep them from getting acquainted. Would they then debate the differences between their respective governments? Or would they find themselves comparing notes about their children and what each other [sic] did for a living?"[3] As far as Reagan was concerned, they would do the latter. The imagined amicable relationship between these two couples was one of his many ways of conveying his sense that all human beings were good and friendly; they all shared the same nature, hopes, and dreams.[4]

Since all human beings were more or less the same—that is, they were more or less American in spirit—Reagan believed that all people desired and deserved to live under liberty and democracy. Various governments around the world, however, were undermining global aspirations for freedom and democratic government by ignoring the will and rights of their peoples. As far as he was concerned, this tension was at the heart of the civil strife and foreign conflicts around the world. On several occasions Reagan claimed that such violence occurred because oppressive governments "got in the way of the dreams of the people."[5] On others he claimed, "People do not make wars; governments do. . . . A people free to choose will always choose peace."[6] This dichotomy between good people, such as Jim, Sally, Ivan, and Anya, and bad government, such as the Soviet Union, was similar to the one he established between the American people and contemporary American government.

With this dichotomy between noble people and tyrannical government in mind, Reagan dedicated himself to promoting freedom and democracy around the world. Perhaps most famously, in his Address to the British Parliament, he called for a global "campaign for democracy" and declared,

"Let us now begin a major effort to secure the best—a crusade for freedom that will engage the faith and fortitude of the next generation."[7] Beyond such general demands, he wanted to advance a number of institutions, including "the system of a free press, unions, political parties, [and] universities," which, in his mind, enabled "a people to choose their own way to develop their own culture, to reconcile their own differences through peaceful means."[8] Because this campaign was meant to secure for the peoples of the world that to which they were naturally entitled, he argued that it was not a manifestation of "cultural imperialism." Those who thought differently were simply exhibiting "cultural condescension, or worse."[9] More than displaying cultural arrogance, opponents of his vision were rejecting one of the noblest parts of America's past.[10]

Reagan often expressed his belief that the United States had a unique and long-standing moral responsibility to undertake this foreign policy. In *An American Life*, he explains, "It was our policy that this great democracy of ours had a special obligation to help bring freedom to other peoples," and "I'd always felt that from our deeds it must be clear to anyone that Americans were a moral people who starting at the birth of our nation had always used our power only as a force of good in the world."[11] He also warned others about the consequences of abandoning this American mission. In his Address to the Nation on the upcoming Summit in Geneva with Soviet leader Mikhail Gorbachev, he argued, "Should the day come when we Americans remain silent in the face of armed aggression, then the cause of America, the cause of freedom, will have been lost and the great heart of this country will have been broken."[12] America's was not the only heart that he feared could break.

Reagan believed the rest of the world was counting on the United States. In remarks given on July 4, 1984, he explained, "You know, throughout the world the persecuted hear the word 'America,' and in that sound they can hear the sunrise, hear the rivers push, hear the cold, swift air at the top of the peak. Yes, you can hear freedom."[13] During a Christmas Day Radio Address to the Nation, Reagan read a letter he had recently received from an American sailor on tour in the Pacific. The letter told of an encounter with a sinking boat full of refugees fleeing Vietnam. As the American ship drew closer to the raft, the refugees began to shout, "'Hello America [sic] sailor! Hello Freedom man!"[14] The refugees were rescued. Reagan explained that this was simply the latest confirmation of how oppressed people around the world saw the United States. He felt that America was morally responsible for their liberty and welfare.

This vision of American leadership shaped Reagan's understanding of his foreign policy practice. It was the primary motivation behind his mission to "transcend communism" and to leave the Soviet Union and "Marxism-Leninism on the ash heap of history."[15] About the message he brought to Europe in the summer of 1982 on how best to deal with the Soviet Union, he writes, "The democracies, I suggested, like the Communists, should adopt a policy of expansionism: We should try to help the new countries of Africa and elsewhere embrace democracy and become evangelists worldwide for freedom, individual liberty, representative government, freedom of the press, self-expression, and the rule of law."[16] Reagan followed his own advice. In an Address to the Nation on the concluded U.S.-Soviet Summit in Iceland, he explained, "We declared the principal objective of American foreign policy to be not just the prevention of war, but the extension of freedom. And we stressed our commitment to the growth of democratic government and democratic institutions around the world."[17] He made such comments on U.S.-Soviet relations repeatedly during his presidency.

This sense of America's mission also formed Reagan's understanding of the American role in Latin America and the Middle East. In April of 1983, Reagan told a joint session of Congress a story he had heard from congressional observers of elections in El Salvador. They told him that El Salvador's hold on democracy was tenuous and that many El Salvadorans had been threatened with violence and death if they voted in upcoming elections. But, they explained to him, one elderly woman told those who would threaten her life because she wanted to be free, "You can kill me, you can kill my family, you can kill my neighbors. You can't kill us all." Commenting on this noble defiance, Reagan argued that the United States was bound both by interest and morality to come to the aid of such brave human beings.[18]

A few months later, Reagan gave a televised address to the nation about recent events in Lebanon and Grenada. The Marine barracks in Beirut had suffered a terrorist attack killing over two hundred American soldiers. He acknowledged that many Americans were now questioning the American presence in Lebanon. He said that America's purpose was to help bring peace to that nation, and he warned against a military withdrawal because "if America were to walk away from Lebanon, what chance would there be for a negotiated settlement, producing a unified democratic Lebanon?"[19] He then related the following story as a way of emphasizing the moral justification for America's presence: "Why are we there? Well, a Lebanese mother told one of our Ambassadors that her little girl had only attended school 2 of the last 8 years. Now, because of our presence there, she said her daughter could live a normal life."[20] Reagan acknowledged that a peaceful Middle East was something that no one then living could recall, but, with resolve and patience, the United States could play a crucial role in creating just such an environment.

Reagan then turned to the events in Grenada. He explained that the small Caribbean island was under martial law imposed by communist insurgents and that a "24-hour shoot-to-kill curfew" was in effect.[21] Not only was the freedom of all native Grenadians in jeopardy, but, of equal importance, nearly one thousand American citizens—mostly young medical students— were trapped on the island. He explained that surrounding countries simply did not have the capacity to restore liberty to Grenada, and thus the Organization of Eastern Caribbean States along with other nations appealed to the United States for military assistance. He argued, "These small, peaceful nations needed our help. Three of them don't have armies at all, and the others have very limited forces. The legitimacy of their request, plus my own concern for our citizens, dictated my decision."[22] By most measures, the intervention in Grenada was a success. Nineteen U.S. soldiers lost their lives, but the American medical students were rescued, and the island was brought back into the fold of free, democratic nations.[23]

Explaining his decision to send armed forces to Grenada as well as the broader significance of the victory on Grenada, Reagan said, "We only did our duty, as a responsible neighbor and a lover of peace, the day we went in and returned the government to the people and rescued our own students. We restored that island to liberty. Yes, it's only a small island, but that's what the world is made of—small islands yearning for freedom."[24] Elsewhere he explains, "The people of Grenada greeted our soldiers much as the people of France and Italy welcomed our GIs after they liberated them from Nazism at the end of World War II. . . . There were no YANKEE GO HOME signs on Grenada, just an outpouring of love and appreciation from tens of thousands of people—most of its population—and banners proclaiming GOD BLESS AMERICA."[25] Grenada was for him another link in the chain of American foreign policy successes that reinforced his belief in America's global mission.

During his presidency Reagan also spoke often about the moral necessity of supporting Nicaraguan freedom fighters, or Contras, in their conflict against the Sandinista government. In his 1985 CPAC speech, he placed his desire for continued assistance to the Contras in the following context: "I've spoken recently of the freedom fighters of Nicaragua. You know the truth about them. You know who they're fighting and why. They are the moral equal of our Founding Fathers and the brave men and women of the French Resistance. We cannot turn away from them, for the struggle here is not right versus left; it is right versus wrong."[26] Reagan himself rather than his speechwriters created this analogy between the Contras and the Continental Army of the American Revolution. It shaped his understanding of the American obligation to support freedom in Nicaragua and strengthened his commitment.[27]

Reagan held this vision with intensity, and he believed it to be an expression of the most noble, longest-standing American foreign policy tradition. Not everyone agreed with him. Although Reagan's cheerful demeanor prevented him from becoming angry with his foreign and domestic political opponents on all but the rarest of occasions, his sense of America's mission and moral obligations abroad made dissenters from his foreign policy difficult for him to understand. He was often flexible about the means of implementing his policies, but he could not accept the possibility of legitimate differences over his foreign policy ends. If America really was a righteous force obligated to extend freedom and democracy abroad, what legitimate opposition could there be?

Reagan believed that some of the opposition to his foreign policy vision was rooted in genuine ignorance of America's mission and history. To remedy this situation, Reagan believed that America and the West needed to overcome their shyness about declaring the moral superiority of their politics and way of life. If some misunderstood America out of genuine ignorance, others understood America and its mission and consciously rejected it. Many such people were "isolationists." During his speech at Point du Hoc, in Normandy, France, Reagan explained that one of the lessons of World War II was that "isolationism never was and never will be an acceptable response to tyrannical governments with an expansionist intent."[28] When imagining the role of America in the world, Reagan believed the United States faced a stark choice between his vision of promoting freedom and democracy on the one hand, and the "isolationist" desire to bury the head of America in the sand regardless of international circumstances on the other. For Reagan, no middle ground existed between these views.

Reagan argued that the moral support and other assistance that America offered the world began to pay dividends during his presidency. In public speeches and private writings, he marveled at the sheer quantity of new democratic governments that emerged during the 1980s. In his 1987 Address to the U.N. General Assembly, he explained that democracy and freedom were growing in Latin America, the Caribbean, the Philippines, South Korea, and elsewhere. As important to him as the quantity of emerging democracies was the view that the "simple, ordinary people" of the world were leading this "worldwide movement to democracy."[29] With American help, the Ivans and Anyas of the world were taking action and claiming the rights to which they were entitled.

About the importance of these ordinary people to the global campaign for liberty and self-government Reagan remarked:

> These simple people are the giants of the Earth, the true builders of the world and shapers of the centuries to come. And if indeed they triumph, as I believe they will, we will at last know a world of peace and freedom, opportunity and hope, and, yes, of democracy—a world in which the spirit of mankind at last conquers the old, familiar enemies of famine, disease, tyranny, and war.[30]

For those in the audience representing governments that stood in the way of the realization of such a world, he had the following advice: "Isn't it better to listen to the people's hopes now rather than their curses later?"[31] He concluded his remarks by saying that for all the differences among the nations present, "there is one common hope that brought us all to make this common pilgrimage: the hope that mankind will one day beat its swords into plowshares, the hope of peace."[32] The terms upon which a peaceful world could be realized formed the core of Reagan's foreign policy vision.

As these comments suggest, Reagan was strongly prone to sweeping, sentimental, even naïve-looking images and ideas when expressing his intuitive sense of America's role in the world. But in his presidential speeches, he sometimes also stressed specific national security concerns, strategic interests, and openness to negotiation with other nations. In the previously mentioned Address to Congress on Central America, for example, he stated that the prospect of political instability in countries such as El Salvador and Nicaragua, closer to the United States than many Americans perhaps realized, was a serious security concern. He also warned of the effects upon U.S. foreign trade and military deployment capabilities should American access to the Panama Canal be compromised.[33] Especially during his second presidential term, he made substantial progress in negotiations with the Soviet Union toward nuclear arms reduction—despite the deep ideological differences between it and the United States. Yet, although considerations of this practical, limited type were sometimes on his mind and were sometimes publicly articulated, they tended to recede behind and be subordinated to the kind of imagination that has been described earlier: the vision of a free, democratic world made possible by American leadership and help.

REAGAN'S FOREIGN POLICY VISION IN HISTORICAL PERSPECTIVE

A clearer understanding of this part of Reagan's imagination can be reached by exploring his claim that his vision represented a long-standing American foreign policy tradition. In his presidential speeches, Reagan repeatedly invoked various figures from the American past—especially Jefferson and Paine—to elaborate his vision of America's moral commitment to global freedom and democracy. Reagan often quoted the following passage from Paine's *Common Sense:* "We have it within our power to begin the world over again."[34] In the foreign policy context, Reagan used this quotation to encourage and inspire his audience with a sense of America's power and opportunity to promote freedom and democracy and transform the world.

Reagan referred even more frequently to Jefferson when expressing this part of his vision. In the Declaration of Independence, which he attributed primarily to Jefferson's mind, he saw both the supreme exposition of America's revolutionary cause and the definitive articulation of the universal rights of all humanity. In a speech Reagan argued, "A great future is ours and the world's if we but remember the power of those words Mr. Jefferson penned not just for Americans but for all humanity: 'that all men are created equal, that they are endowed by their Creator with certain inalienable Rights, that among these are Life, Liberty and the pursuit of Happiness.' "[35] He often quoted from this passage in the Declaration—particularly the human equality clause—when explaining the universality of American ideals and the moral imperative behind his vision of America's mission abroad.

Reagan also quoted from John Quincy Adams on several occasions. In his speech on the Iceland Summit, he quoted from Adams's 1821 Fourth of July Address and explained, " 'Whenever the standard of freedom and independence has been . . . unfurled, there will be America's heart, her benedictions, and her prayers,' John Quincy Adams once said. He spoke well of our destiny as a nation. My fellow Americans, we're honored by history, entrusted by destiny with the oldest dream of humanity—the dream of lasting peace and human freedom."[36] He used these and other quotations to convey to Americans his sense of how deeply ingrained his vision was in their history.

In his efforts to establish a strong historical continuity between his ideas and the American past, Reagan dwelled often upon the American role in World War II. At Point du Hoc in 1984, with veterans before him in the audience, he explained the reasons behind America's sacrifice in the war. He said, "You all knew that some things are worth dying for. One's country is worth dying for, and democracy is worth dying for, because it's the most deeply honorable form of government ever devised by man. All of you loved liberty. All of you were willing to fight tyranny, and you knew the people of your countries were behind you."[37] As he explained it here and elsewhere, Americans died in World War II while liberating oppressed peoples, establishing freedom and democracy, and destroying tyrannical governments. In imagining the war this way, he drained it of much of its historical texture, suggesting instead that it symbolized the victory of one set of abstract political ideas over others. But America's moral commitment to the progress of humanity did not end when armed conflict ceased. In 1985, Reagan gave a radio address to the nation and, via the Voice of America, to the Soviet Union. He explained to Russians listening to his remarks, "Yet after that victory [in World War II], Americans gave generously to help rebuild war-torn countries, even to former enemies, because we had made war on a vicious ideology, not on a people."[38] In the aftermath of the war, when victory over a "vicious ideology" was complete, the United States simply acted according to its natural, moral inclinations. America resumed its selfless, peaceful efforts to bring democracy, free markets, and liberty to peoples and nations around the world.

In Reagan's mind, Americans still acted this way on the international stage. At Kansas State University he explained, "Across the world, Americans are bringing light where there was darkness, heat where there was once only cold, and medicines where there was sickness and disease, food where there was hunger, wealth where humanity was living in squalor, and peace where there was only death and bloodshed."[39] The natural virtues and talents of the American people echoed around the world. In Reagan's imagination, the golden cord running through the American foreign policy tradition, from the Founding, through the nineteenth century, through two world wars, and to the present, was the image of the United States as the dispenser of liberty, champion of democracy, and protector of the world.

A number of scholars have defended Reagan's intuitive sense of America's role in the world by celebrating its moral orientation, identifying what are perceived to be the concrete successes of his diplomatic pursuits, and by pointing out how deeply ingrained such a vision is in the American mind. In *Ronald Reagan*, Dinesh D'Souza argues that Reagan "understood the moral power of the American ideal and saw how it could be realized most effectively in his time."[40] Reflecting upon what he sees as the deep moral foundation of Reagan's concrete diplomatic successes, D'Souza writes, " 'The world,' Woodrow Wilson told a special session of Congress on April 2, 1917, 'must be made safe for democracy.' It was Reagan who finally made it so."[41] Without going too deeply into the issue, D'Souza suggests that Reagan imbibed through lived experience a long-standing view of America in the world.

Paul Kengor argues a number of similar points. In *God and Ronald Reagan*, he suggests that those who criticize Reagan's vision of America's role in the world overlook how deeply such a notion is embedded into the American tradition. He explains that the founder of the Disciples of Christ, Alexander Campbell, viewed the United States as a nation destined to defeat false religion and "autocracy" wherever they existed. America would herald in an era in which the Christian Gospel and democracy reigned over the world, Campbell believed. Kengor speculates that Reagan, an active Disciple as a young man, likely came into contact with such views through his pastor, Ben Cleaver.[42] Kengor also cites John Winthrop, George Washington, Thomas Paine, Woodrow Wilson, and Franklin Roosevelt as figures representing the long-standing tradition of imagining America the way Reagan did. Kengor writes, "Ronald Reagan, then, was not alone in viewing America as specially chosen, as a nation with a divine mandate. He *was* alone in the single-minded passion with which he harnessed and implemented that view in the Cold War."[43]

In an article titled "Neocon Nation: Neoconservatism, c. 1776," Robert Kagan argues for the existence of a strong degree of continuity between a neoconservative foreign policy vision and that of the broader American tradition. He explains that as it relates to American foreign policy the term "neoconservatism" signifies "a potent moralism and idealism in world affairs," and "a belief in America's exceptional role as a promoter of the principles of liberty and democracy."[44] According to Kagan, these ideas have always been appealing to Americans because they are revolutionary and universal. They have the potential to liberate humanity from the constraints of history and tradition, what he calls the "Burkean accretions of the centuries."[45] He invokes the foreign policy thought of a number of Americans to support his argument that individuals from different intellectual and ideological backgrounds have expressed variations of this vision throughout American history. Although the article does not dwell primarily on Reagan, Kagan clearly identifies Reagan's foreign policy vision as existing squarely within this tradition.

Reagan, D'Souza, Kengor, and Kagan all indentify an important dimension of foreign policy thought and imagination in American history. It is certainly true that one can find comments similar to Reagan's on America's role in the world not only in the writings of Jefferson and Paine, but in those of Washington, both Adams, Hamilton, and a number of other Americans who believed strongly in America's future greatness and believed that their nation was special—perhaps even chosen to do or to be something extraordinary in human history. These acknowledgments notwithstanding, it seems as if these scholars, and, above all, Reagan, might not be fully aware of the extent to which their understandings of the American foreign policy past are incomplete and even misleading. To paraphrase the twentieth-century historian John Lukacs, while their claims of historical continuity appear to be true, they are perhaps not true enough.[46] Reagan and these scholars do not seem very sensitive to what another historian, Herbert Butterfield, terms the "unlikenesses" of history.[47] To compare Reagan's foreign policy vision to the views held by leading early Americans is to notice major dissonances.

AN ALTERNATIVE VIEW OF AMERICA'S ROLE IN THE WORLD

It is here helpful to return for a moment to John Quincy Adams and his 1821 Fourth of July Address. In many ways, this address embodies the tensions in American foreign policy thought and action during the early decades of the republic. Reagan correctly quoted Adams as claiming that the United States hoped for the global spread of liberty and democracy and that it would rejoice at each nation's movement in that direction. Further, in a manner similar to Reagan's, Adams described the Declaration of Independence as "the first solemn declaration by a nation of the only *legitimate* foundation of civil government. It was the cornerstone of a new fabric, destined to cover the surface of the globe."[48] Such comments lend credence to Reagan's claims of historical continuity.

But there is another important part to this speech that Reagan does not mention. Immediately following the comments Reagan quoted, Adams stated:

> But [America] goes not abroad, in search of monsters to destroy. She is the well-wisher to the freedom and independence of all. She is the champion and vindicator only of her own. She will commend the general cause by the countenance of her voice, and the benignant sympathy of her example. She well knows that by once enlisting under other banners than her own, were they even the banners of foreign independence, she would involve herself beyond the power of extrication, in all the wars of interest and intrigue, of individual avarice, envy, and ambition, which assume the colors and usurp the standard of freedom. The fundamental maxims of her policy would insensibly change from *liberty* to *force*. . . . She might become the dictatress of the world. She would be no longer the ruler of her own spirit.[49]

Here Adams appears to be *rejecting* just the type of foreign policy mission that Reagan suggested was quintessentially American during this period of history. Adams also seems to be doing so not upon grounds of logistical difficulty or practical inexpediency, but out of deep moral-political concerns. In this instance he argued that an interventionist type of foreign policy should be avoided because it would come at the cost of America's republican soul.

Another American thinker who voiced concerns about America's role in the world similar to those of Adams is Orestes Brownson. In *The American Republic: Its Constitution, Tendencies, and Destiny*, he argues that American promotion of liberty and democracy around the world will actually produce great disorder in foreign lands unprepared for such institutions. This view is based upon his belief that each nation has what he calls written and unwritten constitutions. In the United States, for example, the unwritten constitution is the complex web of historically and organically developed legal precedents and rights, religious and political practices and ideas, and other cultural habits and mores inherited from Britain and the larger Western tradition. According to Brownson, this unwritten constitution is what gives the United States its national identity and makes it a truly sovereign entity. The written constitution is an expression of this preexisting sovereign will in which the people give themselves a government. Examples of America's written constitutions are the Articles of Confederation and the U.S. Constitution.

Brownson holds that America's written constitution has been successful because it is in agreement with the nation's unwritten constitution. But, he claims, it would lead to disaster if other nations, with different unwritten constitutions, tried to adopt it as their own. Brownson writes:

> The constitution of the government must grow out of the constitution of the state, and accord with the genius, the character, the habits, customs, and wants of the people, or it will not work well, or tend to secure the legitimate ends of government. . . . You must take the state as it is, and develop your governmental constitution from it, and harmonize it with it. Where there is a discrepancy between the two constitutions, the government has no support in the state, in the organic people, or nation, and can sustain itself only by corruption or physical force.[50]

There is another side to Brownson's political thought that bears a closer resemblance to Reagan's main beliefs about America's historical significance, but his important, practically very significant view of the relationship between written and unwritten constitutions, which is held intuitively also by the Framers, is absent from Reagan's conception of what U.S. foreign policy and human societies ought to be.

The substantive differences between Reagan's foreign policy vision and those expressed by Adams, Brownson, and other American Framers can be brought into greater clarity with reference to the scholarship of Richard

Gamble and Walter McDougall. In various writings, Gamble explores and analyzes the history of the American belief that the United States is a special, or exceptional, nation. In an article titled "Savior Nation: Woodrow Wilson and the Gospel of Service," he argues that for all the historical, intellectual, and imaginative differences among individuals and epochs in American history, there are essentially two competing visions of American uniqueness. One Gamble calls "New Eden" or "New Israel," and the other he calls "Christ-Nation."[51] Those who believe that the United States is a New Israel tend to view America as a nation chosen by God or Providence "for special blessing."[52] In this view, America is charged with maintaining a particular way of life, one that includes a specific set of political, social, and religious traditions. This vision of the United States informs early American foreign policy thought and practice. Although many Americans hoped that other nations would freely choose to adopt American-style political institutions and principles, they generally practiced what Gamble describes as a "non-ideological, non-interventionist foreign policy to suit this conception of its place in the world."[53]

Beginning in the late nineteenth century, Gamble continues, the idea of America as a New Israel has been supplanted by the vision of the United States as a Christ-Nation. In this view, the United States is not only selected by God for a special blessing, but it is morally responsible for extending that blessing to others around the world.[54] Typically in diplomacy, Gamble writes, such "an 'expansive' mission is predatory, universalist, and even revolutionary."[55] The vision of America as a Christ-Nation charged with redeeming the world from evil was felt deeply by one of its most powerful presidential exponents, Woodrow Wilson. Gamble writes that Wilson continuously "developed the idea that America had been born to perfect and universalize ideals of freedom, democracy, self-government, and love of neighbor."[56] Wilson envisioned the United States as the servant of the world, selflessly sacrificing its own material interests and the lives of its own people for the progress of humanity. This impulse to serve mankind is evident in Wilson's justifications for American intervention in Mexico and in World War I.

According to Gamble, Wilson justified his departure from older views of America's symbolic meaning by reinterpreting American history, especially the Founding and the Civil War, as chapters in a story of the progressive unfolding of liberty and democracy both in the United States and the world. Gamble argues, "Wilson's interpretation of the meaning of the American founding helped transform the United States into a permanently revolutionary nation, dedicated to the fulfillment of universalized abstractions on behalf of others, whatever the cost in blood and wealth."[57] The Civil War, in Wilson's view, was the final test of America's commitment to realizing these ideals within its own borders. Union victory purified the United States and prepared America to emerge as a righteous force in international politics during Wilson's presidency. In holding such ideas about America, history, progress, and world service, Wilson was not alone.

In *The War for Righteousness: Progressive Christians, the Great War, and the Rise of the Messianic Nation*, Gamble explains that this Christ-Nation vision of the United States was widely embraced by members of America's progressive Christian clergy during the late nineteenth and early twentieth centuries. Gamble argues that this vision was at the heart of the American justification for entering into the Spanish-American War in 1898. Many Americans wanted to fight the war, not for national security or territorial ambitions, but because it provided an opportunity to practice "an internationalism guided by abstract notions of universal democracy and permanent peace, a world order benevolently led and dominated by America."[58] As far as progressive American Christians were concerned, the United States was not protecting its own selfish interests in this war. It was working to extend freedom, democracy, progress, and peace to lands suffering under Spanish domination.

The intensity with which Americans believed their nation to be a righteous redeemer state increased by the time World War I began. As a representative example, Gamble cites an article written by Harold Bell Wright, the author of *That Printer of Udell's*, in which Wright compares the salvation of humanity accomplished by the death and resurrection of Jesus Christ to the American mission in Europe during the war. Wright argues, "A man may give his life for humanity in a bloody trench as truly as upon a bloody cross. The world may be saved somewhere in France as truly as in Palestine."[59] Gamble observes that with such a notion, "all distinction between the church and the world, the sacred and the secular, the holy and the profane had been overwhelmed. Metaphors had finally broken down; they had been transformed into reality, and reality had vanished into illusion."[60] Under such a view, the harshness and violence of World War I came into a different light. If America is a force for righteousness, then its opponents must be evil. While lamentable, the carnage of the war was believed to be a necessary payment for a world in which peace and justice were at last secured.

Gamble's scholarship on America's understanding of its mission to the world is both extensive and thoughtful. If he is correct, then the notion that American foreign policy is grounded in a moral obligation to extend freedom and democracy abroad is much more a progressive era departure from an older understanding of America's role in the world than it is the essence of the American diplomatic tradition. If Gamble is right, then at least in foreign policy, Reagan seems to be carrying forward, or conserving, progressive political ideas rather than those of the Founders.

In *Promised Land, Crusader State: The American Encounter with the World since 1776*, Walter McDougall argues that the American encounter with the world can be subsumed under two general categories. He calls the prevailing ways in which Americans thought about and pursued foreign policy from the end of the eighteenth century until the end of the nineteenth century America's "Old Testament." He argues that during this period most Americans, most of the time, were committed to "Liberty at home,

Unilateralism abroad, an American system of states, and Expansion."[61] McDougall notes that the four traditions comprising the Old Testament envisioned the United States as a "promised land," set aside by God, to be a model of liberty for the world's admiration and emulation. In explaining the essence of this Old Testament of American foreign policy, he writes, "These first four traditions were all about Being and Becoming, and were designed by the Founding Fathers to deny the outside world the chance to shape America's future."[62]

McDougall claims that a "New Testament" has dominated American foreign policy thought and practice since the 1890s. This New Testament is "about Doing and Relating, and [was] designed to give America the chance to shape the outside world's future," and it consists of the "doctrines of Progressive Imperialism, Wilsonianism, Containment, and Global Meliorism, or the belief that America has a responsibility to nurture democracy and economic growth around the world."[63] Whereas the Old Testament traditions are coherent and mutually reinforcing, McDougall claims that the New Testament traditions, whatever they may have borrowed from the Old, are much more contradictory and have brought much greater discordance to American diplomacy. McDougall use the image of a crusader state to symbolize the New Testament America.

One component of America's Old Testament foreign policy tradition is "Liberty, or Exceptionalism (so called)." McDougall argues that America's geographical location, political experience, and religious history all contributed to the common belief that the United States was a unique land populated by a chosen people. America was different from the Old World and perhaps superior to it as well. Such notions about America notwithstanding, McDougall argues, "[To] the generation that founded the United States, designed its government, and laid down its policies, the exceptional calling of the American people was not *to do* anything special in foreign affairs, but *to be* a light to enlighten the world."[64] He argues, for example, that none of the Founders seriously invested the American Revolution with the pretensions of an activist global democratic revolution. McDougall claims that Jefferson, even with all his effusive comments on liberty and republican government, falls within the Old Testament tradition of preserving liberty at home. Figures such as Washington, Adams, and Hamilton are even more closely connected to this understanding of American exceptionalism than Jefferson.

Another element of McDougall's Old Testament is "Unilateralism, or Isolationism (so called)." Reagan tended to dismiss many of those who did not subscribe to his vision as "isolationists," although he never quite explained what that term meant. According to McDougall, no one else has made much more of an effort at defining this term. He argues that the term "isolationist" has never accurately described any American foreign policy. The word itself did not come into popular use in America until the 1930s, McDougall explains.[65] He claims that the term first emerged when proponents of a robust, imperial American foreign policy in the late nineteenth century began to label their anti-imperialist opponents as cranks and cowards. McDougall writes, "So, our vaunted tradition of 'isolation*ism*' is no tradition at all, but a dirty word that interventionists, especially since Pearl Harbor, hurl at anyone who questions their policies."[66] Rather than use this term to describe American foreign policy during the late eighteenth and nineteenth centuries, McDougall employs the word "unilateralism."

McDougall explains that the American desire to protect liberty at home rested upon its ability to act with a free hand—i.e., unilaterally. In practice, he claims, this meant implementing the foreign policy principles expressed in Washington's Farewell Address. In this address, Washington stated, "The Great rule of conduct for us, in regard to foreign Nations is in extending our commercial relations to have with them as little *political* connection as possible. . . . 'Tis our true policy to steer clear of permanent Alliances, with any portion of the foreign world."[67] McDougall shows that the United States was deeply involved in the world prior to the end of the nineteenth century, and he cites technology transfers, commerce, labor, and tourism between Europe and North America as some of the more obvious examples. It was only in the context of protecting its neutrality in foreign affairs—i.e., reserving for itself the right to decide under what circumstances it would go to war or use armed forces—that America can be considered to have an "isolationist" history. In this context, American unilateralism was not rooted in the cowardice or stupidity often implied in the term "isolationism." Rather, it meant that America was intent on avoiding disadvantageous political and military alliances.

Some might argue that the Founders likely adhered to these Old Testament positions merely for practical reasons. The argument might be made that as times changed and American power grew, the United States gradually gained the ability to act upon the much grander diplomatic ideas it had held for a long time. It cannot be denied that there was a strong element of practical consideration in what McDougall calls the Old Testament vision of American foreign policy. But the Founders also had deeply felt moral reasons for maintaining their modest vision of America's role in the world. If McDougall's scholarship is correct, then it appears that the early American tradition of foreign policy was rather different from the one Reagan—and, for that matter, D'Souza, Kengor, and Kagan—describe. Although Reagan was much more inclined to quote from and refer to figures from the Old Testament tradition in American diplomacy, many of his most important ideas and images resonate with what McDougall calls the New Testament tradition.

McDougall describes one part of the New Testament tradition as "Progressive Imperialism." He cites a number of examples that represent the changes in American foreign policy thought signified by this term, including one from remarks given by Senator John C. Spooner. In a speech explaining America's reasons for entering into the Spanish-American War, Spooner argued, "We intervene not for conquest . . . not for aggrandizement, not because of the Monroe Doctrine; we intervene for humanity's sake . . . to aid a people who have suffered every form of tyranny and who have made a desperate struggle to be free."[68] About the significance of such a justification for the Spanish-American War, McDougall writes, "Imagine: the American people and government allowed themselves to be swept by a hurricane of militant righteousness into a revolutionary foreign war, determined to slay a dragon and free a damsel in distress."[69] This comment from McDougall captures the intuitive essence of the new direction in which American foreign policy was beginning to travel.

The next tradition in McDougall's New Testament is "Wilsonianism, or Liberal Internationalism (so called)." McDougall holds that Wilsonianism symbolizes the abandonment of many older American foreign policy ideas—largely on the grounds that such notions were immoral. In a 1913 speech given in Mobile, Alabama, Wilson argued, "It is a very perilous thing to determine the foreign policy of a nation in terms of material interest. It not only is unfair to those with whom you are dealing, but it is degrading as regards your own actions."[70] In Wilson's vision, the United States could no longer interact with the world on the basis of defending its own liberty and material interests. Rather, as both Gamble and McDougall claim, Wilson believed America needed to respond to a higher calling of service to humanity by bringing freedom and democracy to the world. In part because of the importance these scholars place upon Wilson, his foreign policy vision needs to be examined in greater detail.

REAGAN, WILSON, AND AMERICAN FOREIGN POLICY

Stability in Mexico was of serious concern to Wilson until the United States entered World War I. In a 1913 address to Congress, he explained, "The peace, prosperity, and contentment of Mexico mean more, much more, to us than merely an enlarged field for our commerce and enterprise."[71] In other words, Wilson was not interested in encouraging stability in Mexico merely to protect American business or other material interests. On the contrary, he wanted to help Mexico achieve peace and prosperity so that "the field of self-government" would be enlarged and "the hopes and rights of a nation" would be realized. Expressing the antithesis of the American foreign policy Old Testament, Wilson continued, "We shall yet prove to the Mexican people that we know how to serve them without first thinking of how we shall serve ourselves."[72] As far as Wilson was concerned, the degree to which the United States ignored or sacrificed its interests in the pursuit of selfless humanitarian service to other nations was the degree to which it possessed a moral foreign policy.

Initially, Wilson did not conceive of using military force in his mission of service to Mexico. In 1913, he thought it likely that America's shining example of goodness would be enough to shame Mexico into better behavior. But less than a year later, Wilson's patience with Mexico expired. McDougall explains that Wilson received intelligence in the spring of 1914 that "a German merchant ship was en route to Mexico with machine guns for [Mexican president] Huerta."[73] Acting on this information in May 1914, the United States sent eight hundred soldiers into Vera Cruz, Mexico. Nineteen Americans and hundreds of Mexicans died as a result of the intervention.[74] In an effort to justify America's military actions on this occasion, Wilson stated the following in a speech at the Brooklyn Navy Yard:

> We have gone down to Mexico to serve mankind if we can find out the way. We do not want to fight the Mexicans. We want to serve the Mexicans if we can, because we know how we would like to be free, and how we would like to be served if there were friends standing by in such a case ready to serve us. A war of aggression is not a war in which it is a proud thing to die, but a war of service is a thing in which it is a proud thing to die.[75]

In conceptualizing his foreign policy activities in this manner, Wilson further departed from the older vision of the United States as a model of liberty defending its own interests, replacing it with an image of America as a selfless, righteous, global apostle and pedagogue of freedom and democracy. This crusading spirit of service on behalf of mankind was also manifest in Wilson's vision of America's role in World War I.

As was the case with Mexico, the war in Europe threatened a number of American interests. Nevertheless, under Wilson's leadership, the United States stayed out of the war until 1917. Why? McDougall writes that although the damage caused by the war to American commerce was serious, it did not seem to matter all that much to Wilson.[76] He was not going to enter into the largest conflict in a century merely to protect what he considered to be selfish American interests. Wilson made clear the conditions upon which the United States would enter World War I. During his 1916 Gridiron Dinner Address, he stated, "America ought to keep out of this war. She ought to keep out of this war at the sacrifice of everything except this single thing upon which her character and history are founded, her sense of humanity and justice."[77] The only basis upon which America would fight was when it perceived its honor, which consisted of commitments to ahistorical notions of justice and sentimental notions of humanity, to be under attack. Wilson concluded these remarks by telling the audience that their restraint would be rewarded. After explaining the meaning of valor in a manner similar to St. Paul's description of love in 1 Corinthians 13, Wilson declared, "Valor withholds itself from all small implications and entanglements and waits for the great opportunity when the sword will flash as if it carried the light of heaven upon its blade."[78] The United States would be using righteous force if only it could wait for its "great opportunity." In Wilson's mind, the sword of America was the sword of God.

As late as January 1917, Wilson was committed to maintaining American neutrality so as to prepare for its role as the mediator of the world. But events in February and early March of that year, especially the discovery of the Zimmermann telegram and Germany's resumption of unrestricted submarine warfare, finally convinced Wilson that war with Germany was the only way in which he could defend America's sense of justice and humanity. On April 2, 1917, he addressed the U.S. Congress and asked them formally to declare war. He argued that Germany was the aggressor forcing war upon a reluctant and neutral United States. He also explained that the United States was going to war, not to avenge the losses of life and treasure from the previous months or years, but for that constant purpose of service to humanity.

Wilson stressed that America was not going to war against the German people, for whom the United States felt nothing but respect and sympathy, but against the autocratic government in Germany that had embroiled Europe in a selfish war without consulting the will of its own people. He argued that in the future only democratic nations could maintain a "concert for peace"; it was only free people who could act upon the interests of the nation and humanity rather than selfish interest.[79] For global peace, freedom, and democracy to succeed, the regime in Germany and all others like it needed to be changed. As the speech drew to a close, Wilson raised the true object of the war to higher level and proclaimed:

> We are glad . . . to fight thus for the ultimate peace of the world and for the liberation of its peoples, the German peoples included: for the rights of nations great and small and the privilege of men everywhere to choose their way of life and of obedience. The world must be made safe for democracy. Its peace must be planted upon the tested foundations of political liberty. We have no selfish ends to serve. We desire no conquest, no dominion. We seek no indemnities for ourselves, no material compensation for the sacrifices we shall freely make. We are but one of the champions of the rights of mankind.[80]

Paraphrasing the Declaration of Independence, Wilson explained that to this mission, "we can dedicate our lives and our fortunes, everything that we are and everything that we have, with the pride of those who know that the day has come when America is privileged to spend her blood and her might for the principles that gave her birth and happiness and the peace which she has treasured. God helping her, she can do no other."[81]

After the United States entered the war, Wilson's bellicosity increased, and his vision of the possibilities for world renewal that would result from the conflict expanded. A year to the day after the United States declared war on Germany, he urged, "Force, Force to the utmost, Force without stint or limit, the righteous and triumphant Force which shall make Right the law of the world, and cast every selfish dominion down in the dust."[82] In the summer of 1918, he declared that peace could not be obtained without "the destruction of every arbitrary power anywhere."[83] He demanded guarantees that all political, social, and economic questions be resolved freely by the people involved, that nations abide by the same code of honor as individuals, and that a league of nations be established to enforce the postwar peace. According to Gamble, America the Good was at this point imagined as fighting in a Manichean type struggle against Evil Germany.[84] As far as Wilson was concerned, Germany could choose to submit to his vision or to perish. After a number of military reversals in the autumn of 1918, Germany made its choice. On the morning of November 11, 1918, Germany signed an armistice. The war was over. Under American guidance, Wilson hoped the principles of freedom and democracy would finally have the opportunity to make the world a better place.

These extended comments on Wilson have served an important purpose insofar as they have brought greater clarity to the shape of Reagan's foreign policy vision as well as its historical resonance. A number of similarities between the foreign policy visions of Wilson and Reagan are immediately apparent. Both men believed that the United States had been founded upon abstract, universal political ideas, including freedom and democracy. Both believed that America was charged with a special mission to spread its political ideas and institutions abroad. They both reinterpreted American history and historical documents in ways that suggested U.S. foreign policy had always sought to realize these ideas. They held that governments, not people, started wars. Hence, America should never wage war against the people of another nation. If the United States had to fight, they believed that it should do so only to liberate people around the world from oppressive and tyrannical governments. Those that opposed their visions were "selfish" or "isolationists." That an interventionist impulse was a salient feature of their foreign policy visions is clear.

Was Reagan, then, a mere carbon copy of Wilson? In one sense, the answer is obviously no. Among other things, they had rather different personalities. McDougall quotes British prime minister David Lloyd George as once saying about Wilson: "he 'believed in mankind . . . but distrusted all men.' "[85] Whatever one may think of Reagan and his ideas, his personal comportment never sanctioned such a remark. There is also a noticeable difference between them concerning the emphasis they place upon America's global mission to extend democracy and freedom. For Wilson, the idea of service was the most important American obligation in foreign policy practice. As far as he was concerned, pursuing other interests was ultimately degrading to the United States and its people. For Reagan, the obligation to spread freedom and democracy was the predominant part of a vision that included more room than did Wilson's for other strategic and national security concerns.

Reagan did not avidly read Wilson's presidential speeches. No claim has been made or implied here that Reagan imbibed Wilson's ideas and vision through rigorous study of primary sources, or that he became a disciple of Wilson's foreign policy thought as an adult. But the notion that it is only under such limited circumstances that visionary similarities can be posited is indicative of an inadequate understanding of the creation of human knowledge. Such an argument could be made only by those with little understanding of the relationship between imagination and life experience as it has been explained in this study.

Gamble's scholarship has shown that Wilson's vision was an especially powerful and persuasive expression of widespread ideas within the larger Protestant progressive Christian world in which Reagan grew up. Reagan was raised as a Disciple of Christ. As Kengor notes, the founder of this sect prophesied America's destiny as world savior in the early 1830s. Kengor also explains that Reagan's mother, Nelle, was highly invested in and publicly promoted prominent progressive ideas about America's role in the world. That Harold Bell Wright, author of the book that persuaded Reagan to become a Disciple, viewed America as a messianic nation literally saving the world in the way Jesus Christ did on the cross is another example of the diffusion of these ideas in the United States. Wilson embodied and expressed a way of seeing and relating to the world that emerged out of this complex set of religious and political ideas. It is with this broader cultural and historical context in mind that Reagan's vision has been compared to Wilson's and can be described accurately as having prominent "Wilsonian" elements.

Both McDougall and Gamble see the legacy of Wilson's vision of America, and the foreign policy ideas it tends to inspire, as problematic on a number of fronts. McDougall argues that although Wilson failed to realize his vision of world peace, democracy, and freedom during World War I and its aftermath, Wilsonianism has remained highly popular in America. He claims that it has informed to varying degrees the foreign policy visions of all of Wilson's presidential successors. About Wilson and his vision, McDougall concludes, "As a blueprint for world order, Wilsonianism has always been a chimera, but as an ideological weapon against 'every arbitrary power everywhere,' it has proved mighty indeed. And that, in the end, is how Wilson did truly imitate Jesus. He brought not peace but a sword."[86] Gamble also ponders the long-term implications of this type of vision for politics. He suggests that the degree to which a foreign policy vision like Wilson's prevails in America is the degree to which war will be total both in its means and ends.[87] Insofar as Reagan's foreign policy imagination has so much in common with Wilson's, Reagan's vision may contain similar potential dangers.

REAGAN AND THE IMAGE OF DEMOCRACY

For Reagan, the image of democracy permeates many important components of his imagination. It symbolizes a number of things including liberty, representative government, elections, unions, free speech and press, universities, and rule of law grounded in a written constitution. In his vision, once these institutions are in place, the spirit of a people will be unleashed and the problems commonly associated with politics will either be greatly diminished or even eliminated over time. Now that the main contexts in which Reagan invokes this image in his speeches have been identified and analyzed, some words directly addressing his understanding of democracy can now be offered.

Reagan's vision of democracy appears to be the political counterpart of his understanding of human nature. In his imagination, the individual is both good and free by nature. Democracy, which is also naturally good, is the only environment in which human freedom and goodness can fully exist and thrive. It seems as if a type of philosophical anthropology is at work in Reagan's vision. If this is true, then Reagan is part of a larger group of statesmen and philosophers who have contemplated the relationship between human nature and politics in anthropological terms.

Plato is one of the earliest Western philosophers to construct a philosophical anthropology that could be applied to the evaluation of political order and disorder, and his insights are worth examining. In a number of his political dialogues, Plato argues that the order of the soul and the order of the *polis*, or society, are reflected in one another. In the *Republic*, Socrates explains, "'You realize, I suppose,' I went on, 'that there must be as many types of individual as of society? Societies aren't made of sticks and stones, but of men whose individual characters, by turning the scale one way or another, determine the direction of the whole.'"[88] By identifying the representative personality type of a particular society, Socrates argues that one can discern the moral qualities of its political order. For Plato, the philosopher embodies the highest degree of order an individual can realize within his or her soul. In the *Republic*, therefore, the city in speech, or *kallipolis*, has the highest degree of order because it is ruled directly by the philosopher.

In contrast to philosophical rule, Plato claims that democracy is one of the worst forms of government. It s nearly devoid of virtue and moderation. This did not surprise Plato insofar as democracy is the democratic man writ large. About democratic man Plato writes:

> "In fact," I said, "he lives from day to day, indulging the pleasure of the moment. One day it's wine, women and song, the next water to drink and a strict diet; one day it's hard physical training, the next indolence and careless ease, and then a period of philosophic study. Often he takes to politics and keeps jumping to his feet and saying or doing whatever comes into his head. Sometimes all his ambitions and efforts are military, sometimes they are all directed to success in business. There's no order or restraint in his life, and he reckons his way of living is pleasant, free and happy, and sticks to it through thick and thin."[89]

In Plato's view, democratic man suffers from a deeply disordered soul. Democratic man's spiritual wounds are self-inflicted. Injustice in a democracy cannot be attributed to poorly arranged political institutions or the insufficient diffusion of democratic principles, such as liberty and popular elections. On the contrary, the ultimate source of disorder in such a society is the ethical immaturity of its symbolic representative. Democratic disorder is a spiritual and existential disease rather than a procedural or institutional problem, as far as Plato is concerned.

If Plato is correct, then the order of a particular society or nation depends most deeply upon the ethical maturity of its individual citizens. There are no institutional shortcuts on the road to a just and ordered society. For Plato, the moral maturity of a people is an issue with which all political thinkers and leaders must deal. As he explains in the *Republic* and other dialogues such as *Gorgias*, order in the soul is achieved only after an individual engages in prolonged efforts to tame his passions and establish a life of moderation through the use of reason. This makes politics a much more difficult enterprise than proclaiming freedom or writing the word "democracy" on paper. That there may be serious problems with aspects of Plato's vision of philosophic-political order is acknowledged. That the remedy for political disorder he proposes in the *Republic* might have significant flaws does not diminish his insights into the relationship between the order of the soul and the order of society and into the existential sources of disorder in certain types of democracy.

That democracy can degenerate into the disordered society described by Plato is always a possibility in politics. Irving Babbitt and Claes G. Ryn are two scholars who have accepted some of Plato's insights into democratic disorder, but they have also articulated conditions within which a just and ordered democratic government can exist. In *Democracy and Leadership*, Babbitt argues that his understanding of human ethical dualism has a governmental analogue in what he calls "constitutional democracy." In contrast to what Babbitt terms "direct democracy," which strives to implement immediately the unfiltered, momentary desires of the numerical majority, constitutional democracy is a form of government that restrains the lower impulses of the people while allowing expressions of the higher ethical will of the political community to become manifest in legislation and governance. Constitutional democracy takes into account the higher and lower inclinations of individuals and societies in ways that direct democracy does not.

For Babbitt, a fundamental difference exists between these forms of democracy. He writes, "There is an opposition of first principles between those who maintain that the popular will should prevail, but only after it has been purified of what is merely impulsive and ephemeral, and those who maintain that this will should prevail immediately and unrestrictedly."[90] As far as Babbitt is concerned, the only type of democracy that can establish a just order, protect liberty, and work toward the common good is the constitutional variety. Genuine constitutional democracy is extremely difficult to achieve and maintain because it can function properly only when a sufficient number of ethically mature people exist within a particular society and actively participate in political life. Although it may claim to be dedicated to realizing the same goals as constitutional democracy, direct democracy inevitably fails to provide liberty, justice, and order. In large part, this is because of its reliance on an incomplete understanding of human nature. It presupposes little or no ethical preparation on the part of citizens for the responsible practice of self-government. Consequently, it is ruled by immature and immoderate democratic souls, such as those whom Plato criticizes in the *Republic*.

In *Democracy and the Ethical Life*, Claes G. Ryn uses a philosophical anthropology similar in some respects to those of Plato and Babbitt to explore the relationship between varieties of democracy and the demands of the ethical life. He writes, "Government derives its shape, strength, and direction from the aspirations of the people it serves. It will reflect and promote the ultimate goals for life that are held by that people and its leaders," and, "Political institutions are indistinguishable from the cultural ethos of a people."[91] Ryn uses these insights to develop a dichotomy between what he calls constitutional democracy and plebiscitary democracy. About the former he argues, "It will be contended here that the idea of democracy, viewed as a realistic statement of human potentiality, is at the same time the idea of constitutional democracy, that is, of popular rule under legal restraints not easily changed. This is so because of the nature of man's moral predicament."[92]

Ryn explains that constitutional democracy includes "a distrust of unhampered action and spontaneous decision."[93] This distrust is equivalent to the practice of individual ethical self-restraint insofar as it includes a similar reluctance to act upon the unchecked impulse of the moment. Ryn claims, "Just as an individual may resolve on the basis of experience of his own moral weakness not to give free rein to his impulses in the future, but to make room for moral scrutiny of his motives before acting, so a people may recognize the need for putting brakes on its own momentary will in the interest of the common good."[94] Ryn believes that constitutional democracy is the most ethically demanding form of government. It requires a great deal of moral maturity on the part of citizens and leaders as well as a culture that nurtures traditions and habits that orient people toward the common ethical purposes of politics.

Ryn contrasts constitutional democracy with what he calls plebiscitary democracy. Whereas a clear understanding of human ethical dualism shapes the idea of constitutional democracy, plebiscitary democracy is based on a belief in the natural goodness of human beings. Ryn claims that Rousseau is one of the earliest and most persuasive expositors of this other form of democracy in the modern era. Ryn argues, "In his effort to reconcile ethics and politics Rousseau becomes the champion of a form of popular rule which may be termed 'plebiscitary democracy,' one which gives maximum freedom and power to the momentary majority of the people by placing no strongly resistant legal obstacles in the way of emerging popular wishes."[95] For Rousseau, constitutional democracy places unnecessary and even immoral restraints upon the naturally good people. Despite their being based on questionable assumptions about politics and human nature, Ryn argues that plebiscitary visions of democracy continue to be immensely popular because they flatter individuals who want to avoid the painful and protracted process of cultivating the ethical maturity demanded by constitutional democracy.

CONCLUSION

These ideas from Plato, Babbitt, and Ryn are deeper philosophical explications of notions expressed by leading American figures such as John Adams, John Quincy Adams, Publius, and Brownson, as well as by Burke. All of these thinkers claim the entire human condition, the moral and immoral inclinations of the human will, must be taken into account when reflecting upon the theoretical conditions for political order and the ethical qualities of an existing regime. For these thinkers, a just order of politics is intimately related to the existence and leadership of ethically mature individuals. They stress the importance of an ethically oriented cultural or civilizational ethos to the existence of any type of responsible government, including democracy. These thinkers are especially skeptical of varieties of democratic self-government that ignore the whole truth about politics and human nature. If the political anthropologies of these thinkers make their respective assessments of the strengths and weaknesses of democracy deeply insightful and more or less correct, then Reagan's vision of democracy, human nature, and the relationship between them may very well contain some profound inadequacies.

8 "A Cathedral of Peace"[1]
Ronald Reagan and Peace among Nations

American power is the indispensable element of a peaceful world.[2]

—Ronald Reagan

Promoting liberty and democracy abroad was essential to what Reagan perceived as the U.S. mission to establish a lasting peace among nations. Although some comments have already been made about how peace is connected to freedom and democracy in Reagan's intuition, it is now time to make the relationship explicit.

REAGAN'S IMAGINATIVE VISIONS OF PEACE

Reagan had a very clear sense of what he thought was a misguided view of peace. In a speech to the American Legion, he remarked, " 'Peace' is a beautiful word, but it is also freely used and sometimes even abused."[3] In his mind, the bad use of this word was captured by the image of Neville Chamberlain, the prime minister of Great Britain during the late 1930s. For Reagan, Chamberlain's foreign policy, especially his pursuit of peace with Nazi Germany during the years before World War II began, symbolized the dangerous consequences of policies of appeasement. He believed that men like Chamberlain actually brought the world "closer to World War II."[4]

Reagan then drew attention to more recent political developments in America and Europe. He was likely thinking of the nuclear freeze movement when he explained, "Today's so-called peace movement—for all its modern hype and theatrics—makes the same old mistake. They would wage peace by weakening the free. And that just doesn't make sense."[5] In his mind, the freeze movement sought to shame the opponents of peace into acting honorably by setting a good example. Despite its good intentions, Reagan thought such an approach to world peace would only embolden the aggressive desires of the numerous enemies of world peace. Nations such as the Soviet Union, Libya, and Nicaragua always interpreted such movements and policies as signs of weakness, not strength. Even though such pacifistic ideas might be highly appealing in theory, to Reagan they were dangerous because they ignored what he felt were important truths about international relations.

What then did Reagan see when he spoke about peace among nations? As is the case in other areas of his imagination, Reagan's understanding of peace consists of distinct, even contradictory, components. In some instances, he described peace in rather modest terms. In his 1982 commencement address at Eureka College, Reagan explained, "Peace is not the absence of conflict, but the ability to cope with conflict by peaceful means. I believe we can cope. I believe that the West can fashion a realistic, durable policy that will protect our interests and keep the peace, not just for this generation but for your children and your grandchildren."[6]

In the speech in which Reagan spoke about Jim, Sally, Ivan, and Anya, he also explained, "I have openly expressed my view of the Soviet system. I don't know why this should come as a surprise to Soviet leaders who've never shied from expressing their view of our system. But this doesn't mean that we can't deal with each other. . . . The fact that neither of us likes the other system is no reason to refuse to talk."[7] Reagan often claimed that his experiences as president of the SAG and governor of California taught him that negotiation was the art of the possible. He knew that he would rarely get everything he wanted in a negotiation, whether it was with Warner Bros. Studio, the California State Legislature, the U.S. Congress, or the Soviet Union. He also knew that rigidity and belligerence were negotiating tactics that did not produce good results. In this part of Reagan's imagination, peace *might* be realized if attempts to reduce existing international political tensions were successful. Success would depend on treating adversaries with some degree of dignity and realizing that one must deal with the world as it is rather than as one might wish it to be.

Never far behind such comments in his presidential speeches were others in which Reagan imagined peace as a potentially permanent achievement connected to the promotion and realization of global democracy and freedom. In his Address on the Geneva Summit, Reagan explained, "When we speak of peace, we should not mean just the absence of war. True peace rests on the pillars of individual freedom, human rights, national self-determination, and respect for rule of law."[8] He knew this because "history has shown that democratic nations do not start wars."[9] The United States itself was proof that this notion was no mere theory. America, after all, was the most peaceful and democratic nation in the world. It never started wars, and it only fought them when there was no other option.[10] In his 1986 State of the Union Address, Reagan explained America's mission of peace as follows: "We know that peace follows in freedom's path and conflicts erupt when the will of the people is denied. So, we must prepare for peace not only by reducing weapons but by bolstering prosperity, liberty, and democracy however and wherever we can."[11]

If this more expansive vision of peace were to become a reality, the world would look very different from the one in which he lived during his presidency. In an Address to the German Bundestag, Reagan encouraged the world to "build a cathedral of peace, where nations are safe from war and where people need not fear for their liberties."[12] In his 1987 Address to the U.N. General Assembly, Reagan argued that if only the world would follow the "will of the people," then "we will at last know a world of peace and freedom, opportunity and hope, and, yes, of democracy—a world in which the spirit of mankind at last conquers the old, familiar enemies of famine, disease, tyranny, and war."[13] He concluded these remarks by explaining that the many differences among nations notwithstanding, all people were united by the common hope that "mankind will one day beat its swords into plowshares, the hope of peace."[14]

Rather than working toward a world in which the tensions among nations were reduced, a goal reflected in his more modest vision of peace, this part of Reagan saw peace as the result of a world fundamentally transformed by the promotion and establishment of certain political ideas and institutions. The culmination of this vision of peace ultimately would be a world without serious political and social tensions and thus without too much need for politics—at least as that term has been generally understood in history. The essence of this part of his vision even appears to invest the spread of liberty and democracy around the world with eschatological significance. The image of beating swords into plowshares, after all, comes from the Prophet Isaiah. It is worth noting that in the original text, this prophesied transformation of the world is brought about not by a nation but by God. In Reagan's imagination, this second, more ambitious vision of peace usually prevailed over its more modest counterpart.

The imagination is not merely the faculty by which human beings daydream. The intuition shapes a person's understanding of the world. The imagination orients the concrete actions of each individual, and it has a direct influence upon a person's political thought and practice. The divergent visions previously mentioned were often present when Reagan expressed his intuitive sense of peace among nations. The tension between them shaped his concrete efforts to pursue peace during his presidency. The different directions in which his visions of peace pulled his presidential activities can be observed more clearly through references to three important representative examples: Reagan's announcement of the Strategic Defense Initiative (SDI) in 1983, his comments about the Geneva Summit with the Soviet Union in 1985, and his thoughts on the Reykjavik Summit with the Soviet Union in 1986.

REAGAN'S IMAGINATIVE VISIONS OF PEACE IN ACTION

On March 23, 1983, only a few weeks after his "evil empire" remarks, Reagan gave a televised speech with the innocuous title "Address to the Nation on Defense and National Security." He began by explaining, "The subject I want to discuss with you, peace and national security, is both timely and important. Timely, because I've reached a decision which offers a new hope for our children in the 21st century, a decision I'll tell you about in a few minutes."[15] Before announcing this decision, Reagan painted a bleak picture of tensions around the world, and he drew attention to the steps the United States needed to take to protect its national security. He explained that although the strategy of deterrence could still work in the Cold War, the United States was not practicing it effectively because America had allowed its military might to decline at the same time that the Soviet Union had increased the size and scope of its armed power. Hence, the United States and the world were much more vulnerable to Soviet aggression than they had been in the past.

Reagan then told the American people about his plans to address this serious threat to national security. He said that his defense budget would address the years of neglect suffered by the American armed forces. He wanted to repair existing equipment and build new items in all branches of the military. He acknowledged that catching up to the Soviets would be expensive, but, because it was necessary, it was non-negotiable. He criticized the supporters of the nuclear freeze movement opposed to his plan because the alternative they offered "would make us less, not more, secure and would raise, not reduce, the risks of war."[16] He stated: "We can't afford to believe that we will never be threatened."[17] Reagan also categorized the calls in Congress for a reduction in defense spending as "the same kind of talk that led the democracies to neglect their defenses in the 1930's and invited the tragedy of World War II. We must not let that grim chapter of history repeat itself through apathy or neglect."[18] In his mind, there were no credible alternatives to his proposals for American security. The world was a dangerous place, and it would remain so. Rather than ignore that reality, Reagan sought to confront it with preparation and strength.

This part of the speech, which comprised most of his remarks, seems to be an expression of Reagan's more moderate vision of peace. But this part of the speech has largely been forgotten. It was the last few paragraphs that grabbed headlines when it was originally delivered. These concluding thoughts from Reagan remain highly relevant to contemporary debates over American national security policy and the meaning of Reagan's vision.

After his account of the need for Congress to accept his defense budget, Reagan reflected upon broader questions and concerns for U.S. national security. He expressed his dissatisfaction with the prevailing strategy for nuclear deterrence between the United States and the Soviet Union, an important piece of which was the threat of nuclear retaliation against an aggressor—the so-called Mutually Assured Destruction (MAD) doctrine. Reagan argued that it was necessary for the United States to "break out of a future that relies solely on offensive retaliation for our security."[19] He claimed that he had reached the conclusion that the "human spirit must be capable of rising above dealing with other nations and human beings by threatening their existence."[20] In offering his vision for breaking out of this strategic impasse, Reagan remarked:

> Wouldn't it be better to save lives than to avenge them? Are we not capable of demonstrating our peaceful intentions by applying all our abilities and our ingenuity to achieving a truly lasting stability? I think we are. Indeed, we must.
>
> After careful consultation with my advisers, including the Joint Chiefs of Staff, I believe there is a way. Let me share with you a vision of the future which offers hope. It is that we embark on a program to counter the awesome Soviet missile threat with measures that are defensive. Let us turn to the very strengths in technology that spawned our great industrial base and that have given us the quality of life we enjoy today.
>
> What if free people could live secure in the knowledge that their security did not rest upon the threat of instant U.S. retaliation to deter a Soviet attack, that we could intercept and destroy strategic ballistic missiles before they reached our own soil or that of our allies?
>
> I know this is a formidable, technical task, one that may not be accomplished before the end of this century. Yet, current technology has attained a level of sophistication where it's reasonable for us to begin this effort. It will take years, probably decades of effort on many fronts. There will be failures and setbacks, just as there will be successes and breakthroughs. And as we proceed, we must remain constant in preserving the nuclear deterrent and maintaining a solid capability for flexible response. But isn't it worth every investment necessary to free the world from the threat of nuclear war? We know it is.[21]

With these words, Reagan clearly and appealingly articulated a vision of the future that was consonant with his more expansive notions of peace. Here, he was not talking about merely reducing the threat of nuclear war— although he explained that at least until this project succeeded he would pursue conventional arms reduction and limitation policies. The driving force behind this part of his speech was the image of permanently freeing the world from the threat of nuclear annihilation. He asked his audience to imagine a world in which the threat of nuclear war was transcended by human ingenuity and technological achievement.

This notion of intercepting and destroying nuclear missiles launched at the United States fit with Reagan's broader understanding of the relationship among democracy, liberty, and peace. After all, he called this technology *defensive*. He did not see it as creating an opportunity for a nation to launch a nuclear attack free from fear of retaliation. Further, he believed that such a technological advance was possible, in large part, because Americans were free to conduct research and develop technology without interference from an intrusive government like the Soviet Union. The same people of genius who gave the world the nuclear bomb—i.e. scientists—were now being asked to develop technologies that would make that discovery obsolete. Thus, besides democracy and liberty, technology would contribute to the establishment of a lasting peace among human beings. Reagan concluded this address with the following words: "My fellow Americans, tonight we're launching an effort which holds the promise of changing the course of human history. There will be risks, and results take time. But I believe we can do it. As we cross this threshold, I ask for your prayers and your support."[22] He then bade America good night.

Reagan's two visions of peace emerged in other moments of his presidency. In 1985, Reagan went to Geneva, Switzerland, for his first summit meeting with a leader of the Soviet Union. Prior to departing, Reagan addressed the nation and explained what he hoped would happen in Geneva. He said, "My mission, simply stated, is a mission for peace."[23] He also explained that he wanted to build a foundation for a "lasting peace." Reagan expressed his desire for more cultural interaction between the Soviet Union and the United States as a means to peace. He said, "Imagine how much good we could accomplish, how the cause of peace would be served, if more individuals and families from our respective countries could come to know each other in a personal way. . . . Imagine if people in our nation could see the Bolshoi Ballet again, while Soviet citizens could see American plays and hear groups like the Beach Boys. And how about Soviet children watching 'Sesame Street.' "[24] These possibilities were not meant to suggest that increased cultural interaction was a panacea for world peace. He explained, "Such proposals will not bridge our differences, but people-to-people contacts can build genuine constituencies for peace in both countries. After all, people don't start wars, governments do."[25] In other words, if real Ivans and Anyas could meet real Jims and Sallys, the cause of peace would be well served.

Although Reagan hoped the summit would be successful, he acknowledged the dearth of significant achievements from previous meetings. He cautioned his audience that they should not even expect the effects of the meeting to be apparent at first glance. He argued, "Only the passage of time will tell us whether we constructed a durable bridge to a safer world."[26] He concluded his remarks with a summarization of his hopes and goals for the summit, and he asked the American people to pray for "God's grace and His guidance for all of us at Geneva, so that the cause of true peace among men will be advanced and all of humanity thereby served."[27] Thirty-six hours later, Reagan departed for Switzerland.

Reagan was told that if all that came out of Geneva was an agreement to meet again in the future, then the summit could be considered a success.[28] He wanted more. He wanted an opportunity to speak candidly with Gorbachev—alone. During the first official meeting between the two nations, in which professional diplomats talked about a variety of technical issues, Reagan asked Gorbachev if he would like to go for a walk outside. The two leaders retired to a nearby boathouse, warm with the heat of a roaring fire, and they began to have the candid discussion for which Reagan had hoped.

During their conversation, Reagan explained his view that both he and Gorbachev were capable either of starting World War III or of bringing about world peace.[29] With these possibilities in mind, Reagan continued, it was imperative that they work toward an enduring peace between their nations.

As their conversation continued, Reagan observed that although Gorbachev was fully committed to Soviet ideology, he was also willing to listen to Reagan.[30] They talked frankly about a wide range of issues, the most important and most controversial of which was SDI. Gorbachev claimed that the United States was pursuing SDI research in order to obtain a strategic advantage over the Soviet Union. Reagan explained to Gorbachev that if SDI began to look as if it could actually work, then the United States would be willing to share this technology with the Soviets and the rest of the world.[31] Gorbachev was incredulous. Although this fireside meeting afforded them the important opportunity to become acquainted, no major breakthroughs on arms reduction or SDI were reached. But, as they walked back to the official meeting from which they had escaped, each leader invited the other to visit his respective nation. On this level at least, the summit was already a success.

On the one hand, this summit shows just how difficult it is to make even the smallest amount of progress toward a more peaceful world. It was preceded by a number of candid letters between the two leaders in which they established their ideological visions, addressed what they perceived as the other nation's insincere desire for serious progress toward arms reduction and other strategic objectives, and expressed their hopes for a future peace. This correspondence continued after Geneva. Furthermore, representatives from each nation spent a great deal of time and thought in preliminary negotiations on a number of diplomatic and arms-control issues. During actual meetings, negotiations were prolonged and replete with the same candor and vigor of the pre-summit activities. But the discussions between Reagan and Gorbachev were also conducted with a high degree of genuine civility and respect. Both men stood their ground, and on certain issues and ideas they were unwilling to compromise. Nevertheless, they were also willing to address their differences and search for any peaceful common ground they could find.[32]

On the other hand, Reagan also imagined that the summit was a small step in the direction that history must inevitably move—the direction of peace, freedom, and democracy. Reagan believed that a new foundation for realizing this part of his vision of peace had been created during his private meeting with Gorbachev. Among other things, the meeting was a microcosm of the fruits that could be reaped by increased cultural interaction between the people of America and the Soviet Union. In Reagan's recollection of these events, he and Gorbachev were not so much the leaders of the two most powerful nations on earth as they were ordinary people who, unlike the professional diplomats they both brought with them to Geneva, were making real progress toward peace.

In *An American Life*, Reagan reflects upon how it was that he, the man who had called the Soviet Union an "evil empire" two years earlier, could meet with a Soviet leader and take something meaningful away from the experience. Perhaps in an attempt to dispel the notion that he had changed his ideas about the Soviet Union and had "gone soft" on communism, as it were, he writes, "Yet I knew I hadn't changed. If anything, the world was changing, and it was changing for the better. The world was approaching the threshold of a new day."[33] Reagan knew there were still major differences between the two nations. Nevertheless, it was because the world was beginning to align with the chimeric side of Reagan's imagination that he believed peace was truly possible.

Reagan's satisfaction with U.S.-Soviet relations plummeted when the two leaders met in 1986, this time in Reykjavik, Iceland. During the summit, Gorbachev agreed to U.S. proposals to eliminate nuclear weapons in Europe and ultimately the world in ten years. Reagan wondered if it was the recent nuclear disasters at Chernobyl and on a Soviet submarine that had made Gorbachev more receptive to the American position on nuclear weapons.[34] The next day, Sunday, even more incredible concessions came from Gorbachev. In response to NATO fears that a reduction in European nuclear weapons would embolden the conventional forces of the Warsaw Pact to act aggressively, Gorbachev offered to reduce drastically the number of forces in Eastern Europe. Reagan could not believe that these unprecedented concessions were being made.[35] The Sunday meeting was scheduled to end at noon, but under these extraordinary circumstances, Reagan ignored the deadline and worked with Gorbachev until the evening.

Reagan's hopes about the summit were suddenly dashed when Gorbachev demanded the United States give up its research on SDI in exchange for his concessions.[36] Reagan felt that he was being played for a fool and lost his temper. He told Gorbachev that SDI never was and never would be a bargaining chip. He then reiterated his position in Geneva that he would share SDI with the Soviets. Gorbachev's skepticism about this possibility was as strong as it had been in Geneva. In *Ronald Reagan: Fate, Freedom, and the Making of History*, John Patrick Diggins relates the following exchange between Reagan and Gorbachev over SDI during the Iceland Summit:

GORBACHEV: You will take the arms race into space, and could be tempted to launch a first strike from space.

REAGAN: That's why I propose to eliminate ballistic missiles and share SDI with you.

GORBACHEV: If you will not share oil-drilling equipment or even milk processing factories, I do not believe you will share SDI.

REAGAN: We are willing to eliminate all ballistic missiles before SDI is deployed, so a first strike would be impossible.[37]

Despite his best efforts, Reagan could not convince Gorbachev of his honest desire to share SDI. When the futility of further argument became apparent,

Reagan abruptly ended the meeting.[38] He returned home and addressed the nation about the hopes and disappointments of his recent visit with Gorbachev.

In his address, Reagan explained that he viewed the American people as "full participants" in the negotiations with the Soviet Union and that he went to Iceland with the view that to obtain peace, "everything was negotiable except two things: our freedom and our future."[39] He said that he and Gorbachev had made great progress in arms reduction, and he explained that the abolition of nuclear weapons within a decade appeared to be within reach. Then Gorbachev told him that all the progress they had made was contingent upon the United States accepting the Soviet position on SDI. Reagan then asked a rhetorical question that was likely on the minds of many members of his audience: "Why not give up SDI for this agreement?" He explained that SDI was "America's insurance policy" against a change back to a more aggressive Soviet foreign policy. It was SDI and the general reconstitution of the American military during the previous five years that had brought forth fruitful negotiations with the USSR. More importantly, "SDI is the key to a world without nuclear weapons."[40] For these reasons, Reagan would not abandon the project.

In the aftermath of the Iceland Summit's failure, Reagan told the American people that there were no specific future meetings scheduled between him and Gorbachev.[41] But Reagan still sounded a note of optimism about the future. He stated, "I'm ultimately hopeful about the prospects for progress at the summit and for world peace and freedom."[42] He was optimistic because the world was a very different place, in his mind, than it had been in the past. The world had changed much for the better because the American people had restored America's economy, military, and national unity. American courage and success were sources of hope and inspiration for the world. The world's democracies drew strength and purpose from the United States, and the rest of the world was turning to "democratic ideas and the principles of the free market."[43] America could be hopeful about a peaceful future because it was now dealing from a position of strength. It would only be a matter of time before the Soviets came back to the negotiating table and the movement toward peace resumed.

The Iceland Summit, perhaps more than any other event during his presidency, symbolizes the tension between Reagan's two visions of peace. Reagan once told Gorbachev that they must seize existing opportunities for peace rather than wait for ideal negotiating conditions to materialize, and yet Reagan walked away from agreements he himself described in the most grandiose terms. Why? During his speech about the Iceland Summit, he told the American people that SDI could not be abandoned because it had brought the Soviets back to the negotiating table. It was an "insurance policy" in case the Soviet Union decided to renege on its commitments to arm reductions after the United States had stopped SDI research. For Reagan, SDI was both a symbol of renewed American strength and

Reagan's recognition that blind trust in negotiated agreements with the Soviet Union was not a wise policy. In part, SDI was an expression of Reagan's favorite Russian proverb: "Trust, but verify." In this light, Reagan's attachment to SDI might appear to be rooted in his more realistic vision of peace. But he had other reasons for protecting SDI in which he believed more deeply.

The night before Reagan gave his 1983 address announcing SDI, he wrote in his diary: "On my desk was a draft of the speech on defense to be delivered tomorrow night on TV. . . . I did a lot of re-writing. Much of it was to change bureaucratic into people talk."[44] His personal investment in this speech and his desire to communicate clearly *his* vision, rather than one crafted for him by members of his administration, is indicative of his strong attachment to SDI. In *President Reagan*, Lou Cannon writes, "More than any other specific program of the administration, SDI was a product of Reagan's imagination and Reagan's priorities."[45] Long before he became president, Reagan had found appealing the possibility that the United States and the world could be protected from a nuclear attack with defensive measures. In *The Crusader: Ronald Reagan and the Fall of Communism*, Paul Kengor explains that Reagan was first acquainted with such an idea as governor of California in the late 1960s. Kengor also indicates that the appeal of a defense against nuclear attack was intensified during a 1979 visit to NORAD in which Reagan was told that the United States simply had no defense against a Soviet nuclear attack.[46]

That Reagan had a long-standing attachment to something like SDI does not explain very much about *why* he found it so appealing. Some scholars and journalists have attributed Reagan's affinity for SDI to its resonance with ideas and images from movies in which he starred. *Murder in the Air* (1940) is often cited as a representative example of the alleged connections between Reagan's political thought and acting career. In *Way Out There in the Blue: Ronald Reagan, Star Wars and the End of the Cold War*, Frances FitzGerald explains that in the movie Reagan played a "secret agent charged with protecting a newly invented superweapon, the 'Inertia Projector,' " which could destroy all enemy aircraft. In the film, FitzGerald writes, "a Navy admiral claims that the weapon 'not only makes the United States invincible in war, but, in doing so, promises to become the greatest force for world peace ever discovered.' "[47] Still other arguments draw attention to Reagan's religious views on Armageddon and the possibility that it could be delayed if technologies such as SDI could be developed. Lou Cannon writes, "Reagan was convinced that American ingenuity could find a way to protect the American people from the nightmare of Armageddon. As he saw it, the Strategic Defense Initiative was a dream come true."[48] Appeals to Reagan's acting career and religious ideas about the end times as explanations of his support for SDI are not wholly without merit, but there seem to be other, more important reasons explaining Reagan's deep commitment to SDI.

Reagan was very uncomfortable with the so-called MAD doctrine of nuclear deterrence. In *Ronald Reagan*, Dinesh D'Souza writes, "Reagan's main reason for supporting the concept of SDI was that he believed it was immoral for a nation to have an official policy of leaving its citizens defenseless against Soviet nuclear attack."[49] There is an important sense in which Reagan believed nuclear weapons were *immoral.* Part of the appeal to him of SDI was that, unlike MAD, technology promised to provide protection against a nuclear attack that would be effective and *moral.* In the Iceland speech, Reagan devoted an entire paragraph to asking rhetorical questions about the Soviets' desire to prohibit the United States from protecting itself and the world against nuclear attacks. After all, SDI was a *defensive* weapon. Gorbachev objected to SDI on one level because, even if Reagan would not use it in conjunction with offensive nuclear weapons to gain a strategic advantage over the Soviet Union, Gorbachev felt it was possible that a future American leader might. This type of objection did not resonate with Reagan at all. In Reagan's mind, democratic nations never start wars.

Reagan told Americans there were two things that were non-negotiable in Iceland: America's freedom and America's *future.* When the possible reduction of a large number of nuclear weapons was at hand, Reagan was unwilling to relinquish his vision of a world protected by SDI from nuclear attacks. SDI was too important to be given away in negotiation.[50] The *image* of a world in which human beings had used technology to eliminate the fear of nuclear weapons seems to have been more important than the *reality* of a world in which the number of nuclear weapons was significantly reduced. Ultimately, Reagan's support for SDI was an expression of his more expansive vision of peace. Along with liberty and democracy, technology promised to bring forth a peaceful world the likes of which no human beings had thought possible. SDI was morally superior to MAD and needed to be protected at all costs. Reykjavik seems to symbolize the triumph of a dream over practical politics in Reagan's mind.

Reagan's comments announcing SDI, his thoughts on the Geneva Summit, and his remarks about Reykjavik have clarified further how two different conceptions of peace fit together in his political thought and practice. In his speech to the British Parliament, Reagan declared, "While we must be cautious about forcing the pace of change, we must not hesitate to declare our ultimate objectives and to take concrete actions to move toward them. We must be staunch in our conviction that freedom is not the sole prerogative of a lucky few, but the inalienable and universal right of all human beings."[51] It appears that at least on some occasions the image of a world changing in conformity with his vision of the inexorable triumph of global freedom and democracy is the intuitive lens through which Reagan interpreted the more practical steps he took toward realizing a more peaceful world. Perhaps these comments about choosing practical means to make progress toward the inevitable end of history provide grounds for a partial synthesis of the two apparently divergent visions of peace held by Reagan.

REAGAN'S VISION OF LIBERTY, DEMOCRACY, AND PEACE: A THEORETICAL PERSPECTIVE

At this time, a difficult and important set of issues need to be raised concerning Reagan's vision of democracy, liberty, and peace. A number of scholars have called into question the theoretical adequacy of foreign policy ideas similar to those expressed by Reagan. Some argue that Western attempts to establish democracies around the world often cause more harm than good for the people upon which this type of political arrangement is forced. Others suggest that promoting liberty and democracy as the means to a more peaceful world reveals an incomplete understanding of how tensions among nations can be successfully managed. Still others claim that expressions of concern for the suffering of people around the globe, when combined with the desire to bestow freedom and democracy upon the world, are often pretexts for the emergence of a nation's will to power in international politics. Exploring briefly these types of theoretical concerns will help clarify further this part of Reagan's imagination.

Eric Voegelin, a noted twentieth-century philosophical historian and political theorist, holds that many in the West err when treating constitutional democracy and the good society as synonymous concepts. In "Liberalism and Its History," he argues, "A constitutional model that is so manifestly historically contingent must lead unavoidably to difficulties and cause severe damage when it is dogmatized into a worldview and its elements are raised to articles of faith. The catastrophe of its exportation to non-Western societies plays itself out for all to see, but we need not look that far."[52] Like Orestes Brownson and, of course, Aristotle, Voegelin believes that goodness can inhere in different types of societies and be advanced through various forms of government. He also claims that some societies—not just their leaders—are not good or otherwise ready for constitutional government. They cannot be made so merely by becoming democracies on parchment. In "Industrial Society in Search of Reason," Voegelin writes, "Unconscionable damage to millions of people throughout the world has resulted from ill-considered constitutional experiments modeled after the West."[53] If these comments are correct, then they raise the possibility of serious theoretical and practical flaws in Reagan's central vision of promoting freedom and democracy as the best means to a peaceful world.

Claes G. Ryn has also criticized what he considers the lack of depth and realism in the kind of dreamy globalism promoted by Reagan. In *A Common Human Ground: Universality and Particularity in a Multicultural World*, Ryn contends that such a view places unwarranted faith in the ability of abstract and sentimental notions of liberty and democracy to bring about

world peace. But neither are international agreements and institutions sufficient for averting conflict. This belief, too, overlooks the most important prerequisites for peace. Ryn also criticizes trust in technological developments as
the means to eliminating tensions among nations. He argues:

> Many in the West and elsewhere trust in scientific progress and general
> enlightenment to reduce the danger of conflict, but we need only look
> to the century preceding this one—the most murderous and inhumane
> in the history of mankind—to recognize that the spread of science and
> allegedly sophisticated modern ideas does not reduce the self-absorption
> or belligerence of human beings. It only provides them with new means
> of asserting their will.[54]

About the genuine conditions for peace, Ryn writes, "In the long run,
political, economic, scientific, and other contacts need to be informed and
shaped by a morality of self-control and by corresponding cultural disci-
pline and sensibility."[55] Ryn concedes that this emphasis does not make
the achievement of peace among nations easy. Discovering and cultivating
the aesthetic, moral, intellectual, and spiritual common ground among different countries and civilizations presupposes a deep knowledge of one's
own culture and history as well as of those of others. It also requires an
understanding and acknowledgement that there is no single model of the
good society; good can be realized in a variety of forms in different cultural
and political situations. Whatever the circumstances, there is for Ryn no
plausible substitute for moral and cultural effort. He writes, "Peace will
not emerge spontaneously. . . . There are no shortcuts, such as narrowly
political or economic measures, to creating genuine respect and friendliness
among peoples."[56] But if Ryn is generally correct, then the paths to peace
advocated by Reagan may be incapable of achieving the objective and may
even be counterproductive.

In *Democracy and Leadership*, Irving Babbitt draws the seemingly
counterintuitive conclusion that allegedly disinterested desires to serve the
world often culminate in some form of empire. With sentimental humanitarians such as Woodrow Wilson in mind, Babbitt writes, "We have heard
asserted in our own time the abstract right of whole populations to self-
determination as something anterior to their degree of moral development.
To put forward a supposed right of this kind as a part of a program for world
peace is to sink to the ultimate depth of humanitarian self-deception."[57] By
self-deception Babbitt meant that the humanitarians misunderstood both
the possibilities of politics in the real world and their own motives. He
draws their motives out into the open when he explains, "The humanitarian would, of course, have us meddle in foreign affairs as part of his
program of world service. Unfortunately, it is more difficult than he sup-
poses to engage in such a program without getting involved in a program
of world empire."[58] Babbitt argues that, in practice, the supposedly high

idealism of most humanitarians translates into an idealistic or sentimental type of imperialism.

Reagan had conflicting thoughts on the relationship between his vision of America's role in the world and empire. He often protested against charges of imperialism in his presidential speeches. In one respect, he did not see his vision as imperial because that term meant a foreign policy of conquest benefiting one's nation at the expense of other countries and peoples. This is a rather conventional way of thinking about imperialism. The activities of various past empires carving out colonies around the globe correspond to this notion. Reagan was never interested in acquiring colonies in that sense. In supporting democratic movements around the world, he rarely committed the U.S. military to combat. When he did, as was the case in Lebanon and Grenada, it lasted for months, not years, and he deployed a few thousand, not a few hundred thousand, American soldiers.

But is it not possible that a different type of imperialism might be present in his imagination? In his 1992 speech to the Republican National Convention, Reagan himself actually conceded the imperialism in question, admitting a good deal more than he and many of his listeners probably realized. He said, "There was a time when empires were defined by land mass, subjugated peoples, and military might. But the United States is unique, because we are an empire of ideals."[59] The image of America as an empire of ideals captures the essence of the predominant part of his sense of America's role in the world, unifying its various images and ideas into a complete and captivating whole. It is a symbol of his strong desire for the global diffusion of a certain way of life. The symbol demands the acceptance of certain abstract ideas and the establishment of corresponding political and social institutions. A longing for this new world pervaded Reagan's statements on foreign policy and peace in presidential speeches and other writings.

In a presidential speech, Reagan claimed, "It's not an arrogant demand that others adopt our ways. It's a realistic belief in the relative and proven success of the American experiment."[60] About those who were hesitant to undertake his campaign for liberty and democracy, he made the following remarks:

> Some people argue that any attempt to do that represents interference in the affairs of others, an attempt to impose our way of life. Well, it's nothing of the kind. Every nation has the right to determine its own destiny. But to deny the democratic values and that they have any relevance to the developing world today, or to the millions of people who are oppressed by Communist domination, is to reject the universal significance of the basic, timeless credo that all men are created equal and that they're endowed by their Creator with certain inalienable rights.
>
> People living today in Africa, in Latin America, in Central Asia, possess the same inalienable right to choose their own governors and decide their own destiny as we do.[61]

Reagan combined his thoughts about the universal significance and sovereignty of the Declaration of Independence, which he often referred to in this manner, with similar notions about the global importance and authority of the U.S. Constitution. In a speech given at the 1987 "We the People" Celebration, he argued:

> One scholar described our Constitution as a kind of covenant. It is a covenant we've made not only with ourselves but with all of mankind. . . . It is an oath of allegiance to that in man that is truly universal, that core of being that exists before and beyond distinctions of class, race, or national origin. It is a dedication of faith to the humanity we all share, that part of each man and woman that most closely touches on the divine.[62]

CONCLUSION

In Reagan's chimeric imagination, the United States has a mandate, a moral obligation, to make real the possibilities for global political and social order. No one needs to fear American power because it will only be used to serve the true interests of all and to realize the dreams of the world. This is what Reagan has in mind when referring to America as an empire of ideals. The image does in fact suggest a *sentimental* variety of imperialism, which, as any student of Babbitt will readily recognize, is often easily transformed into a justification for asserting American military might. If the insights of Babbitt, Voegelin, and Ryn are more or less correct, then Reagan's vision of global democracy, freedom, technology, and peace is incomplete and in important respects flawed. Reagan's vision of America's role in the world might even undermine genuine opportunities for peaceful international relations, thus making the world more dangerous.

9 "The Land of Limitless Possibilities"[1]
Ronald Reagan, Progress, Technology, and America

> Emerson was right. We are the country of tomorrow. Our revolution did not end at Yorktown. More than two centuries later, America remains on a voyage of discovery, a land that has never become, but is always in the act of becoming.[2]
>
> —Ronald Reagan

In many of his presidential speeches, Reagan spoke about technological progress and how it was improving numerous aspects of human life. He linked the various manifestations of material progress to the continued global progress of freedom, democracy, and free markets. By liberating people from many of the restraints imposed on them by their various governments, progress could continue at an ever more rapid pace. In Reagan's view, progress was a vital component in promoting global community, brotherhood, and peace. He also believed that progress did not draw Americans or the world away from traditional religious and moral beliefs. Progress did not spell cultural or spiritual decline. Rather, progress and religion went hand in hand. "Progress" is one of the most frequently used words in Reagan's presidential speeches, and it is one of the most important symbols in his imagination. Obtaining a clearer understanding of what this word symbolizes in his vision will shed more light upon his broader imagination. Reagan's intuitive understanding of the past, present, and future as well as the relationship between his vision and conservatism can then be further clarified.

REAGAN AND THE MANIFOLD FORMS OF PROGRESS

In his presidential speeches, Reagan drew frequent attention to one of his favorite types of progress—technological progress. He often stated that the speed of technological progress was staggering. In his 1983 State of the Union Address, he explained, "To many of us now, computers, silicon chips, data processing, cybernetics, and all the other innovations of the dawning high technology age are as mystifying as the workings of the combustion engine must have been when that first Model T rattled down Main Street,

U.S.A."[3] Reagan spoke many times about the wonder of technology from his personal experience. During remarks at Tuskegee University, he stated, "The goals Americans set for themselves in the days of my youth seem so modest: indoor plumbing, electricity, a family car, having a telephone or a radio crystal set. Traveling to distant cities was rare; traveling overseas was within reach of only a few. For my family, even going to a movie was not always within reach."[4] Indeed, it was during his lifetime that the automobile emerged as a primary means of transportation, and radio, movies, and television were invented or came into prominence. In a number of ways, American life in the 1980s looked very different from the turn-of-the-century Dixon, Illinois, in which Reagan grew up. The pace of technological progress during the twentieth century made the modest expectations of his childhood unnecessary for the United States as well as the world. After all, Regan argued that since the time of his youth, "the evolution of technology has become evermore rapid—each step of the way—making a better life for man on Earth."[5]

Early in his presidency, Reagan observed that progress was once again on the march in America. In a 1983 radio address to the nation, he told Americans that the quality of their lives was dramatically improving. He explained that Americans had more purchasing power than in years past. Inflation was dropping, and food and other commodity prices were climbing at slower speeds. Interest rates and federal income taxes were also falling, driving down the cost of starting a business, financing higher education, and obtaining a home mortgage. The number of employed Americans was the highest in its history, and Reagan argued that Americans not only had more jobs than ever before—they had *better* jobs. In addition to these economic indicators of progress, he said, "Life expectancy reached a record high last year, climbing to 74.5 years. Infant mortality declined to an all-time low with only 11.2 deaths per 1,000 live births."[6] In a different speech, he argued, "Medical technology is conquering one by one the diseases that have plagued mankind for centuries."[7] In remarks at the Goddard Space Flight Center, Reagan said, "I've also been shown a hand-held x-ray machine and the Programmable Implantable Medication System, called PIMS, that administers medication automatically within the body. It would be difficult to put a pricetag on the value of these human benefits."[8] Such evidence proved that progress was allowing people to live longer, more productive, and happier lives than ever before.

Medical technological progress and longer life expectancy would enable Americans and others around the world to take advantage of other technological achievements. In remarks at Tuskegee University, Reagan explained:

> While jet airliners carry passengers, even those of modest means, from coast to coast and overseas, our engineers are busy developing crafts that one day will take off from a runway and carry us into space, aerospace planes that will deliver us anywhere in the world in just a few

hours' time. Discoveries in the field of superconductivity are coming so rapidly that research results are often out of date before they're in print. Scientists are bringing us to the day of pollution-free electric cars and magnetic trains that carry cargo and travelers at speeds of 300 or 400 miles per hour.[9]

American agriculture had also found ways to increase output and thereby the quantity and quality of food in the United States and around the world. Reagan argued that in his youth, "It took one farmer then to feed four Americans in those days. Today that same farmer can feed 60 Americans and 15 foreigners."[10] In a different speech, he explained, "Biotechnology has invented new grains that are a winning weapon in the war against hunger."[11] Although all these advances were important examples of technological progress, nothing was more so in Reagan's imagination than the American space program.

On July 4, 1982, Reagan delivered remarks at Edwards Air Force Base during a celebration of the completion of the space shuttle test flights. He stated that both the space program and the space shuttle had made strong contributions to the restoration of American optimism. But the program and the shuttle were doing more than this. He explained, "We've only peered over the edge of our accomplishment, yet already the space program has improved the lives of every American." [12] He claimed that it had created jobs in aerospace and aviation-related industries for "over a million of our citizens."[13] It had also contributed to vast technological developments in "communications, computers, health care, energy efficiency, consumer products, and environmental protection."[14] These were only a few of the ways in which the space program contributed to American technological and economic progress.

Reagan knew there were people who were skeptical of the types of progress he extolled, believing these forms of progress to perpetuate selfishness, greed, immorality, the fragmentation of society, and cultural decay. Reagan believed the United States had shown that such developments were not inevitable or even likely. During his 1983 remarks to the National Association of Evangelicals, he said, "One recent survey by a Washington-based research council concluded that Americans were far more religious than the people of other nations; 95 percent of those surveyed expressed a belief in God and a huge majority believed the Ten Commandments had real meaning in their lives."[15] He claimed another study concluded "an overwhelming majority of Americans" disapproved of "adultery, teenage sex, pornography, abortion, and hard drugs."[16] In a Radio Address to the Nation on Voluntarism, Reagan celebrated "an unprecedented outpouring of charity and good will" in America.[17] He remarked, "Last year alone, individuals, corporations, bequests, and foundations gave nearly $80 billion to good causes. . . . And according to a recent study, some 89 million Americans perform volunteer work every year."[18] By all these measurements, it was clear to Reagan that Americans were more than capable of maintaining their moral bearings in the midst of the progress that was changing everything else around them. Those who feared or rejected progress simply did not understand progress.

Reagan's vision of progress in America had many implications for the rest of the world. He believed that the world admired and wanted to emulate the American tradition of progress. In his mind, global political and economic progress was the key to unlocking the world's full potential for progress in other areas. In his Second Inaugural Address, Reagan explained, "Freedom is one of the deepest and noblest aspirations of the human spirit. People, worldwide, hunger for the right of self-determination, for those inalienable rights that make for human dignity and progress."[19] During his presidency, Reagan was satisfied that democracy, freedom, and free markets were growing around the world. He often touted the growth of democracy in Asia and Latin America. He repeatedly described the stirrings of liberty in the Soviet Union and Eastern Europe, especially Poland, as signs of hope for more peace and freedom in those lands in the future. Reagan claimed new free market policies in countries such as India and China had led to an "explosion in production."[20] Taiwan, the Republic of Korea, and Japan had "created the true economic miracle" of the era.[21] Their decisions to open their markets led to "a soaring of growth and standards of living" in their respective nations and in the Pacific Rim region.[22] He cited other nations and regions around the world that were opening their economies to the free market, cutting taxes and regulations, and freeing their citizens to pursue their hopes. About this global progress he remarked, "Yes, policies that release to flight ordinary people's dreams are spreading around the world."[23]

REAGAN, PROGRESS, AND TIME

Reagan's vision of progress also had a strong influence upon his intuitive sense of time—that is, his understanding of how the past, present, and future held together. References to the dangers of the present and to the pessimism of the recent American past were numerous in Reagan's presidential speeches. Even after the economy had improved in the mid- and late 1980s, he reminded his audience of how dangerous the previous decades had truly been. In his 1986 State of the Union Address, he said, "But it wasn't long ago that we looked out on a different land: locked factory gates, long gasoline lines, intolerable prices, and interest rates turning the greatest country on Earth into a land of broken dreams. Government growing beyond our consent had become a lumbering giant, slamming shut the gates of opportunity, threatening to crush the very roots of our freedom."[24] The combination of political blundering and governmental mismanagement on the one hand, and the growing sense of pessimism about the future on the other, had presented grave threats to progress.[25]

But if the present was a time of great peril, it was also a time of great hope and possibilities. The path to progress could be reestablished and made brighter than before if only government would get out of the way, trust the people, and encourage them to dream and imagine a world in which anything is possible. In his 1981 nationally televised address on the economy, Reagan said, "We must not be timid. We will restore the freedom of all men and women to excel and to create. We will *unleash* the energy and genius of the American people, traits which have never failed us."[26] Reagan frequently expressed his desire to free the American people from governmental restraints that impeded their natural goodness. This notion of unchaining Americans was also a fundamental part of his desire to increase the rate and types of progress in America and the world.

In Reagan's imagination, the prospects for letting Americans loose were tied to a reorientation of the American mind toward hope for the future. In other words, Reagan needed to help Americans rediscover their natural optimism. In his 1985 State of the Union Address, he said:

> My fellow citizens, this nation is poised for greatness. The time has come to proceed toward a great new challenge—*a second American Revolution of hope and opportunity*; a revolution carrying us to new heights of progress by pushing back frontiers of knowledge and space; a revolution of spirit that taps the soul of America, enabling us to summon greater strength than we've ever known; and a revolution that carries beyond our shores the golden promise of human freedom in a world of peace.
>
> Let us begin by challenging our conventional wisdom. There are no constraints on the human mind, no walls around the human spirit, no barriers to our progress except those we ourselves erect.[27]

Reagan's new revolution meant getting Americans to start dreaming again. In a speech he argued, "Our vision is not an impossible dream; it's a waking dream. As Americans, let us cultivate the art of seeing things invisible. Only by challenging the limits of growth will we have the strength and knowledge to make America a rocket of hope shooting to the stars."[28] The notion that one's imagination and dreams were the only limits upon human achievement and progress was one he expressed frequently. Reagan believed that if his message were taken to heart, then the future would be one of unlimited possibilities.

To stimulate the American capacity to dream, Reagan often referred to the progress future technological developments would provide. In remarks at the United States Air Force Academy, Reagan told the new graduates, "Your generation stands on the verge of greater advances than humankind has ever known. America's future will be determined by your dreams and your visions."[29] He told them this would be nowhere more obvious than in the conquest of America's newest frontier—"the vast frontier of space."[30] He said, "The benefits to be reaped from our work in space literally dazzle the imagination."[31] He argued that space travel and technological research would produce new "life-saving medicines" and "superchips" that would extend human life and make America a stronger economic power.[32] In this vision of the future, "space observatories" would be constructed "enabling scientists to see out to the edge of the universe."[33] The only limits upon these and other developments were the "courage and imagination" of the next generation.[34]

Reagan used his 1984 State of the Union Address to announce the future plans of his administration for space exploration and development. He stated, "We can follow our dreams to distant stars, living and working in space for peaceful, economic, and scientific gain."[35] He then announced his decision to direct the National Aeronautics and Space Administration (NASA) to construct a manned space station within a decade. He claimed:

> A space station will permit quantum leaps in our research in science, communications, in metals, and in lifesaving medicines which could be manufactured only in space. We want our friends to help us meet these challenges and share in their benefits. NASA will invite other countries to participate so we can strengthen peace, build prosperity, and expand freedom for all who share our goals.[36]

With the right guidance and vision, space exploration, space shuttles, and space stations could unlock an age of limitless progress. Various technology-driven industries could reap unimaginable benefits from doing research in space. International cooperation in space exploration would advance the cause of world peace. From Reagan's point of view, the future was already being realized in the present. As he said in a 1988 speech, "Technology in these last decades has reshaped our lives. It's opened vast opportunity for the common man and has brought all of mankind into one community."[37]

Reagan believed his sentiments about progress and hope for the future were quintessentially American. In a 1984 radio address, he explained, "Just as the Yankee Clipper ships of the last century symbolized American vitality, our space shuttles today capture the optimistic spirit of our times," and, "We've always prided ourselves on the pioneer spirit that built America. Well, that spirit is a key to our future as well as our past. Once again we're on a frontier."[38] In a speech given a year earlier, he remarked, "We're a nation that lionizes pathfinders, whether they be Daniel Boone or Charles Lindbergh. Many of tomorrow's heroes, the men and women who will inspire our people and exemplify what it means to be an American, will be individuals who are part of our conquest of the vast frontier of space—a frontier that's always been in sight, but that only now is coming within reach."[39]

Providing progress was one of the important ways in which America remained the "New World," as well as "future's child, the golden hope for all mankind."[40] In remarks at the Opening Ceremonies of the 1982 World's Fair, Reagan said, "I'm sure that patriots in every country believe that their nation holds the key to world progress. But I have long believed the United States of America and her people have a special destiny. Abraham Lincoln said, 'God would never cease to call America to her true service, not only for her sake, but for the sake of the world.' "[41] For Reagan, the space shuttle and space exploration were the newest parts of a long-standing American tradition of progress. Astronauts were the latest versions of American adventurers. In these instances, current and future technological developments were drawing upon the same spirit that had made America the envy of the world in days past. For Reagan, time itself was held together by the image of progress.

Beyond his general references to more and better medical technology, scientific research and discovery, space exploration, and international cooperation and unity, Reagan left the content of the future open and vague. After all, how could he define a future that was limited only by the imagination and dreams of individuals in America and around the world? Although the future could be anything, he was certain it would be both good in itself and better than the past and present of human existence.

All these ideas and images represent the predominant strain of Reagan's vision of progress. But, in rare instances in his presidential speeches, Reagan seemed to intuit that the types of progress he often celebrated might also degrade civilized life. In a speech Reagan said, "Now, there are those who see a dark side to our technological progress."[42] He explained that such people often admitted that technological progress had brought humanity many benefits. And yet, according to Reagan, these critics usually pointed out, "as man has advanced into this new age, so has his capability to kill and destroy; and it's no longer just those in uniform who are victimized."[43] He then reflected upon his days as an undergraduate student at Eureka College. He recalled a discussion in one of his classes in which the moral authority of Americans to bomb cities and civilians was debated. He explained, "Half felt it might be necessary. The others felt bombing civilians would always be beyond the pale of decency, totally unacceptable human conduct, no matter how heinous the enemy."[44] Reagan went on to say that only a decade later, presumably during World War II, "few, if any, who had been in that room objected to our country's wholesale bombing of cities. Civilization's standards of morality had changed. The thought of killing more and more people, noncombatants, became more and more acceptable."[45] He immediately went on to explain how new technologies, such as those associated with his Strategic Defense Initiative (SDI), would provide an escape from such ethical dilemmas. New technologies, he promised, were going to provide the next generation with "a chance to raise the moral standards of mankind."[46]

Such questions and concerns about the potential moral consequences of progress were seldom raised in Reagan's public remarks. Nevertheless, in those rare instances, Reagan sensed the possibility that material and technological progress might not be synonymous with moral and spiritual progress. In other words, he entertained, however briefly, the possibility that

146 "An Empire of Ideals"

progress in one area of existence may not guarantee progress in other areas that make for civilization.

REAGAN'S VISION OF PROGRESS: PHILOSOPHICAL AND AESTHETIC PERSPECTIVES

Various thinkers in the twentieth century have raised concerns that the vast technological achievements of the Western world during the modern era have, for all of their benefits, created a number of problems for civilized life. The sociologist and communitarian writer Robert Nisbet explains, "The modern release of the individual from traditional ties of class, religion, and kinship has made him free; but, on the testimony of innumerable works in our age, this freedom is accompanied not by the sense of creative release but by the sense of disenchantment and alienation."[47] Nisbet argues that technological changes, in conjunction with political, economic, and social developments, have contributed mightily to a strong sense of individual isolation from other human beings. He writes, "It has become obvious, surely, that technological progress and the relative satisfaction of material needs in a population offer no guarantee of the resolution of all deprivations and frustrations."[48] He considers this to be the irony of ironies because "man's belief in himself has become weakest in the very age when his control of environment is greatest."[49] Overall, Nisbet's analysis suggests that the varieties of progress often celebrated by Reagan tend to undermine human community, individual identity, and happiness.

The economist Wilhelm Röpke argues that the same developments described by Nisbet have also contributed to the rise of an impoverished culture and the "enmassment" of modern life. He states:

> As we increasingly become mere passively activated mass particles or social molecules, all poetry and dignity, and with them the very spice of life and its human content, go out of life. Even the dramatic episodes of existence—birth, sickness, and death—take place in collectivized institutions. Our hospitals are medical factories, with division of labor between all sorts of health mechanics and technicians dealing with the body. People live in mass quarters, superimposed upon each other vertically and extending horizontally as far as the eye can see; they work in mass factories or offices in hierarchical subordination; they spend their Sundays and vacations in masses, flood the universities, lecture halls, and laboratories in masses, read books and newspapers printed in millions and of a level that usually corresponds to these mass sales, are assailed at every turn by the same billboards, submit, with millions of others, to the same movie, radio, and television programs, get caught up in some mass organization or other, flock in hundreds of thousands as thrilled spectators to the same sports stadiums.[50]

Reagan often used various quantifiable measurements, such as more jobs, more and better gadgets, lower taxes, higher salaries, and longer life expectancy, to prove the progress of civilization. Röpke suggests that focusing mainly upon such quantifiable examples provides an incomplete and dubious account of progress. He argues, "Man simply does not live by radio, automobiles, and refrigerators alone, but by the whole unpurchasable world beyond the market and turnover figures, the world of dignity, beauty, poetry, grace, chivalry, love, and friendship, the world of community, variety of life, freedom, and fullness of personality."[51] If the question were put to him directly, Reagan would no doubt agree with this statement. Nevertheless, the predominant part of his vision of progress seems to undermine these parts of civilized life.

Both Nisbet and Röpke identify social problems caused by modern developments commonly associated with the term "progress." Irving Babbitt dwells deeply upon the nature of these types of civilizational problems. Although he wrote *Democracy and Leadership* when Reagan was barely a teenager, Babbitt concedes many of the points Reagan would later make about the extent and types of progress in America. Babbitt writes, "Judged by any quantitative test, the American achievement is impressive."[52] Here he is referring to America's then-overwhelming superiority in the output of oil, steel, copper, telephones, and typewriters as evidence of this quantitative progress. Babbitt thought that such measurements of progress overlooked more disconcerting changes in the United States. He argues, "If quantitatively the American achievement is impressive, qualitatively it is somewhat less satisfying."[53] He identifies numerous qualitative indicators similar to those mentioned by Nisbet and Röpke to support this argument. Babbitt believes this tension between quantitative and qualitative progress reflects a growing confusion in America between scientific progress and spiritual progress.

Babbitt argues that many Americans believe technological and scientific advances immediately confer a commensurate growth in moral standards. He explains:

> We assume that because we are advancing rapidly in one direction we are advancing in all directions; yet from what we know of man in history we should rather be justified in assuming the exact opposite. Whatever may be true of the doctrine of progress in the abstract, it is likely, as held by the average American, to prove a dangerous infatuation. We reason that science must have created a new heaven because it has so plainly created a new earth. And so we are led to think lightly of the knowledge of human nature possessed by a past that was so palpably ignorant of the laws of electricity; and in the meanwhile we are blinded to the fact that we have men who are learned in the laws of electricity and ignorant of the laws of human nature.[54]

To Babbitt's mind, assumptions about the convergence of moral and material progress are ill founded. He argues, "One may be aided in detecting the nature of this confusion by the Emersonian distinction . . . between a 'law for man' and a 'law for thing.'"[55] By "law for thing," which Babbitt also somewhat confusingly calls the "natural law," he means the laws of nature commonly associated with modern science. By "law for man," which he also calls the "human law," he means the moral laws, cultural norms, and insights into the human condition commonly associated with ancient Greek and Roman philosophy as well as with religions such as Judaism, Christianity, and Buddhism. Babbitt never categorically condemns all technological advances, but he believes an understanding of *both* laws is vital. He maintains, "Progress according to the natural law must, if it is to make for civilization, be subordinated to some adequate end; and the natural law does not in itself supply this end."[56] Making the "natural law" dependent on the "human law" is where many modern individuals come up short. Modern man's mastery of the "law for thing" is impressive, but it has enabled him more easily to avoid the painful self-scrutiny engendered by the pursuit of realizing the "law for man." Babbitt writes, "What leads the man of to-day to work with such energy according to the natural law and to be idle according to the human law is his intoxication with material success."[57] Babbitt claims it is humanity's material progress that has progressively detached many people from "the past and its traditional standards of good and evil."[58] Thus, although modern individuals expend great effort in working toward scientific progress, many of them become merely productive without becoming ethically centered.[59]

In his efforts to explain how the balance between these two laws may be maintained, Babbitt looks to various ideas from the West and East. For all their differences, Babbitt argues the ancient Greeks and Romans, the Christians, Buddha, and Confucius all believe that human beings suffer from a divided will. Generally speaking, these traditions claim moral progress according to the "human law" comes only after individuals make strenuous efforts to restrain the lower impulses of the will while allowing those of the higher, ethical variety to become realized in action. Such ethical work is always difficult. Yet no real alternative to such labor exists if the individual and society desire to live in accordance with true justice. Babbitt agues, "Civilization is something that must be deliberately willed; it is not something that gushes up spontaneously from the depths of the unconscious. Furthermore, it is something that must be willed first of all by the individual in his own heart."[60] But it is precisely this type of individual striving that Babbitt claims is deemed unnecessary by many modern proponents of progress.

Babbitt holds that if his insights are accurate and human ethical dualism is a truth that cannot be ignored, and if the greatest danger of the modern obsession with progress is its tendency to detach individuals from the experiential reality of the "law for man," then visions of the future promising unprecedented progress, mainly through scientific achievement, will sow the seeds of civilizational disorder. About the dreams and disillusionment experienced by many American proponents of progress during the early twentieth century, he writes, "An age that thought it was progressing toward a 'far-off divine event,' and turned out instead to be progressing toward Armageddon, suffered, one cannot help surmising, from some fundamental confusion in its notions of progress."[61] For Babbitt, such dubious visions of progress tend to produce efficient megalomaniacs who call themselves by more flattering names, but who do not create or sustain genuine order, happiness, or peace.[62]

Similar thoughts about the perils of a certain type of progress found aesthetic expression in the fiction of Nathaniel Hawthorne. In 1844, Hawthorne published a short story titled "Earth's Holocaust." The story begins with the narrator stating, "Once upon a time—but whether in time past or time to come, is a matter of little or no moment—this wide world had become so overburthened [sic] with an accumulation of worn-out trumpery, that the inhabitants determined to rid themselves of it by a general bonfire."[63] He explains his reasons for traveling to see this grand conflagration and says, "Having a taste for sights of this kind, and imagining, likewise, that the illumination of the bonfire might reveal some profundity of moral truth, heretofore hidden in mist or darkness, I made it convenient to journey thither and be present."[64] As the story develops, family coats of arms, royal mantles, alcohol, tobacco, weapons, written constitutions, literature, philosophy, money, deeds to property, marriage certificates, churches, and the Bible are all flung into the bonfire. The bonfire is consuming civilization itself.

Many figures at the bonfire celebrate the event as a sign of human progress. One character, who seems to be a stand-in for Ralph Waldo Emerson, exclaims, " 'That's just the thing,' said a modern philosopher. 'Now we shall get rid of the weight of dead men's thought, which has hitherto pressed so heavily on the living intellect, that it has been incompetent to any effectual self-exertion. Well done, my lads! Into the fire with them! Now you are enlightening the world, indeed!' "[65] Other characters are not happy about the situation. A hangman, a drunkard, a murderer, and a pickpocket have all lost their reasons to live. Sharing one of the world's last bottles of alcohol, they decide to hang themselves rather than live in the world being created by the flames. Just then, a man with a dark complexion and glowing red eyes approaches. The Devil has come to offer them comfort. He tells this miserable group not to worry about the bonfire because its participants forgot to burn the most important element that constitutes the world they are trying to escape. When asked what it was that they forgot to burn, the Devil explains:

> "What, but the human heart itself!" said the dark-visaged stranger, with a portentous grin. "And, unless they hit upon some method of purifying that foul cavern, forth from it will re-issue all the shapes of wrong and misery—the same old shapes, or worse ones—which they have taken such a vast deal of trouble to consume to ashes. I have stood by, this

live-long night, and laughed in my sleeve at the whole business. Oh, take my word for it, it will be the old world yet!"[66]

In "Earth's Holocaust," Hawthorne raises the mid-nineteenth-century American obsession with progress, reform, and innovation in politics, economics, and social life to farcical heights. Most of the people at the bonfire expect the world to be transformed—as if by magic—through their efforts to erase the past. The admirers of the bonfire imagine that the world can be reformed and made truly just merely through external reorganization. Hawthorne intuits both the ridiculousness and the dangers of the ideas he satirizes. The advocates of progress and enlightenment in the story do not realize that the primary source of disorder and injustice in the world is human beings, not the political and social institutions they create. The enthusiasts at the bonfire refuse to come to grips with the permanent flaws in the human condition; this is the reason the Devil is confident that their efforts will end in complete failure. In beginning his story by noting that this event might have happened in the past or could happen in the future, Hawthorne suggests that the essence of his tale, especially its insights into the perils of the modern obsession with reform as well as the naiveté of proponents of progress, transcends his specific encounters with such movements in the United States of the 1840s and 1850s.

REAGAN, PROGRESS, AND CONSERVATISM

Especially in the United States, "conservatism" has become an increasingly difficult word to define. Since the end of World War II, it has been used to describe such a wide variety of political, economic, religious, and intellectual movements in America that the term appears to mean everything and nothing at the same time. The confusion surrounding this term is particularly acute when it is applied to Reagan. Scholars as different as Dinesh D'Souza and Russell Kirk have described Reagan as a conservative. Looking at the same evidence, other scholars, such as John Patrick Diggins, have labeled Reagan a type of political radical. An exhaustive account of the numerous, often contradictory, definitions of the word "conservatism" cannot be provided here. Neither is it possible to offer a definitive explanation of the relationship between Reagan and conservatism. The term "conservatism" can be reflected upon here only insofar as it sheds greater light upon the chimeric quality of Reagan's imagination.

Russell Kirk is considered by many to be one of the leading American conservative intellectuals of the twentieth century. In an essay titled "What is Conservatism?" Kirk argues, "Strictly speaking, conservatism is not a political system, and certainly not an ideology. . . . Instead, conservatism is a way of looking at the civil social order."[67] He claims that unlike other modern "-isms" such as socialism and liberalism, genuine conservatism offers no abstract, universal template for the arrangement of political and social life around the world. He writes, "On the contrary, conservatives reason that social institutions always must differ considerably from nation to nation, since any land's politics must be the product of that country's dominant religion, ancient customs, and historic experience."[68] Kirk also explains that true conservatives admire social traditions and have strong attachments to historical and social continuity because "human society is no machine, to be treated mechanically. The continuity, the lifeblood, of a society must not be interrupted."[69] Kirk argues that conservatives eschew revolution and radical changes because such efforts inevitably have terrible consequences for genuine political and social order. He states, "Revolution slices through the arteries of a culture, a cure that kills."[70]

Based on Kirk's description of conservatism, one might conclude that a conservative is a rigid antiquarian, a lover of old things simply because they are old. Perhaps some people that describe themselves as conservatives fit such a definition. Kirk's brand of conservatism does not. Kirk, after all, was a student of other leading figures in modern conservatism, including Irving Babbitt and Edmund Burke. In *Democracy and Leadership*, Babbitt argues, "I have said that the only effective conservatism is an imaginative conservatism."[71] In his *Reflections on the Revolution in France*, Burke explains, "A state without the means of some change is without the means of its conservation. Without such means it might even risk the loss of that part of the constitution which it wished the most religiously to preserve."[72] Neither Kirk, nor Babbitt, nor Burke opposed political change or social reform in the abstract. All of them were advocates of reform in politics and social life—when such changes were guided by necessity and prudence and informed by a deep knowledge of and respect for tradition and culture.

A disposition to refrain from altering traditions and institutions that ennoble the human spirit combined with an ability to reform elements of social and political life that no longer function properly is the essence of conservative politics, according to Kirk, Burke, and Babbitt. Burke expresses this view of conservative change well when he writes, "Thus, by preserving the method of nature in the conduct of the state, in what we improve we are never wholly new; in what we retain we are never wholly obsolete."[73] All three of these thinkers hold in low regard individuals and mass movements that promote frequent and sweeping social and political change on the basis of ahistorical or sentimental ideas. These thinkers believe that a mania for reform betrays a high degree of ethical immaturity on the part of its promoters. On this point, Burke is again instructive when he states, "A spirit of innovation is generally the result of a selfish temper and confined views. People will not look forward to posterity, who never look backward to their ancestors."[74] These innovators, as Burke describes them, are the same people Kirk has in mind when he is thinking of the leaders of revolutions who kill civilization in the name of progress.

Another leading twentieth-century American conservative intellectual, Peter Viereck, has many ideas in common with Babbitt and Burke. His thoughts on conservatism and on the differences between conservatism and antiquarianism on the one hand, and conservatism and liberalism on the other hand, are well expressed and deserve to be quoted at length for those that might be unfamiliar with his views. In *Conservatism Revisited: The Revolt against Ideology*, Viereck contrasts antiquarianism and conservatism thusly:

> Conservatism is a treasure house, sometimes an infuriatingly dusty one, of generations of accumulated experience, which any ephemeral rebellious generation has a right to disregard—at its peril. To vary the metaphor: conservatism is a social and cultural cement, holding together what western man has built and by that very fact providing a base for orderly change and improvement.
>
> But not all the past is worth keeping. The conservative conserves discriminately, the reactionary indiscriminately. Though the events of the past are often shameful and bloody, its lessons are indispensable. By "tradition" the conservative means not all the lessons of the past but only the ethically acceptable events. The reactionary means all the events. Thereby he misses all the lessons.[75]

Viereck also contrasts conservatism with liberalism. In *Unadjusted Man in the Age of Overadjustment: Where History and Literature Intersect*, he argues:

> The liberal sees outer, removable institutions as the ultimate source of evil; sees man's social task as creating a world in which evil will disappear. His tools for this task are progress and enlightenment. The conservative sees the inner, unremovable nature of man as the ultimate source of evil; sees man's social task as coming to terms with a world in which evil is perpetual and in which justice and compassion will both be perpetually necessary. His tools for this task are the maintenance of ethical restraints inside the individual and the maintenance of unbroken, continuous social patterns inside the given culture as a whole.[76]

According to Viereck, figures such as Thomas Paine and Thomas Jefferson represent this type of liberalism. Figures such as Edmund Burke and John Adams embody conservatism, as defined by Viereck.

It is certainly true that Reagan understood himself to be a conservative. On occasion, Reagan made comments that sounded very similar to those quoted here from Kirk. At the 1977 CPAC, Reagan explained, "Conservatism is the antithesis of the kind of ideological fanaticism that has brought so much horror and destruction to the world. . . . Whatever the word may have meant in the past, today conservatism means principles evolving from experience and a belief in change when necessary, but not just for the sake of change."[77] Many scholars and journalists have described Reagan as a conservative. Further, if by conservative one means a member of the Republican Party, then Reagan truly was a conservative. And yet, Reagan imagined human nature as naturally good. He celebrated the radical and revolutionary heritage of the United States. He believed political reform consisted largely of rearranging external institutions. He extolled progress and often drew attention to what he believed was America's unbroken tradition of technological change, innovation, and revolution. In his mind, a narrative about progress united past, present, and future. He preached the transformative powers of free markets, technology, liberty, and democracy in the United States and around the world. He rarely seemed interested in preserving or defending authentic, historically developed modes of life in the United States or around the world.

CONCLUSION

Reagan's vision of progress is not entirely problematic. He does draw some attention to specific political, economic, material, and technological advances that have benefited Americans and people around the world. At the same time, the insights of Babbitt, Nisbet, Röpke, and Hawthorne suggest that the underlying quality of Reagan's intuitive sense of progress is chimeric and mixed with a high degree of unreality. Reagan imagined progress as a type of mystical, transformative process that always works to the benefit of America and the world. He seldom expressed awareness of the dangers lurking beneath the types of progress he so effusively celebrated. Reagan may be correct when he claims that modern human beings are more comfortable, healthy, and prosperous than ever before, but he did not see, as others have seen, that many of these same people are also suffering from social isolation, the bland commodification of life, and spiritual emptiness. Progress of the type Reagan promoted has a pronounced tendency to become an intoxication that distracts people caught in its thrall from the more important demands of the ethical life. When all this is taken into account, it is difficult to reconcile the primary strain of Reagan's imagination with the notions of conservatism expressed by Kirk, Babbitt, Burke, and Viereck. The main parts of Reagan's vision all seem to celebrate ideas that these conservative figures abhorred and rejected. These conservative theorists likely would have repudiated much of Reagan's chimeric vision as philosophically questionable and ultimately destructive of the genuine, organic traditions and cultures they were deeply interested in conserving in their specific historical contexts.

10 "A Shining City upon a Hill"[1]
Ronald Reagan, Religion, and America

If you take away the belief in a greater future, you cannot explain America—that we're a people who believed there was a promised land; we were a people who believed we were chosen by God to create a greater world.[2]

—Ronald Reagan

In *Democracy and Leadership*, Irving Babbitt writes, "When studied with any degree of thoroughness, the economic problem will be found to run into the political problem, the political problem in turn into the philosophical problem, and the philosophical problem itself to be almost indissolubly bound up at last with the religious problem."[3] Even a cursory examination makes clear that Reagan's presidential speeches are replete with references to God, Jesus (or "the man from Galilee"), religion, prayer, the Ten Commandments, the parables of the Good Samaritan and the Talents, and the Bible. Religion and religious ideas—especially those Reagan associates with Christianity—are of great importance to Reagan and are therefore vital to understanding his imagination. This point has not always been well understood, but recent scholarship has begun to draw serious attention to the centrality of religion to Reagan's mind.[4]

Although Reagan's vision has a strong religious dimension, at least in some sense of that word, its connection to the broader American and Western Christian tradition he often invokes is more complex and tenuous than he realizes. In some instances, he seems to suggest that the relationship between politics and religion is one of fruitful tension. In this view, religion and politics are seen as needing the other to thrive, but they remain distinct entities serving different, though not incompatible, ends. Much more frequently, Reagan appears to blur the distinctions between these realms, and he even expresses a longing for the abolition of the tension between them. This latter strain of his imagination includes Reagan's view that God has chosen the United States and its people to complete a mission suffused with eschatological importance and millennial expectation. This far more prominent side of Reagan's religious sensibilities, which will be the focus of this chapter, finds its most powerful and seductive expression in the image of America as a shining city upon a hill.

The central part of Reagan's religious vision has deep roots in American and Western political and religious thought. Elaborating this crucial dimension of his imagination requires that it be placed within wider historical, theological, and philosophical contexts. Insights from Claes G. Ryn, Irving Babbitt, and Richard Gamble will elucidate the implications of such a vision for politics. Ideas from Eric Voegelin will shed further light upon the existential motivation and attraction of Reagan's primary way of imagining the relationship between religion and politics and between God and America. Voegelin's scholarship will also draw attention to the type of appeal Reagan makes when he expresses the predominant side of his religious imagination. Given the difficult nature of the following explication and analysis, a few words must be said about the conceptual framework of this chapter.

THE THINGS OF GOD AND CAESAR: A BRIEF NOTE ON CHRISTIANITY AND POLITICAL THOUGHT

At a conference on religious liberty, Reagan argued, "One of the great shared characteristics of all religions is the distinction they draw between the temporal world and the spiritual world."[5] He then claimed, "All religions, in effect, echo the words of the Gospel of St. Matthew: 'Render, therefore, unto Caesar the things which are Caesar's; and unto God the things that are God's.' "[6] Reagan held that this admonition, spoken by Jesus of Nazareth, taught that there was an "almost mysterious" realm of being that transcended the political and which could not be subjected entirely to political control. Furthermore, he explained, "Only in an intellectual climate which distinguishes between the city of God and the city of man and which explicitly affirms the independence of God's realm and forbids any infringement by the state on its prerogatives, only in such a climate could the idea of individual human rights take root, grow, and eventually flourish."[7] In making such comments about the relationship and tension between politics and religion—that is, between the things of God and the things of Caesar—Reagan identified one of the most important contributions of Christianity to political thought.

Among other things, Jesus's words about rendering unto Caesar and God the things they were owed expressed his view that no inherent conflict existed between the responsibilities of citizenship and membership in the fledgling Christian community. In the same spirit, St. Paul later commanded Christians to obey both the spiritual and secular authorities because "there is no power but of God: the powers that be are ordained of God."[8] Several centuries later, Pope Gelasius I explained the government and the church have different though not conflicting responsibilities to minister to the temporal and spiritual needs of people.[9] This understanding of the relationship between politics and religion, one in which church and state need each other to survive and thrive, has been affirmed by of other Christian figures, including St. Augustine and Thomas Aquinas.

In the speech quoted earlier, Reagan also referred to the "city of God" and "city of man." These symbols are most closely associated with St. Augustine, and they are related to the God and Caesar distinction in Christian political thought. In *The City of God*, St. Augustine argues that despite the multiplicity of civilizations and nations, there exist only two cities throughout history, the City of God and the earthly city. Citizenship in either city is determined by the quality of love in each member's heart. Members of the city of God are animated by the *amor Dei*, or love of God. Those belonging to the earthly city, in contrast, are driven by the *amor sui*, or love of self. The two cities symbolize a permanent division between two types of human beings and communities; they have no earthly analogues, but rather serve as eschatological symbols encompassing the full range of human historical existence.

In St. Augustine's mind, the two cities are related to two types of history, sacred and profane. Sacred history is the story of the City of God. It is the tale of humanity's separation from and reconciliation to God. It began with the Fall, continued with the Israelite exodus from Egypt, and culminated in the birth, death, and resurrection of Jesus. Sacred history is the source of knowledge about human nature, God, existence, and salvation. In contrast, profane history is a catalog of mundane historical events, beads on a string marking the rise and fall of civilizations, devoid of meaning, signifying nothing. Further, although sacred history remains relevant until the end of time, the major events comprising it have already occurred. Since the Resurrection of Jesus, in St. Augustine's view, humanity has lived in the last stage of history, in the millennial period. Since the Resurrection, Christians have been waiting patiently for the Second Coming of Christ. Life on earth, in other words, will remain more or less the same until the Last Judgment.

St. Augustine seems to push Christian indifference to politics and profane history to an extreme. From his writings, one could get the impression that politics is so corrupting, so "dirty," that it is almost impossible to be both a good Christian and a just and competent political leader. This should not be surprising, given that he believed that politics is not natural; it is only a consequence of the Fall. Political authority, in his view, serves no greater purpose than to restrain human depravity. His views seem to suggest that God and Caesar really do not have a meaningful relationship. These are common criticisms of St. Augustine's understanding of politics and history. Although some scholars exaggerate these tendencies in St. Augustine's writings, such assessments have some merit.

Thomas Aquinas, a theologian whose importance to the development of Western Christianity matches St. Augustine's, affirms the distinction between God and Caesar. But he has a different view than St. Augustine on the possibilities of politics. In the *Summa Theologicæ*, Aquinas argues noncoercive political society would have emerged in the state of innocence and that this could not happen "unless someone is in authority to look after the common good" as well as the good of each individual.[10] Even though politics is later compelled to use coercion as a means for achieving its ends, it has an important, secondary role in promoting virtue.[11] Political life cannot provide the ultimate in human happiness, Aquinas maintains, but it can make a substantive contribution toward this end.

These comments indicate that traditional Christianity does not see the relationship between God and Caesar as inherently acrimonious. Jesus, St. Paul, Gelasius I, St. Augustine, and Thomas Aquinas each give wide latitude to the political realm. Christianity is compatible with a number of regime types and political structures because politics is of secondary importance in the Christian tradition here represented. These thinkers are not overly concerned with articulating systematic theories of politics, or with prescribing specific political policies. This should not be surprising. Christianity is a religious movement, not a political philosophy. It seeks to shed light upon the relationship between God and humanity, not to promote an ideology that seeks a transformation of the world through political action. After all, in St. John's Gospel, "My Kingdom is not of this world," was Jesus's response to Pontius Pilate's question about the nature of his kingship.[12] That Christianity ought to shape the spirit in which politics is conducted is a notion these figures affirmed. That it is a political religion is something they rejected.

This foray into Christian political thought has served the important purpose of establishing a conceptual framework for analyzing Reagan's religious vision. It must be noted that one need not be a Christian to affirm (or reject) the philosophical importance of the distinction between God and Caesar. In "The Things of Caesar: Toward the Delimitation of Politics," Claes G. Ryn writes, "I am intimating that an adequate theory of politics may have to incorporate in some form a grasp of the divine. This is not to suggest that the politician must become a theologian or embrace a particular religious creed, but that he be willing to examine on its own ground the general quality of life which has given rise to such concepts as 'the holy,' 'the sacred,' or 'the divine.'"[13] In this chapter, the distinction between God and Caesar, and the relationship it recommends between religion and politics, will be dealt with as a *philosophical* rather than religious concept. The purpose is to determine with the help of theoretical rather than dogmatic tools the extent to which Reagan appears to embrace or reject this distinction and what this might indicate about his chimeric imagination. The argument to be advanced is not that certain portions of Reagan's vision are problematic because they are not sufficiently "Christian."

REAGAN, AMERICA, AND THE SHINING CITY ON A HILL

The city on the hill image originally comes from the Sermon on the Mount. Reagan appropriated the image from John Winthrop's 1630 sermon "A Modell of Christian Charity." He started using it as early as the late 1960s—adding the word "shining" to Winthrop's language—and he often referred to it in his presidential speeches. In his imagination, the shining city stood as an overarching symbol for a complex mixture of ideas about politics, God, human history, America, its people, and its mission or calling. In a 1986 speech, Reagan argued that Winthrop's sermon served to remind the Puritans that "they must keep faith with their God, that the eyes of all the world were upon them, and that they must not forsake the mission that God had sent them on, and they must be a light unto the nations of all the world—a shining city upon a hill."[14] For Reagan, Winthrop's sermon was still relevant. The United States both was and was still becoming the shining city.

Whatever the historical epoch, it was clear to Reagan that America's glory and success were attributable to God's will and blessing and to the holiness of the American people. In his 1982 proclamation establishing the National Day of Prayer, he explained, "Through the storms of Revolution, Civil War, and the great World Wars, as well as during times of disillusionment and dis-array, the nation has turned to God in prayer for deliverance. We thank Him for answering our call, for, surely, He has. As a nation, we have been richly blessed with His love and generosity."[15] In a 1983 proclamation on the same topic, he stated, "From General Washington's struggle at Valley Forge to the present, this Nation has fervently sought and received diving guidance as it pursued the course of history."[16] God uniquely favored Americans, in part, because they called upon him often for help and guidance.

To Reagan, it was no coincidence that Americans were both pious and strongly influenced by the Christian Bible and its teachings. They were des-tined to be a people who would worship God and practice his preferred political ideas, thereby serving as a spiritual and political model for the rest of the world. At Kansas State University, Reagan argued:

> I said that we were a nation under God. I've always believed that this blessed land was set apart in a special way, that some divine plan placed this great continent here between the oceans to be found by people from every corner of the Earth who had a special love for freedom and the courage to uproot themselves, leave homeland and friends to come to a strange land, and where, coming here, they have created something new in all the history of mankind—a land where man is not beholden to government; government is beholden to man.[17]

Reagan frequently expressed such ideas about God's plan for the United States. He offered this thought in nearly identical language on numerous occasions before and during his presidency.

Did Reagan then think that America and its people were perfect? Or, to put the question in religious terms, did he think that Americans were granted a special reprieve from the human inclination to sin, or that America, some-how, was immune to the tendencies of politics to degenerate into disorder? Answering these questions about Reagan's vision is not easy. On the one hand, the obvious response Reagan would have given to this question was that no, Americans were not incapable of sinning or acting immorally. In his 1983 Address to the National Association of Evangelicals, he even stated: "[We] must never forget that no government schemes are going to perfect man. We know that living in this world means dealing with what philosophers would call the phenomenology of evil, or, as theologians would put it, the doctrine of sin."[18] In some speeches he identified slavery as a particularly awful scar on the American soul. In others he cited a number of social problems, ranging from abortion, to high divorce rates, to drug usage, as evidence that the United States and its people were not perfect.

More frequently, Reagan suggested that America and its people, although they were not perfect, were still different from and perhaps morally superior to the peoples of the rest of the world. In a 1982 speech, he acknowledged, "Hatred, envy, and bigotry are as old as the human race itself, as too many tragic passages in the history of the world bear witness."[19] But, immediately following this comment on the chronic weaknesses of human beings, he argued:

> What is new and daring and encouraging about the American experiment is that from the beginning, men and women strove mightily to undo these evils and to overcome the prejudice and injustice of the old world in the virgin soil of the new. . . . Nowhere does history offer a parallel to this vast undertaking. With all its flaws, America remains a unique achievement for human dignity on a scale unequaled anywhere in the world.[20]

Reagan then stated, "America has already succeeded where so many other historic attempts at freedom have failed. Already, we've made this cherished land the last best hope of mankind."[21] Thus, although the United States was not without failings, its special status as a place set aside by God to be populated by a chosen people allowed America to come the closest to perfection out of all nations in history. This tension between acknowledging that Americans, like all other human beings, acted upon their lower impulses, and the desire to downplay the pervasiveness or even existence of these tendencies in the United States, was present in many of his presidential speeches.

Reagan's sense of America as a shining city contributed to his belief that the American president was obligated to play an active role in cultivating and maintaining the spiritual health of the American people.[22] In an interview he explained, "There is a great hunger for a kind of spiritual revival in this country, for people to believe again in things that they once believed in—basic truths and all."[23] Furthermore, he argued that as president he felt personally responsible for using, "as Teddy Roosevelt called it, 'a bully pulpit'" to facilitate and encourage such revival. He also felt a sense of urgency about undertaking this mission because "if you look back at the fall of any empire, any great civilization, it has been preceded by their forsaking their gods. . . . I don't want us to be another great civilization that began its decline by forsaking its God."[24] Reagan seemed to believe Americans were capable of forfeiting their inheritance as a chosen people. He even considered the possibility that the nascent stages of this type of decline might already have begun. In his mind, the ultimate survival of the United States was tied to the continuation and expansion of a religious awakening for which he, the president of the United States, bore the primary responsibility. The shining city could not be rejuvenated if the American people were not worthy of citizenship.

The shining city image informed to a great extent Reagan's vision of America's mission to promote progress and reform in the United States and around the world. Referring to his first presidential victory at the 1988 Republican National Convention, Reagan explained that in 1980, "it was our dream that together we could rescue America and make a new beginning, to create anew that shining city on a hill."[25] On domestic politics, he stated in a different speech that the United States had been "blessed with a sacred opportunity and a sacred quest."[26] He argued in yet another speech that to fulfill America's "higher mission," Americans must "build together a society of opportunity, a society that rewards excellence, bound by a body of laws nourished with the spirit of faith, equity, responsibility, and compassion."[27] If the United States succeeded in its quest, what would the country look like? He explained, "The streets of America would not be paved with gold; they would be paved with opportunity." Reform was the only way to preserve the American dream, which was a gift from God and not an American creation.[28] It was the only way to revitalize the shining city. And yet a number of economic, social, and political problems stood in the way.

Reagan believed that the excessive growth of the national government had stifled American freedom and creativity. High taxes and the expansion of federal bureaucracy and regulation had nearly strangled the U.S. economy to death. As president, Reagan wanted to lower taxes, reduce the size of government, and reestablish the constitutional distinctions between the national government and the various state governments. Ideas of this type are some of the most widely recognized as expressions of Reagan's political thought. Less well known is the degree to which these views were shaped by Reagan's religious ideas, including his understanding of the Bible and certain Christian parables.

Reagan referred to the parable of the Good Samaritan in many of his presidential speeches. In the parable, a lawyer asks Jesus what he must do to inherit eternal life. Jesus replies by asking, "What is written in the law? how readest thou?" The lawyer says that he is to love God and neighbor as self. "Thou hast answered right: this do, and thou shalt live," Jesus answers. But the lawyer then asks him who is his neighbor. By way of answering, Jesus tells the story of a man on a journey from Jerusalem to Jericho. The traveler is set upon by thieves and beaten. A priest and a Levite pass by this man while he lies in the road "half dead," but they do not help him. Then a Samaritan passes by this injured man, and he has compassion upon him. The Samaritan tends to the traveler's wounds and takes him to an inn where he pays the innkeeper to administer further care. The Samaritan then leaves the inn, but he promises the innkeeper that he will pay for any additional costs upon his return. Upon concluding the parable, Jesus asks the lawyer, "Which now of these three, thinkest thou, was neighbor unto him that fell among the thieves?" The lawyer answers that it was the Samaritan. "Go, and do thou likewise," is the command that Jesus gave to the lawyer.[29]

In the standard Christian interpretation of this parable, the Samaritan symbolizes Jesus, the beaten man is humanity, and the inn is the church. Among other things, the parable indicates that human beings truly love their neighbors, and thus themselves and God, only insofar as they demonstrate it through concrete moral action. This emphasis on actions as evidence of virtue permeates the Christian scriptures. In the Epistle of James it is written, "But be ye doers of the word, and not hearers only, deceiving your own selves."[30] About telling the difference between true and false prophets, Jesus says, "Wherefore by their fruits ye shall know them."[31] But the parable of the Good Samaritan also suggests that individuals are permanently morally flawed. All people are lying "half dead" on the road, so to speak. Further, the possibilities for alleviating the self-inflicted physical and spiritual wounds of human beings are limited. In the Christian view here represented, humanity must await the return of the Samaritan in order to receive a complete cure, to be made whole again. As it is told in the Bible, the parable has no direct reference to government. The views expressed may have important contributions to make to the sound practice of politics, but such effects are ultimately indirect and secondary.

In Reagan's imagination, the parable of the Good Samaritan was given a rather different interpretation and emphasis. On occasion he explained:

> And I've always believed that the meaning and the importance of that parable is not so much the good that was done to the beaten pilgrim, it was to the Samaritan who crossed the road, who knelt down and bound up the wounds of the beaten traveler, and then carried him into the nearest town. He didn't take a look and hurry on by into that town and then find a caseworker and say, "There's somebody out there on the road I think needs help."[32]

In a different speech, Reagan argued, "In recent years, too many of us have tended to forget that government can't properly substitute for the helping hand of neighbor to neighbor. And in trying to do so, government has, to a great extent, brought on the economic distress that mires us down in recession."[33] As interpreted by Reagan, the parable's injunction to love one's neighbor demands protection against the meddling of government, which is capable only of hindering each individual's ability to act upon Samaritan impulses. For him the parable of the Good Samaritan is as much a *political* lesson about the dangers of big government as it is a lesson about the obligations of human beings to love and care for each other.

Reagan also referred to the parable of the talents on many occasions. In it, Jesus says, *"For the kingdom of heaven is* as a man traveling into a far country, *who* called his own servants, and delivered unto them his goods." The man portions out talents, which was a measure of considerable wealth, to three of his servants "according to his several ability." The man then leaves his estate and returns after a long absence. A servant to whom he had given five talents used them to make another five talents, giving ten talents back to his master. A servant to whom he had given two talents likewise made another two talents, giving four talents back when the master returned. In each case, the master saw what the industry of these two servants had accomplished and says, "Well *done*, good and faithful servant; thou hast been faithful over a few *things*, I will make thee ruler over many *things:* Enter into the joy of thy lord." But the last servant did not increase the one talent his master had given him. Thinking his master a "hard man," this servant simply hid his talent in the ground in order to give it back. This servant was rebuked as "wicked and slothful" because he chose not to increase that which he was given. This single talent was then given to the good servant who already had ten. The "unprofitable servant" was cast into "the outer darkness."[34]

In the traditional Christian interpretation, the talents symbolize gifts given by Jesus to his disciples that will help them work toward their salvation and spread his message. What are these gifts? In 1 Corinthians St. Paul provides examples and writes, "Now there are diversities of gifts, but the same Spirit. . . . For to one is given by the Spirit the word of wisdom; to another the word of knowledge by the same Spirit; To another faith by the same Spirit; to another the gifts of healing by the same Spirit."[35] In this view, one Spirit pursues and accomplishes its will by acting through a diverse body of individuals, giving to each member the virtues or graces he or she can bear and multiply. The parable of the talents thus conveys the Christian sense of a unity of spirit and purpose realized through a diversity of members and faculties. It describes an active life of love and virtue inspired by a vision of and a longing for the kingdom of heaven, which, as Jesus points out, is not of this world. The use of monetary imagery is symbolic and incidental to the main point of the parable. The parable has no explicitly political or economic message.

Reagan interpreted the parable of the talents as a story primarily concerned with extolling the virtues of entrepreneurship. It was a reminder of the necessity of freedom for human happiness and progress, and it was another warning about the dangers of excessive governmental taxation and economic regulation. In a national radio address on small business, he argued that entrepreneurs did not fit the stereotypes commonly associated with greed and selfishness. Rather, they were "men and women who had the spirit to dream impossible dreams, take great risks, and work long hours to make their dreams come true," and "owners of that store down the street, the faithfuls [sic] who support our churches, schools, and communities, the brave people everywhere who produce our goods, feed a hungry world, and keep our homes and families warm while they invest in the future to build a better America."[36] These heroes were proof that free markets were as much about making great personal sacrifices for the happiness of others as they were about accumulating private wealth.

According to Reagan, this understanding of wealth and responsibility was based on the Christian scriptures. In this radio address, he explained, "In the Parable of the Talents, the man who invests and multiplies his money is praised. But the rich who horde their wealth are rebuked in scripture."[37] In Reagan's mind, multiplying talents meant that Americans were able to invent new technologies and start new businesses, which led to corresponding increases in manufacturing and agricultural production as well as increases in wealth and progress for all people. But Americans could not use their talents efficiently if government hindered them. They needed tax and regulatory relief in order to use their talents for their own benefit and the benefit of others.

The shining city symbol also had implications for the world and for peace among nations. Reagan often spoke in religious terms about the obligation of the United States to spread freedom throughout the world. In his 1982 speech to the British Parliament, he announced a *crusade* for freedom. Elsewhere, he encouraged America and the West to become evangelists for liberty. In a 1984 speech, he informed the audience: "We stand for freedom in the world. . . . We're blessed by God with the right to say of our country: This is where freedom is."[38] In his Second Inaugural Address, Reagan concluded with a reflection on what he called "the American sound." This sound was "hopeful, big-hearted, idealistic, daring, decent, and fair."[39] It resounded through American history, and it would guide the United States as it charted a path to the future. He said, "We raise our voices to the God who is the Author of this most tender music. And may He continue to hold us close as we fill the world with our sound—in unity, affection, and love—one people under God, dedicated to the dream of freedom that He has placed in the human heart, called upon now to pass that dream on to a waiting and hopeful world."[40]

Reagan also invoked religious imagery when promoting global democracy. During a speech given on the Fourth of July, he argued, "Democracy is just a political reading of the Bible."[41] In his mind, the divine preference for democracy was another reason it should be embraced by the world and advanced by God's new chosen people. In the same speech in which Reagan described the Constitution as a covenant with mankind, he reflected upon George Washington's First Inaugural Address and claimed, "But [Washington] knew . . . that the guiding hand of providence did not create this new nation of America for ourselves alone, but for a higher cause: the preservation and extension of the sacred fire of human liberty. This is America's solemn duty."[42] In Reagan's imagination, a strong connection existed between God's preferences for politics and the American obligation as a shining city to spread freedom and democracy abroad.

Beyond the general demand to export these political institutions, Reagan believed that as a shining city the United States was bound by God and morality to share its abundance with the world. At Kansas State University Reagan borrowed from Winthrop and said, "The eyes of mankind are on us, counting on us to protect the peace, promote new prosperity, and provide for them a better world."[43] In his view, Americans were fulfilling this mission: "Bringing light where there was darkness, heat where there was once only cold, and medicines where there was sickness and disease, food where there was hunger, wealth where humanity was living in squalor, and peace where there was only death and bloodshed."[44]

A few months before these comments, in a speech given during a visit to the Vatican to meet Pope John Paul II, Reagan remarked, "We know that God has blessed America with the freedom and abundance many of our less fortunate brothers and sisters around the world have been denied. Since the end of World War II, we have done our best to provide assistance to them, assistance amounting to billions of dollars worth of food, medicine, and materials."[45] He went on to explain that his administration would be committed to continuing this general program of global benevolence because "Americans have always believed that in the words of the Scripture, 'Unto whomsoever much is given, of him shall be much required.' "[46] To paraphrase a comment from Richard Gamble about Woodrow Wilson, this line of thought suggests that Reagan's vision of America as a shining city included the image of the United States as a Good Samaritan with the entire world as its neighbor.

The notion that America had been chosen to bring about the universal realization of certain political institutions also contributed to Reagan's broader understanding of the Soviet Union. In his mind, the USSR was an evil empire primarily because it stood in direct and prideful opposition to God and his will for politics. This was also the reason it was doomed to inevitable failure. In his 1983 speech to the National Association of Evangelicals, Reagan argued, "I believe that communism is another sad, bizarre chapter in human history whose last pages even now are being written. I believe this because the source of our strength in the quest for human freedom is not material, but spiritual."[47] Reagan believed that the United States and its citizens needed to "reassert our commitment as a nation to a law higher than our own, to renew our spiritual strength" in order to "leave Marxism-Leninism on the ash heap of history."[48] In this way, his desire for spiritual revival in America was directly related to the prospects for the growth of liberty, democracy, and religious freedom around the world.[49]

Reagan expressed many aspects of his religious vision during his 1988 trip to the Soviet Union. In remarks he made at a recently reopened Russian Orthodox monastery, he celebrated Russian Christians such as Alexander Solzhenitsyn who came to know God and worshiped him even in the midst of suffering the horrors of the gulag. He also praised the Russian people for the fact that despite constant persecution, religion had survived and was beginning to grow again in the late 1980s. They were proof that freedom and faith could not be extinguished by any government.[50] He also spoke to a group of Soviet dissidents at the Spaso House in Moscow. He told his listeners that as "a head of government," he was committed to promoting a robust agenda with the Soviet Union that included "freedom of religion," "freedom of speech," "freedom of travel," and "institutional changes to make progress permanent."[51] But he also wanted to speak to them "as a man," and he explained his vision of the future in the Soviet Union and around the world in the following terms: "I want to give you one thought from my heart. Coming here, being with you, looking into your faces, I have to believe that the history of this troubled century will indeed be redeemed in the eyes of God and man, and that freedom will truly come to all."[52] Reagan's shining city had been given a unique role to play in this redemptive drama.

When Reagan described his sense of a peaceful world, he often quoted parts of the following passage from the Prophet Isaiah: "And he shall judge among the nations, and shall rebuke many people: and they shall beat their swords into plowshares, and their spears into pruning hooks: nation shall not lift up sword against nation, neither shall they learn war any more."[53] Repeatedly during his presidency, Reagan associated the ultimate goal of America's role in the world with this particular image as well as with others of a similar nature. These types of religious images led Reagan to imagine the possibility of "a world of peace and freedom, opportunity and hope, and, yes, of democracy—a world in which the spirit of mankind at last conquers the old, familiar enemies of famine, disease, tyranny, and war."[54] Reagan believed deeply in the power of a pious United States to transform the world. This was another reason why spiritual renewal in America was important. In general, his thinking about the shining city's role in securing world democracy, liberty, and peace contained a high dose of apocalyptic expectation.

Throughout his presidency, Reagan cited empirical evidence as proof that his general vision was a realistic description of the world and its possibilities. He often pointed to quantitative economic data, including declines in unemployment, taxation, regulation, and interest rates and increases in production and technological development, as evidence of the soundness of his vision. In foreign policy, he frequently cited the increase in the quantities of democracies and free markets in Asia, Europe, and Latin America as evidence that he understood the world and the direction in which the tide of history flowed. Reagan also cited evidence of what he perceived as a profound spiritual revival in the United States during his presidency. In remarks to the Student Congress on Evangelism in 1988, for example, he claimed, "An overwhelming 9 out of 10 Americans pray. Audiences for religious books are growing. The modern communications media are being used for evangelism."[55] In a different speech, he gave further evidence of America's resurgent piety. He explained, "Americans are turning back to God. Church attendance is up. . . . On college campuses, students have stopped shunning religion and started going to church."[56] On the basis of many different measures, Reagan believed he had succeeded in bringing about the spiritual revival that was critical to revitalizing the shining city and changing the world. In his mind, this spiritual awakening in the United States contributed greatly to the various political, economic, and international achievements of his presidency.

REAGAN'S SHINING CITY IN AMERICAN HISTORICAL PERSPECTIVE

Reagan's intuitive belief in America as a shining city on a hill has deep historical roots. But before taking up an historical analysis, a few words of caution are in order. There are different conceptions of America as a chosen nation within the American tradition of political and religious thought. Some are politically passive and some are politically activist. Some are religiously grounded and others are mainly secular. No claims are here being made that the long-standing tradition of thinking about America as a special or exceptional nation is uniform, or that Reagan's interpretation of the shining city is the inexorable product of past thought. Further, the ways in which these images might influence the practice of politics is not the same for all individuals or historical periods. No two people or historical epochs are identical. Figures who might appear to share intuitive visions of America as a chosen nation would not necessarily have the same policy ideas. Even where common ground exists between Reagan and the American past regarding the religious underpinnings of America's destiny, it should not be assumed that Reagan's policies would have met with the unequivocal approval of the various figures to be discussed here.

Despite their having different views on a number of topics, many of the Founders believed that the United States had a special status in history and a special mission to the world. One obvious example from the Founding period is the world-transforming zeal in the comment from Thomas Paine's *Common Sense* about beginning the world over again. Thomas Jefferson held a similar view about America and its destiny. In his First Inaugural Address, Jefferson referred to the United States as "the world's best hope" and "a chosen country."[57] Even John Adams was not entirely immune to the appeal of the vision of a chosen America. In an early version of his "A Dissertation on the Canon and Feudal Law," he explained, "I always consider the settlement of America with reverence and wonder, as the opening of a grand scene and design in Providence for the illumination of the ignorant, and the emancipation of the slavish part of mankind all over the earth."[58] Adams's comment has a stronger, traditionally religious tone than those expressed by either Paine or Jefferson, but all three figures invested America with eschatological hope.

George Washington also saw the hand of Providence in the events of the revolutionary and Framing periods. The special status granted to the United States by Providence came with a responsibility that Americans owed to themselves and the rest of the world. Washington argued, "The preservation of the sacred fire of liberty, and the destiny of the Republican model of Government, are justly considered as *deeply*, perhaps as *finally* staked, on the experiment entrusted to the hands of the American people."[59] In these comments, Washington seems to see America as possibly the last, best hope of mankind.

The idea that America was destined to play a crucial role in the unfolding of a divine plan for all of humanity was also expressed during the colonial period. Jonathan Edwards, perhaps colonial New England's most insightful religious thinker, believed that America was a providential land. He wrote that it was *probable* that the regeneration of the world would begin in the British North America of the mid-eighteenth century. With the Great Awakening in mind, he argued, "It is not unlikely that this work of God's spirit, so extraordinary and wonderful, is the dawning, or at least a prelude of that glorious work of God, so often foretold in scripture, which, in the progress and issue of it, shall renew the world of mankind."[60] Edwards was one among many who felt this way about America's divine destiny. As did many others, he devoted a substantial amount of time interpreting the apocalyptic symbolism of the Bible, especially the Book of Revelation, with reference to recent political and religious events in order to determine when the Christian Eschaton, or end times, might begin.

These similarities notwithstanding, important differences exist between Reagan's religious sensibilities and those of the colonial and Framing periods. For John Winthrop, the city on a hill image meant something different than it did to Reagan. In the original sermon, Winthrop said, "For wee must Consider that wee shall be as a Citty upon a Hill, the eies of all people are uppon us; soe that if wee shall deale falsely with our god in this worke wee have undertaken and soe cause him to withdrawe his present help from us, wee shall shame the faces of many of gods worthy servants, and cause theire prayers to be turned into Cursses upon us."[61] In this context, being a city on the hill seems to impart as much anxiety about failure as it does hope for success. On occasion, Reagan quoted or paraphrased some of these admonishments. Much more frequently, Reagan assumed that the United States was good by nature and thus ultimately incapable of failing to live up to the responsibility of being a city on a hill.

Jonathan Edwards was also deeply concerned about the possibility and consequences of America's failure to live up to this image. In a sermon titled "A City on a Hill," he explained that God indeed raised nations and peoples up as cities upon hills for the observation of others. But, he reminded his parishioners, such election was *"a very great obligation upon them to honor religion in their practice."*[62] He said:

> As they are thus set up on an hill, so they are under advantage to do
> either more good or more hurt than any people in the world, that are

not set on an hill as they are. If they carry themselves unsuitably, and unchristianly, and contrary to their profession, their carriage will do vastly more hurt than the like ill carriages of other people.[63]

Edwards delivered this sermon precisely because he felt that New England had been chosen as a city upon a hill. The rest of the world was watching, waiting to see how New England would fair under this burden. Edwards felt that the outcome was by no means certain. With Winthrop and Edwards in mind, it appears that Reagan's shining city was a different place than the Puritan ideal he invoked.

When compared with Reagan, it seems that many early American thinkers and leaders, especially Washington, Adams, and Edwards, were relatively cautious when contemplating and describing America's providential identity and millennial role. Unlike the fortieth president, many colonial and early republican political and religious leaders expressed much more anxiety about the ability of the United States to live up to this responsibility. Sin was for them a serious and permanent problem. They tended to place much stronger emphases on the need to maintain high levels of individual and public virtue and piety. To use Walter McDougall's terms, they tended to view America as a "promised land," looking to perfect liberty, Christianity, and self-government at home, rather than as a "crusader state" exporting these ideas and institutions abroad. These differences notwithstanding, these representative examples show that, as Richard Gamble writes in *The War for Righteousness*, "With surprising consistency, though to varying degrees over time and with shifting emphases, Americans have been habitually drawn to language that is redemptive, apocalyptic, and expansive."[64]

In *Redeemer Nation: The Idea of America's Millennial Role*, Ernest Lee Tuveson explores the historical American and European roots of many of the ideas about religion and politics that were expressed by Reagan. He writes: "To the belief that history, under divine guidance, will bring about the triumph of Christian principles, and that a holy utopia will come into being, I have assigned the name 'millennialist.' "[65] He continues, "It has not been generally realized that some version of the 'millennialist' doctrine has probably been predominant among English-speaking Protestants since the later seventeenth century."[66] Tuveson claims American religious thinkers such as Jonathan Edwards and Timothy Dwight and British religious thinkers such as Thomas Goodwin and Daniel Whitby belong to this millennialist category. Tuveson explains that millennialist religious thought rejects various ideas and concepts derived from traditional Christian theology including the allegorical interpretation of the Christian millennium, the difference between sacred and profane history, and the division between the City of God and the earthly city.

About the appeal of millennialism, Tuveson writes, "Christians need no longer lead the furtive existence of Augustine's City of God; militant action against the remaining wrongs had now a great promise of success."[67] For people persuaded by these ideas, Tuveson continues, "The Reformation became the assurance that the long era of superstition, injustice, and poverty was ending and that light was breaking over the world."[68] No longer would Christians be forced to wait for a Last Judgment that would come like a thief in the night. Now they could work incrementally towards the redemption of the world in time. Millennialist ideas encouraged speculation about which nation or nations had been chosen to carry out God's will on earth. Tuveson argues that Englishmen and other Europeans carried various types of millennialism to the New World during the colonization of North America.

It was not long thereafter that America became viewed as the chosen land. It is out of this historical religious context, one in which the distinction between God and Caesar became increasingly difficult to discern, that many of the claims about America's status as a chosen nation emerged. Many of Reagan's ideas about America as a shining city were rooted in a particular strain of thought in the Western political and religious past that is strongly at odds with the mainstream of Christianity, whether Eastern Orthodox, Catholic (Roman or Anglican), or Protestant. But the tendency to interpret history, American or otherwise, in this manner is not simply an American, English, or Protestant phenomenon. It is a possibility that extends back into the earliest history of the Christian church.

REAGAN'S SHINING CITY AND EARLY CHRISTIANITY

Jesus gave his Apostles a general account of the events that would culminate in end of the world and his Second Coming. After telling them about the end times, he said, "For as the lightning cometh out of the east, and shineth *even* unto the west; so shall also the coming of the Son of man be."[69] The unpredictability of this event was reaffirmed by St. Peter, who writes, "But the day of the Lord will come as a thief in the night."[70] He reminded his readers that this was because "one day is with the Lord as a thousand years, and a thousand years as one day."[71] Even the Book of Revelation, which offers a vivid account of the "events" of the Christian apocalypse, was mainly interpreted as an allegory since at least the time of St. Augustine. Thus, although Christians were taught that history someday would end, they were not supposed to spend their lives attempting to decipher the date of Jesus's return by interpreting pragmatic events through a millennial filter.

These traditional ideas about the end of history did not go unchallenged. During the first and second centuries, some Christians interpreted historical events, especially the various persecutions they suffered at the hands of the Roman Empire, as signs of the looming apocalypse. St. Augustine, who perhaps went further than any other early Christian theologian in separating Christianity and its transcendent eschatology from the events of the mundane world, was prompted to protect sacred history and the City of

God from profane history and the earthly city in part because this type of confusion was not uncommon during his lifetime.

As Christianity gained acceptance in the Roman Empire, a number of Christians, including political rulers and clergy, began to describe the empire as having a unique relationship to God and a special role in the unfolding of his providence in history. In "A Speech on the Dedication of the Holy Sepulchure Church," Eusebius of Caesarea, a bishop and early church historian, argued that it was not a coincidence that the Incarnation of Christ, heralding the one true religion for all of humanity, occurred at approximately the same time as the declaration of the *Pax Romana*, a proclamation made possible by Rome's dominion over the known world. Prior to these events, Eusebius argued, the world was primarily a place of suffering in which tyranny, war, injustice, and the worship of false gods were common. In his view, Christianity was the spiritual liberator of humanity. It allowed all people to worship the one true God. The empire too, especially after it established Christianity as its official religion, was destined to accomplish great and holy things on earth. Through its enormous power, Rome would put an end to human suffering and establish order and peace throughout the world.[72] Working together, the church and the empire, God and Caesar, would bring about a dramatic improvement in the living conditions of humanity that would eventually amount to a transfiguration of reality itself. In Eusebius's view, the empire is an equal partner with the church in bringing about this divinely willed change in human existence.

In *The City of God*, St. Augustine devotes much time and care to exploding what he perceived as an impermissible assertion of human knowledge about the movements of Providence in human history contained in views like the one expressed by Eusebius. He reminds his contemporaries that the Roman Empire served God's will both when it established Christianity as its official religion and when it persecuted Christians. He also argues that God admits only the righteous into the City of God, but, "Earthly kingdoms, however, He gives to the godly and the ungodly alike, as it may please Him, whose pleasure is never unjust."[73] Thus, for reasons known only to him, God gave an empire not only to the Romans, but also to the Persians, the Assyrians, the Babylonians, and others. Speculation about the meaning of the events in profane history is not a Christian concern, according to St. Augustine. He explains, "The New Testament clearly reveals what is veiled in the Old: that the one true God is to be worshipped not for the sake of those earthly and temporal goods which divine providence grants to good and evil men alike, but for the sake of eternal life and everlasting rewards, and the fellowship of the supernal City itself."[74]

St. Augustine also dismantles the Eusebian view of the *Pax Romana* by reminding his readers of its transitory nature and high cost. He acknowledges that the Roman Empire established a modicum of order and stability throughout much of the known world. But he feels that many of those who assign the empire a prophetic destiny overlooked the manner in which this peace was achieved. In *The City of God*, he argues, "[This peace] was to be accomplished only at the expense of titanic hazards, hair-raising exertion, and much mutual devastation—for by this time the other peoples of the earth had also become stout-hearted and strong, practiced in the use of weapons, and unwilling to yield."[75]

Nor did St. Augustine consider this peace to be the permanent achievement that Eusebius suggested. In a sober assessment of the fragility of political order on earth, he states, "There never has been, nor, is there today, any absence of hostile foreign powers to provoke war. What is worse, the very development of the empire accruing from their incorporation has begotten still worse wars within. I refer to the civil wars and social uprisings that involve even more wretched anxieties for human beings, either shaken by their actual impact, or living in fear of their renewal."[76] For St. Augustine, the ever-present threat of conflict without and within the empire was a permanent feature of life on earth. All his comments were directed at reminding Roman Christians that earthly life is transitory, that their true home is not of this world, and that even the best arrangements of politics can make only the most modest progress toward a just and ordered society.

These comments about a connection between dissident forms of the Reformation and a dubious tendency in early Christianity should not be interpreted as definitive statements about any of the mentioned thinkers and epochs. They have been offered to impart a sufficient awareness of how deeply rooted in Christianity is the propensity to conflate earthly living and eschatological expectation. This tendency is not incidental to Christianity. It appears that it is a permanent problem of human existence that Christianity may even exacerbate. In other words, Reagan's tendency to combine God and Caesar is at least as old as Christianity itself. Eric Voegelin explains this seemingly inevitable tendency in Christianity in many of his political and philosophical writings. His thoughts will shed more light upon Reagan's religious-political beliefs.

ERIC VOEGELIN ON CHRISTIANITY AND THE PROBLEM OF HISTORICAL EXISTENCE

Voegelin devoted much of his scholarship to recovering and interpreting experiences and symbols of religious, political, and philosophical order. He dwelt a great deal upon the philosophy of Plato and the theology of St. Augustine, and he drew much inspiration for his writings and philosophical ideas from these two thinkers. He also spent time diagnosing the existential causes of spiritual, intellectual, and political disorder in the modern era. Voegelin used a number of highly specialized terms and concepts to express his ideas, and dictionaries and glossaries of his terminology abound in his collected works and in the secondary literature. Here, the usage of Voegelin's technical terminology will be reduced to a minimum. Definitions will be provided when possible or appropriate.

Voegelin argues that individuals and societies experience a reality beyond the mundane or ephemeral modes of existence. He holds that words such as love, good, evil, reason, beauty, God, soul, and death, when described in a philosophically serious manner, do not refer to static objects completely known to or under the total control of human beings or societies. On the contrary, such words are symbols, providing societies and individuals with as much clarity as possible about a realm of existence of which they have some experience, but that ultimately transcends human consciousness. Symbols of great power and clarity often become authoritative for individuals and societies because they express deep understandings of order in the human soul and politics. In many writings, Voegelin claims that Christianity either refined or transcended a number of earlier insights into the human condition and the structure of reality, such as those articulated by the ancient Israelites and by cosmological societies such as ancient Egypt and prephilosophical ancient Greece. He believes that Christianity brought the greatest clarity to human consciousness.

At the same time, Voegelin claims that the Christian breakthrough into a more complete, or "differentiated," understanding of the structure of reality does not imply a transformation of earthly existence. The mundane world remained for Voegelin, as for St. Augustine, the place in which human beings are born, feel joy and sorrow, experience order and chaos, and die. The tension between the new heightened awareness of transcendent reality and the continuation of earthly life more or less as it was before produces anxiety in a number of individual Christians. In *The New Science of Politics*, Voegelin argues that this is not a surprising experience because "uncertainty is the very essence of Christianity."[77] He claims that with Christianity the security previously derived from a belief in a cosmos populated by immanent, or intraworldly, gods is lost, and "communication with the world-transcendent God is reduced to the tenuous bond of faith, in the sense of Heb. 11:1, as the substance of things hoped for and the proof of things unseen."[78]

As Christianity expanded, and as its insights into human nature, God, and history gained authority, it began to reshape Western civilization. Many Christians endured the heightened uncertainty about existence ushered in by Christianity—especially if they realized that God, who was infinite, could not be dominated by the human intellect or will, both of which were finite. But a number of human beings, both Christian and non-Christian, were not willing to accept this tenuous hold upon reality. Voegelin explains, "The very lightness of this fabric [of Christian faith] may prove too heavy a burden for men who lust for massively possessive experience."[79] Indeed, one consequence of Christianity's formative influence upon Western civilization is that an increasing number of people ill equipped to bear Christianity's uncertainty are nevertheless brought under the dominion of Christian symbolism. This led to a development within Christianity, which was discernible from the beginning and was amplified during and after the Reformation, which Voegelin calls "gnosticism."

In Voegelin's view, gnosticism is the essence of the disorder of modernity. He uses this technical term to describe what he sees as a common response to the pressure of living in the de-divinized, mundane world of Christianity. In his view, gnosticism encompasses a wide range of religious and secular political movements, ranging from Christian millennial movements, such as those described earlier, to Marxism and various totalitarian political and ideological movements. Gnosticism attracts and unites individuals who have common experiences of the world as a defective and deeply disappointing place, a state of affairs that they attribute to the world's poor organization. The typical gnostic believes that this dissatisfaction will dissolve as soon as he conjures and implements a plan for politics or society that promises a transformation of reality. In this view, there is no need to wait for a divine event or force to bring about this type of change. The key to regenerating the world and humanity lies in human action itself. Gnostics of all types, religious and secular, are animated by desires to re-divinize the world and immanentize, or bring into history, the Christian Eschaton, or its secular equivalent. According to Voegelin, gnosticism, as a development in political thought, has both a highly utopian and revolutionary cast.[80]

For Voegelin, the appeal of such a vision to spiritually immature individuals is not difficult to understand. Gnosticism requires little to no effort on the part of the individual to adjust his soul to a transcendent realm of order or to restrain his will's lower impulses. As Voegelin argues, "The spiritual strength of the soul which in Christianity was devoted to the sanctification of life could now be diverted into the more appealing, more tangible, and, above all, so much easier creation of the terrestrial paradise."[81] Such a vision also satisfies, at least for a time, psychological and existential needs to feel secure, certain, and in control of reality. For the typical gnostic, the moral purity of his vision to transform reality demands universal assent; objections to his vision are heresy. To Voegelin, gnostic visions, regardless of the fervency with which they are promoted by individuals or societies, are pneumopathological disorders, or spiritual diseases. When they serve as the organizing ideas for political activity, they wreak horrendous havoc.

Voegelin's efforts to understand the root causes of modern political and spiritual disorder are not confined to his gnostic thesis. In *Israel and Revelation*, he explores and analyzes the desires of the Israelite prophets for a change in the constitution of being, or the structure of reality. In so doing, he develops a number of interpretive concepts, including "metastatic faith" and "metastatic apocalypse," which are derived from the word "metastasis" (meaning "change" or "transformation"). He uses these terms to interpret an episode he recounts from the Old Testament in which the Prophet Isaiah counseled the king of Judah that faith in Yahweh was sufficient protection against an imminent invasion. With a strong enough faith in God, Isaiah claimed, the Lord would disperse the enemies. The king rejected this advice and made the practical arrangements one would expect of a monarch charged with defending the realm.

Voegelin argues that this encounter is important because "an aura of magic undeniably surrounds the counsel: It is due to the fact that the divine plan itself has been brought within the knowledge of man, in as much as Isaiah knows that God wants the survival of Judah as an organized people in pragmatic history."[82] The act of faith Isaiah demanded, based on his unique knowledge of God's plan for Israel, promised a fundamental change in the entire structure of existence. It had the allure of a reprieve from the perpetual, mundane responsibilities of political life. In this sense, it promised a metastatic apocalypse produced by an act of metastatic faith.

About this episode Voegelin writes, "Isaiah, we may say, had tried the impossible: to make the leap in being a leap out of existence into a divinely transfigured world beyond the laws of mundane existence."[83] Voegelin admits that there are important differences between the metastatic desires of Isaiah and those of later gnostic figures. But these differences, however large, are of degrees rather than kind. Voegelin explains, "The constitution of being is what it is, and cannot be affected by human fancies."[84] The structure of being is fixed, he says, and "the will to transform reality into something which by essence it is not is the rebellion against the nature of things as ordained by God."[85] Voegelin believes that Christianity is successful in the main in transforming the various metastatic symbols of the Old and New Testaments into "eschatological events beyond history," but he also stresses that movements desiring transformations of reality never entirely disappeared.[86] In a manner similar to Tuveson, Voegelin holds that new versions of these old symbols and of religious and political movements devoted to their propagation reemerged during the Reformation.

In an essay titled "Man in Society and History," Voegelin claims that metastatic political movements remained active in the twentieth century. He argues, "The metastatic ideas that determine politics until our day, for example, in the idea of a final Communist empire, move in the tradition of apocalyptic thought."[87] He also believes that gnostic variants of symbols such as "chosen nation" and "chosen people" still linger in the present. He writes that although various ancient empires destroyed the political organization of the historical chosen people of Israel, "that does not mean that the idea of a Chosen People is dead. Still today it dominates the political scene in which more than one people feels itself chosen to enter into leadership of world society."[88]

Elsewhere, Voegelin draws attention to a problem in political thought that is poorly understood by many Western theorists and political figures. In a review of Hannah Arendt's *The Origins of Totalitarianism*, Voegelin argues that a tendency to juxtapose good liberal-democratic order with evil totalitarian order provides an inadequate explanation for the disorder and violence of the twentieth century. He writes, "The true dividing line in the contemporary crisis does not run between liberals and totalitarians, but between the religious and philosophical transcendentalists on the one side and the liberal and totalitarian immanentist sectarians on the other side."[89] That many defenders of liberalism, such as Arendt, were also committed to transforming the world and human nature through political activity, he suggests, "reveals how much ground liberals and totalitarians have in common; the essential immanentism that unites them overrides the differences of ethos that separate them."[90]

Voegelin considered Karl Marx to be one of the most influential modern gnostic thinkers. A brief summary of Marx's understanding of human nature, the historical process, and the end of history will help draw out the gnostic tendencies of Marx's thought and communist ideology. For Marx, human beings are unique because they possess the freedom to engage in creative labor. Unfortunately, history is the story of the development and evolution of social classes, property relationships, and the means of production—all of which increasingly alienate individuals from their natural selves. This story moved through many stages and had arrived at the penultimate epoch of capitalism, which happened to be the time in which Marx lived. In capitalism, the working class, or proletariat, is completely alienated from its labor. Thus, it is able to develop a revolutionary consciousness. With Marx's vision in mind, the proletariat can unite on a global scale, rise up, destroy the bourgeoisie and their capitalist superstructure, and complete the final stage of history, which produces communism.

In *The German Ideology*, Marx explains the following about human existence before and after this revolution:

> For as soon as the distribution of labour comes into being, each man has a particular, exclusive sphere of activity, which is forced upon him and from which he cannot escape. He is a hunter, a fisherman, a shepherd, or a critical critic, and must remain so if he does not wish to lose his means of livelihood; while in communist society, where nobody has one exclusive sphere of activity but each can become accomplished in any branch he wishes, society regulates the general production and thus makes it possible for me to do one thing today and another tomorrow, to hunt in the morning, fish in the afternoon, rear cattle in the evening, criticize after dinner, just as I have a mind, without ever becoming hunter, fisherman, shepherd or critic.[91]

When history is complete, Marx claims, politics as it has theretofore been known in human history will no longer be necessary. Through the revolutionary process itself, all human beings, or, more specifically, everyone who survives the revolution, will be free and equal. They will have overcome their historical alienation. The belief that this future paradise is on the brink of being realized permits the proletariat to use any means necessary both to ignite and complete the revolution.

As this brief account suggests, Marx's revolutionary and apocalyptic vision of communism is global in scope and has a highly utopian character. It is possible, he thought, to transform completely both human nature and the rest of reality. It is this part of the Marxist imagination that drove many people, including Whittaker Chambers, to embrace communism.

These ideas from Voegelin shed a different, perhaps unexpected light upon the quality of Reagan's religious vision as expressed in the image of America as a shining city upon a hill. It is well known that Reagan was no intellectual friend of Karl Marx. On virtually every conceivable topic, they seem to be deeply at odds. Unlike Marx, Reagan believed in God as the creator of the world and humanity. In Reagan's mind, human life is sacred. Reagan was an advocate of free markets, private property, liberty, and democracy. For him, these are not only practical but also moral institutions. Notwithstanding these and other important specific differences, one should not overlook the fact that Marx and Reagan seem to share certain broader imaginative tendencies.

Like Reagan, Marx was enthralled by a vision in which political activity fundamentally changed human nature and the world. They both imagined a future in which politics would no longer be necessary. Reagan, it is true, promoted a peaceful type of democratic apocalypse. In many ways, his self-appointed role in the drama of history was similar to the one played by the Prophet Isaiah as described by Voegelin. Both Reagan and Isaiah relied upon the nonviolent appeal of their words to act as a catalyst for the metastatic transformation of the world. Marx's notion of how to bring change, in contrast, involved destruction and violence. Nevertheless, both Reagan and Marx saw the structure of reality as malleable. They saw the process of history as intelligible and as working toward a culmination in time. This part of Reagan's imagination used Christian symbols, whereas Marx categorically rejected such images. This difference should not obscure what, to use Voegelin's term, appears to be the underlying gnostic character of their ostensibly different visions. In their efforts to obtain and communicate certainty about the structure of reality, both figures seem to have lost sight of the distinctive nature of the divine realm, collapsing God into Caesar.

Voegelin's description of modernity as permeated by gnostic and metastatic movements has provided philosophical support for Babbitt's claim that political and economic problems are ultimately expressions of deeper spiritual disorders. Voegelin's scholarship has also provided a more rigorous philosophical context for interpreting the millenarian religious and political movements described by Tuveson. In penetrating to the essence of the gnostic and metastatic attitudes toward Being and history, Voegelin identifies similarities between liberalism and totalitarianism that have helped uncover what some might consider to be startling similarities between the ideological structure of Marxism and Reagan's religious sensibilities. Voegelin's research has also shown how deeply gnostic and metastatic tendencies run in the Western mind and in Christianity; this might make the predominant side of Reagan's religious imagination more forgivable, if not more philosophically acceptable.

Voegelin's writings also shed light upon the types of intellectual and political debates and movements that emerged in the aftermath of World War II. It is worth noting that *The New Science of Politics, Israel and*

Revelation, his review of *The Origins of Totalitarianism*, and "Man in Society and History" were written during a period from the late 1940s until the mid 1960s. At the same time that Voegelin was developing theoretical tools with which to diagnose the spiritual and political disorder of the age, Reagan was constructing and refining his vision of politics. Voegelin's work during this period is but one indication that alternatives to the vision Reagan ultimately adopted were available. Were Reagan to have encountered Voegelin's work—which is not an implausible idea since Voegelin became widely associated with the so-called American conservative intellectual movement—it is unlikely, however, that he would have adopted Voegelin's views. Such a step would have required a fundamental reorientation of Reagan's imagination. His basic intuitive sensibilities were already deeply ingrained and would have strongly predisposed him against a transformation of beliefs in the direction of traditional Christianity and the distinction between the things of God and the things of Caesar.

As helpful as Voegelin's scholarship has been to analyzing Reagan's religious views, it should be noted that Voegelin's thoughts on Christianity are not without ambiguities. Some of his critics suggest he has either an incomplete or a flawed understanding of Christianity. David Walsh, a scholar sympathetic to Voegelin, writes, "Voegelin left the Christian dimension of his thought in a relatively undeveloped stage."[92] In "Immortality: Experience and Symbol," for example, Voegelin declares, "History is Christ written large."[93] Yet in his many writings Voegelin does not seem to realize the full implications of his own statement. Voegelin's "underdeveloped" interpretation of Christianity actually exaggerates the distance between the transcendent and the immanent. He does not sufficiently understand that the Christian God, who was incarnated in history, has an intimate connection with creation. To that limited extent, Christianity can be said to have "divinized" the "mundane" world. Contrary to Voegelin's suggestions, mainstream Christianity does not understand itself as having drained earthly existence of mystery or the divine presence. God is thought to work through history.

The idea that universality is present in history has serious implications for politics that can only be briefly touched upon here. Edmund Burke, an Anglican Christian, sees society at its best as an attempt to articulate and maintain a connection with the divine mystery. In the *Reflections* he argues, "They conceive that He who gave our nature to be perfected by our virtue willed also the necessary means of its perfection. He willed therefore the state—He willed its connection with the source and original archetype of all perfection."[94] That Burke observes this relationship between politics and the divine does not mean that he believes England is sacred in the way that Reagan thinks America is holy. Burke's defense of tradition and his belief in Providence are indistinguishable from his view that human nature is chronically fallen and that even the most admirable society is deeply flawed. Like Voegelin, Burke is a sharp critic of movements that promise a transformation of the human condition and that advocate abstract principles like "freedom" and "democracy" as the salvation of mankind. At the same time, Burke has a clearer sense than does Voegelin of the degree to which the universal dwells in the particular. Burke understands more fully than Voegelin the ways in which the divine can raise the moral standards of politics.[95]

CONCLUSION

Although Reagan sometimes expressed a fairly traditional understanding of the Christian distinction between God and Caesar, the primary side of his religious sensibilities is permeated by millennial expectations and gnostic elements. In "Ronald Reagan and the American Public Philosophy," Hugh Heclo seems to have the main part of Reagan's religious beliefs in mind when he claims, "Finally, I think it is fair to say that Reagan was unable to recognize that his faith and redemptive vision of America sailed dangerously close to idolatry, if not quite landing there."[96] Reagan's inclination to confuse or synthesize God and Caesar strongly affects both religion and politics. Claes G. Ryn argues that those who seek to turn the highest moral standards of Christianity into programs for political action have an understanding of politics that "is symptomatic of not having discovered the spiritual life in its highest manifestation. An exaggerated notion of the moral potential of politics reveals a contracted and distorted awareness of the holy."[97] According to Ryn, those who hold these ideas fail to realize that *the deification of politics requires the politization, and hence devaluation, of the divine.*"[98] If Ryn is right, then Reagan's strong propensity to blur the things of God and Caesar and even to let the religious realm collapse into the political may actually degrade the very religious ideas that Reagan claimed to represent and defend.

Irving Babbitt develops a number of dichotomies to explain what he sees as the growing political and spiritual disorder of the West. One of his dichotomies is between the "missionary spirit" and "the crusading spirit." About the difference between the two he writes, "The missionary spirit, the purely spiritual appeal from man to man, is unquestionably Christian. By the crusading spirit I mean, on the other hand, the attempt to achieve spiritual ends collectively through the machinery of the secular order."[99] Babbitt believed the crusading spirit is not only a profound distortion of Christianity but also highly dangerous when put into political practice. About the Christian crusader of the twelfth and thirteenth centuries, he states, "By his confusion of the things of God with the things of Caesar the crusader was in danger of substituting a will to power for the will to peace that is at the heart of genuine Christianity."[100] The danger of confusing the will to power with the will of God did not disappear with the end of the Western European crusades. Babbitt believed that this spirit increasingly came to define the America of his time. He writes, "It is becoming the dangerous privilege of the United States to display more of the crusading temper than any other country in both its domestic and its foreign policies."[101] The apocalyptic structure of the millennial dimension of Reagan's imagination, captured most powerfully in his symbol of America as a shining city on a hill, appears to be imbued with the type of crusading spirit condemned by Babbitt. When the ideas of Voegelin, Heclo, Babbitt, and Ryn are all taken into account, it seems that Reagan's predominant religious imagination contains many highly problematic components that often spell great trouble for practical politics.

Conclusion: An Empire of Illusions?
The Chimeric Imagination of Ronald Reagan

> They called it the Reagan revolution. Well, I'll accept that, but for me it always seemed more like the great rediscovery, a rediscovery of our values and our common sense.[1]
>
> —Ronald Reagan

Ronald Reagan has cast a long shadow over the United States. In one sense, Reagan's enduring relevance to understanding American political thought and practice is so ubiquitous that commentary upon the topic feels like stating the obvious. As Will Bunch documents in *Tear Down This Myth*, in the United States there are airports, highways, and schools named after Reagan. Some U.S. states have declared the former president's birthday, February 6, Ronald Reagan Day. Groups have sought to replace the image of Alexander Hamilton on the ten-dollar bill, or Franklin Roosevelt on the dime, with one of Reagan. Even more ambitiously, Bunch writes, "Since 1999, some Republican members of Congress have pushed to add Reagan's face to Mount Rushmore—appropriately to the far right side of the South Dakota monument."[2]

Other evidence of Reagan's legacy comes easily to mind. The Republican Party's Contract with America and Democratic president Bill Clinton's declaration that "the era of big Government is over" are two representative examples of Reagan's imprint upon American politics in the 1990s.[3] Reagan's reach extended into the early twenty-first century with the election of Republican president George W. Bush. Bush actively sought to associate himself with the Reagan legacy during his presidential campaigns and presidency. A number of Bush supporters as well as journalists drew conclusions early in Bush's first term that he was Reagan's heir. As president Bush's popularity plummeted in his second term, some criticized him on the grounds that he was *not* following Reagan closely enough. More recently, one has only to think of the many Republican presidential primary candidates who tried to appropriate the mantle of Reagan during the 2008 and 2012 presidential campaigns. In Republican presidential primary debates, invocations of Reagan's name have become increasingly contrived, even absurd. But Republicans are not the only politicians talking about Reagan. On important occasions, Barack Obama has used Reaganesque language. Comparisons between Reagan and Obama have been made as the Obama presidency has developed. Obama and members of his administration have even sought some guidance and perhaps inspiration from the Reagan presidency.

The most recent writings on Reagan's legacy have focused upon a wide range of issues and have drawn various, often incompatible, conclusions about Reagan's accomplishments and ideas. It seems as if the only thing various scholars and journalists agree upon is the importance of Reagan's legacy for understanding the American present. In *Tear Down This Myth*, Will Bunch argues that while Reagan remains highly popular in America, the Reagan Americans remember is mostly an illusion concocted by nefarious forces dedicated to using the former president's image and popularity for clandestine purposes.[4] In *The Man Who Sold the World: Ronald Reagan and the Betrayal of Main Street America*, William Kleinknecht paints a picture of Reagan as equal parts imbecile and demon; he sees Reagan as Chance the Gardener one moment and Mephistopheles the next.[5] Both authors express a profound disappointment and exasperation with Reagan's enduring popularity in the United States. They do not understand how Reagan and his legacy minders have hoodwinked so many Americans.

Other authors have offered more sympathetic treatments of Reagan. In "The Mixed Legacies of Ronald Reagan," in *The Enduring Reagan*, Hugh Heclo provides a fair and concise assessment of Reagan's foreign and domestic policy successes and failures.[6] In *Upstream: The Ascendance of American Conservatism*, Alfred Regnery celebrates a number of Reagan's presidential achievements. He wants Reagan to be a source of inspiration for the American conservative movement in the future. Even as he praises Reagan as a conservative who successfully combined important ideas and the demands of practical politics, Regnery is relatively silent on why Reagan's vision is sound or worth remembering. To him, the importance of free markets, democracy, liberty, and moral values is self-evident. Overall, Regnery's book reflects an increasing lack of intellectual curiosity in the broader American conservative movement.[7]

In *Reagan's Disciple: George W. Bush's Troubled Quest for a Presidential Legacy*, Lou Cannon and Carl Cannon see Reagan's legacy as one of practical foreign and domestic policy successes in which ideology was an important, but ultimately secondary concern. Especially when he is compared to Bush, Cannon and Cannon praise Reagan for his willingness to adjust ideology to practical concerns and limitations on action. On the one hand, the authors offer interesting if ultimately cursory insights into the practical side of Reagan's presidency. On the other hand, in their efforts to distance Reagan from Bush, they downplay too much the deep ideological similarities between the two presidents.[8]

Whereas Regnery and Cannon and Cannon side with Reagan over Bush, Michael Gerson sides with Bush over Reagan. In *Heroic Conservatism: Why Republicans Need to Embrace America's Ideals (And Why They Deserve to*

Fail If They Don't), Gerson acknowledges Reagan's influence upon Bush, especially in foreign policy. Gerson justifies the War on Terror and the Iraq War as manifestations of the American spirit and as parts of the historical U.S. obligation to bring justice, freedom, and democracy to the world. Reagan expressed similar ideas when he spoke about the Cold War. Despite these similarities, Gerson celebrates Bush as superior to Reagan because he believes Bush developed a vision of America and of the world that was more compassionate, moral, and Christian than the one held by Reagan.[9]

All these authors offer different perspectives on the Reagan legacy. Although some of these treatments have genuine strengths, they all tend to avoid a serious and sustained discussion of what Reagan himself saw as his most important legacy: his success in getting Americans to embrace his vision of America, its people, and the world.

On January 11, 1989, Ronald Reagan addressed the American people for the last time as president of the United States. He began his remarks by expressing his deep and sincere gratitude to the American people for allowing him to serve as their president. He then drew his audience's attention to an incident he first described to the nation on Christmas Day, 1982, in which the *USS Midway* rescued a sinking boat of refugees shouting "Hello, American sailor. Hello, freedom man." About this event Reagan explained, "A small moment with a big meaning, a moment the sailor, who wrote it in a letter, couldn't get out of his mind. And, when I saw it, neither could I. Because that's what it was to be an American in the 1980's. We stood, again, for freedom. I know we always have, but in the past few years the world again—and in a way, we ourselves—rediscovered it."[10] The theme of rediscovering the American spirit permeated his address as his remarks alternated among the past, the present, and the future, and between celebrating his foreign policy successes and his domestic policy achievements.

Reagan stated, "The way I see it, there were two great triumphs, two things that I'm proudest of. One is the economic recovery, in which the people of America created—and filled—19 million new jobs. The other is the recovery of our morale. America is respected again in the world and looked to for leadership."[11] He argued that during his 1980 campaign, some people claimed that his vision for America and the world "would result in catastrophe."[12] Some predicted that his foreign policy vision would lead to war, others that his approach to fixing the economy would lead to economic dislocation and collapse. In Reagan's mind, critics had been proved wrong on both fronts. In terms of his success in reviving the American economy, he related an anecdote about attending an international economic summit early in his presidency. He said that when the opening meeting convened, everyone stared at him without saying a word. As Reagan explained, "And then one of them broke the silence. 'Tell us about the American miracle,' he said."[13]

To Reagan, however, America's economic recovery was not miraculous. It was simply the result of applying American common sense to politics. He argued, "Common sense told us that when you put a big tax on something, the people will produce less of it. So, we cut the people's tax rates, and the people produced more than ever before. The economy bloomed like a plant that had been cut back and could now grow quicker and stronger."[14] He explained that as a result of his prudent economic and tax-cutting policies, the United States was in the midst of the largest period of peacetime economic expansion in American history. He claimed that income levels were up, poverty was down, entrepreneurship was thriving, and technology was developing at unprecedented levels. All this allowed the United States to be more competitive, to export more goods abroad, and to break down international barriers to free trade among nations.[15] The economic growth of the 1980s provided stability and prosperity at home and respect and admiration abroad. It also provided the United States with the opportunity to rebuild its national defenses and reassert its role as a defender of freedom in the world.

Transitioning to an assessment of his foreign policy achievements, Reagan picked up his theme of common sense and said, "Common sense also told us that to preserve the peace, we'd have to become strong again after years of weakness and confusion. So, we rebuilt our defenses, and this New Year we toasted the new peacefulness around the globe."[16] As evidence of this new peacefulness, Reagan cited the beginnings of nuclear weapons reductions by the United States and the Soviet Union, the Soviet withdrawal from Afghanistan, the Vietnamese withdrawal from Cambodia, and the departure of Cuban troops from Angola. Even more importantly, Reagan remarked, "Countries across the globe are turning to free markets and free speech and turning away from the ideologies of the past. For them, the great discovery of the 1980's has been that, lo and behold, the moral way of government is the practical way of government: Democracy, the profoundly good, is also the profoundly productive."[17] These sentiments did not obscure Reagan's understanding of the delicate nature of these accomplishments. About future relations with the Soviet Union, which was still in existence when Reagan left the White House, he argued, "We must keep up our guard, but we must also continue to work together to lessen and eliminate tension and mistrust."[18]

The main focus of Reagan's Farewell Address was explaining the significance of the rejuvenation of the American spirit that had occurred during his presidency. He reminded Americans of their history, spirit, and future. He said that during his time in office he had earned the nickname "The Great Communicator." He disagreed with the criticism of him implicit in this epithet. About this label Reagan said:

> But I never thought it was my style or the words I used that made a difference: it was the content. I wasn't a great communicator, but I communicated great things, and they didn't spring full bloom from my brow, they came from the heart of a great nation—from our experience, our wisdom, and our belief in the principles that have guided us for two centuries.[19]

Immediately after these remarks, he acknowledged that many had described his presidency as "the Reagan Revolution." To Reagan, the rekindling of the American spirit was not a revolution so much as it was a rediscovery.

What had the United States rediscovered? For the last time as president, Reagan explained to Americans that the United States was a unique nation. He stated:

> Ours was the first revolution in the history of mankind that truly reversed the course of government, and with three little words: "We the people." "We the people" tell the government what to do, it doesn't tell us. "We the people" are the driver, the government is the car. And we decide where it should go, and by what route, and how fast. Almost all the world's constitutions are documents in which governments tell the people what their privileges are. Our Constitution is a document in which "We the people" tell the government what it is allowed to do. "We the people" are free. This belief has been the underlying basis for everything I've tried to do these past 8 years.[20]

A central element of Reagan's lifelong political crusade was reminding Americans about the unlimited beauty and power of liberty and democratic government. In his Farewell Address, he stated that his mission began in the 1960s when he, like so many other Americans, began to feel that government was growing too large and eroding too much of America's prosperity and liberty. He argued that someone had to tell the government to stop traveling down the road of higher taxes and more interference in American life. In his mind, "I was a citizen politician, and it seemed the right thing for a citizen to do."[21] Reagan the citizen politician viewed his presidency as one that "stopped a lot of what needed stopping."[22] He felt that his presidency had been fairly successful.

Reagan's estimation of his success in reinvigorating Americans with patriotism and pride was qualified. He was particularly concerned that there were not enough younger Americans who believed in the America Reagan had talked about for the last eight years. He said, "Our spirit is back, but we haven't reinstitutionalized it. We've got to do a better job of getting across that America is freedom—freedom of speech, freedom of religion, freedom of enterprise. And freedom is special and rare. It's fragile; it needs production [protection]."[23] A few moments later, Reagan's warning about the future became more dire. He explained, "If we forget what we did, we won't know who we are. I'm warning of an eradication of the American memory that could result, ultimately, in an erosion of the American spirit."[24] He counseled Americans to pay more attention to American history and civic ritual. He also encouraged American children to hold their parents accountable for teaching them about the United States and its ideals. He stated, "If your parents haven't been teaching you what it means to be an American, let 'em know and nail 'em on it. That would be a very American thing to do."[25]

As he concluded his address, Reagan reflected upon one of the most important images in his imagination, the shining city upon a hill symbol. He said:

> I've spoken of the shining city all my political life, but I don't know if I ever quite communicated what I saw when I said it. But in my mind it was a tall proud city built on rocks stronger than oceans, wind-swept, God-blessed, and teeming with people of all kinds living in harmony and peace; a city with free ports that hummed with commerce and creativity. And if there had to be city walls, the walls had doors and the doors were open to anyone with the will and the heart to get there. That's how I saw it, and see it still.[26]

He said that the city had become happier, more prosperous, and more secure during his time in office. This did not surprise him because, as he explained, the shining city had triumphed over every challenge it had encountered for more than two centuries. In his mind, the shining city remained a proud and strong achievement of the American people; the United States was still a beacon of hope calling the world to liberty and democracy. Then he asked that God bless his audience and the United States. President Ronald Reagan said goodbye to the American people.

In these remarks, Reagan extolled the virtues of democracy and liberty in America and around the world. He expressed his sense of the United States and its people as free and unique in history. He celebrated the American Revolution for its world-historic achievement of reversing the relationship between government and the governed. In his mind, Americans were the first people on earth to establish limited democratic government built on a foundation of liberty. By mentioning these views about the American Revolution and American history, Reagan drew attention to what he considered the conservative nature of his imagination. He celebrated the economic prosperity, political progress, and resurgent morale that had occurred in the United States during his presidency. Reagan warned Americans that it would take their conscious efforts to retain their hold upon this new sense of pride and national strength. By recalling the image of America as a shining city, Reagan reminded Americans of their religious heritage and of their special relationship with Providence.

These are the most important images and ideas that constitute Reagan's chimeric vision of America as an empire of ideals. This is the side of his mind that has been explained and analyzed in depth throughout this study. A clearer understanding of Reagan's vision has been obtained by comparing and contrasting its central elements with relevant ideas in the broader traditions of American political thought, Western political theory, and aesthetic theory. It has been shown that Reagan was not an "amiable dunce." The exigencies of the Cold War notwithstanding, the possibility that Reagan spoke frequently to Americans in highly sentimental and ahistorical terms merely for rhetorical convenience or out of conventional necessity cannot be maintained. He believed deeply in the vision he expressed as president. It is now both possible and appropriate to draw final conclusions about the quality of Reagan's imaginative vision, and about what the enduring appeal of his imagination tells Americans about themselves.

The idea of progress was just beneath the surface during parts of Reagan's Farewell Address. In countless speeches, Reagan provided vivid images of progress. He explained that progress could be made at any moment, and he argued that freedom, democracy, and free markets were its best facilitators. With these political and economic institutions in place, human creativity would be unleashed and civilization would be improved. The United States proved his point and confirmed his faith in progress. It was the exemplar of the free market. The United States was the birthplace of liberty, and Americans were constantly progressing toward ever more individual freedom. Political and economic progress in America created the environment for technological developments such as the automobile, the radio, the television, the space shuttle, and numerous pieces of life-saving medical technology. Reagan knew the wonder of these developments because he had lived with them all his life. Reagan seldom expressed a deep awareness of potential dangers lurking beneath these types of progress. On occasion, he seemed to intuit that his sanguine view of progress, particularly of its technological varieties, might not convey a complete picture. His anxiety over experiencing a nuclear holocaust, and his disgust at the horrors of modern warfare, represent the limited instances in which he grasped for a more sober and complete understanding of progress.

Robert Nisbet, Wilhelm Röpke, and Irving Babbitt are only three of many scholars who have articulated more nuanced, complex, and thoughtful views of modern notions of progress and the dangers to civilization presented by such ideas. In different ways, Nisbet and Röpke both argue that fundamental aspects of modern political and economic life have exacted a great price for all of the conveniences and progress they have provided. Röpke expresses an important truth about modernity when he argues that its fixation on technological progress has acted as a type of Novocain upon the human spirit. He argues with vigor and persuasiveness that the tendency of the modern world toward an "enmassment" of social life is one that is destructive of the "unpurchasable" world otherwise known as civilization. Nisbet also observes a number of harmful consequences resulting from the types of progress Reagan frequently describes. In his view, progress of the kind celebrated by Reagan actually weakens the organic bonds of community that are of great importance to human happiness.

In various writings, Babbitt freely admits that by the standards of the "law for thing," the world, especially the United States, has made great progress in the modern era. But for him, the typical modern individual's unwavering focus upon the "law for thing" is ultimately a dangerous form of moral escapism. In Babbitt's view, the types of modern technological innovation and progress extolled by Reagan often become obsessions, intoxications, and diversions for individuals seeking to avoid the demands of the ethical life. However well organized human beings might become at this utilitarian level of existence, Babbitt refuses to downplay or dismiss the instability produced in a world populated by a number of efficient egotists. According to Babbitt, modern human beings might be deeply disciplined according to the "law for thing," but, when measured by the higher, more important standard of the "law for man," they can be seen as leading lives of great disorder and hence miserable where it counts the most. Babbitt, Röpke, and Nisbet are attuned to the dehumanizing tendencies of modern notions of progress. They rightly observe the dangers immature visions of progress can present to societies and individuals. Reagan's overall lack of awareness of these manifold problems reflects a serious deficiency in his imagination.

Reagan did not believe that his understanding of progress was in conflict with or a threat to genuine religious faith and piety. Reagan's views on religion are extremely complex and difficult to discuss precisely because they permeate many other aspects of his intuition. In countless presidential speeches, he referred to God, Jesus of Nazareth, the Bible, and the Ten Commandments to explain his understanding of America, Americans, the Declaration of Independence, the Constitution, the world, history, democracy, and freedom. He often argued for the practical and moral superiority of democracy over communism. The United States allowed its citizens to practice a variety of religions, and the country drew strength from religious diversity and toleration. The Soviet Union, in contrast, persecuted religious believers of all faiths and was officially atheist.

Sometimes, Reagan articulated his notion of religion in such a way as to suggest that human beings are morally flawed creatures. The other, more prevalent side of Reagan's view of religion expressed a rather different vision of politics, America, human nature, and the world. The essence of this side of his imagination was contained in his vision of the United States as a shining city upon a hill. In this side of his mind, the United States is a vehicle through which God works his will on earth. Reagan believed the United States had been set aside by Providence to be discovered by a chosen people called Americans. The United States was intended to be a model of piety, democracy, and liberty. It was also obligated to share and extend these blessings at home and abroad.

Reagan even seemed to suggest that by encouraging crusades for democracy, faith, and freedom in America and around the world, the United States had a millennial role to play in human history. He often borrowed language from the Old Testament, especially the Prophet Isaiah, to convey his vision of the world after the United States had succeeded in promoting providentially approved political, economic, and religious ideals. This side of Reagan's imagination suggested that the United States was a temporal manifestation of the City of God. It was an intuition filled with apocalyptic expectation, making the things of God essentially indistinguishable from the things of Caesar. Such sentiments have roots in the broader traditions of American and Christian political thought.

Ernest Lee Tuveson has examined a number of millenarian movements that emerged in Europe during the Reformation. Some of these ideas were brought to the New World by English and other European colonists in the early seventeenth century, and millenarian religious and political speculation has been a part of the American tradition ever since. The ideas of John Winthrop and Jonathan Edwards represent different ways in which colonial Americans interpreted their new land as a New Israel or New Jerusalem. When compared to Reagan, these figures each expressed rather modest understandings of America as a chosen land and of Americans as a chosen people. It has been shown that speculation about the roles nations or other civilizational units might play in bringing about the millennium extends even further into Western history than the Reformation. As the historical contexts of the writings of St. Augustine reveal, such religious expectation was already present a few centuries after Christianity first emerged. St. Augustine's preoccupation with explaining the differences between the City of God and the city of man arose in part because he too was confronted with arguments that a world transformed into heaven on earth was not only possible, but probable.

In many writings, Eric Voegelin provides penetrating insights into the spiritual and psychological factors that have allowed individuals and mass movements to create order and disorder throughout human history. Voegelin argues that Christianity brings to humanity the utmost clarity about the relationship between the transcendent and mundane levels of existence. In his view, this clarification effectively drains the world of its divine presence. Hence, the Christian differentiation of human consciousness produces an anxiety and uncertainty about earthly existence that is too much for some people to bear. Since Christianity emerged in history, some Christians, and even some non-Christians, have attempted to re-divinize the world, reinvigorating it with possibilities for transformative political action, thereby giving themselves the illusion of mastery over their lives and Being. Voegelin's gnostic thesis is one way in which he attempts to understand the structure of this type of derailment in human consciousness. He also draws attention to other elements of this type of derailment when he discusses ideas such as "metastatic faith" and "metastatic apocalypse" in his treatments of the Old Testament and the Prophet Isaiah.

For Voegelin, gnosticism, immanentism, and metastatic faith are all symptoms of a pneumopathological disorder, a spiritual disease, afflicting a number of individuals and ideological movements in the modern era. He sees such a spiritual disorder at the heart of Marxism. Applying Voegelin's analysis, one discovers a similar problem in the more expansive side of Reagan's religious vision. The details of the stories of history, politics, and the future told by Reagan and Marx are very different. The hard edge of Marxism is absent from the seemingly humble and optimistic vision promoted by Reagan. Marx sought to establish a substitute for religion. Reagan used Christian and other traditional religious imagery to articulate his sense of the world. In spite of these obvious and important differences between Marx and Reagan, the structures of their competing ideological narratives are essentially the same. Each thinker presents himself as one who has profound, even secret knowledge about the historical process, its culminating events, and the actions that human beings can take to bring about a political apocalypse within time. Voegelin's insights into the deeper structural similarities between totalitarianism and certain varieties of liberalism have provided additional analytical tools for examining Reagan's religious imagination.

Claes Ryn and Irving Babbitt have drawn important conclusions about the consequences for politics when guided by the type of religious vision expressed by Reagan in his shining city image. Ryn argues that those who blur the lines between religion and politics have inadequate conceptions of the divine. In Ryn's view, politicizing religion degrades that which is genuinely holy and diminishes the true contributions religion can and should make to political life. Babbitt draws attention to the ways in which confusing authentic religious sentiments with their political counterfeit makes the practice of politics even more uncompromising and violent than it would otherwise be. He suggests that the presence of a crusading spirit in politics often masks a dark, lurking ambition for domination in the people at large and in statesmen.

It is clear that these arguments from Voegelin, Ryn, and Babbitt do not apply to Reagan unqualifiedly. What has become clear about Reagan's religious imagination in this study is that its predominant mode of expression consists of images and ideas that are antithetical to genuine religion and, specifically, to Christianity, as defined by scholars such as Ryn, Babbitt, and Voegelin, and by Christian theologians and political theorists such as St. Augustine and Thomas Aquinas. The more expansive elements in Reagan's religious vision also appear to create profound problems insofar as they make the limits of politics more difficult to know and respect. Blending God and Caesar to the extent that Reagan often did serves neither God nor Caesar well. Politics and religion both suffer because the relationship between them is unbalanced and poorly conceived.

In numerous presidential speeches, Reagan expressed his vision of the role of the United States in the world. Reagan's view of American foreign policy and the conditions for peace among nations was not all of one part. Sometimes he articulated a rather modest vision of foreign policy and peace based on a sober understanding of human nature and a realistic sense of the possibilities of politics. Far more often, Reagan's way of thinking about the role of the United States in the world was sentimental and even simplistic. This side of his imagination saw human beings as naturally good and more or less "American." In this side of his mind, he heard the world crying out to America to provide democracy and liberty. He believed the United States was obligated by its sense of morality and by its history to contribute to the establishment of these and other political institutions around the world, thereby helping humanity realize its dreams. Reagan held that the degree to which liberty and democracy took root around the world was the degree to which true, lasting peace among nations could be realized.

The chimeric side of Reagan's foreign policy vision has much in common with the political theories of Thomas Jefferson, Thomas Paine, and Woodrow Wilson. A number of scholars, including Dinesh D'Souza, Paul Kengor, and Robert Kagan, agree with Reagan when he claims that the expansive elements in his foreign policy imagination are in tune with the dominant aspects of the American foreign policy tradition. It has been shown, however, that the most prominent parts of Reagan's view of America's role in the world are mostly at odds with the foreign policy ideas that prevailed in the early American republic. John Quincy Adams represents a widespread older view when he argues the United States would be forced to embrace empire if it embarked upon a mission of promoting democracy and liberty abroad. According to him, America would lose its republican soul in the process. Orestes Brownson's descriptions of written and unwritten constitutions are vital to understanding the theoretical inadequacies of key elements of Reagan's desire to promote freedom and democracy throughout the world. When the scholarship of Walter McDougall and Richard Gamble is taken into account, it becomes clear that many of Reagan's most deeply cherished foreign policy ideas originate in the late nineteenth and early twentieth centuries, rather than in the early decades of the American republic. Reagan's ideas are more correctly associated with the American progressive movement than with the Founding era.

Reagan imagined that America's role in the world would ultimately create the conditions for a lasting peace among nations. The scholarship of Claes Ryn, Eric Voegelin, and Irving Babbitt has shown that views about peace like Reagan's convey serious misunderstandings of politics and human nature. Voegelin draws important attention in several places to the differences between a good society and democratic society. He also identifies the dangerous consequences for politics when the two terms are viewed as inherently synonymous. Ryn argues that simply establishing more democracy, developing more technology, or proclaiming more freedom cannot create peace among nations. True peace, Ryn maintains, is possible only when ahistorical and romantic visions of peace are abandoned and the actual limits of politics, as well as the ignoble aspects of human nature, are fully understood and taken into account in the practice of international affairs. Babbitt provides convincing arguments that a vision of peace among nations similar to the one expressed by Reagan is often but a pretense for the will to power. Despite his affable personality, Reagan was inclined to talk about American political ideas, the Declaration of Independence, and the U.S. Constitution as the guarantors of peace and as having universal authority, which exemplifies the sentimental imperialism of

Reagan's chimeric imagination. It has been shown that Reagan occasionally conceded this point in public speeches.

That this part of Reagan's imagination is particularly popular in the United States is well known. Subsequent presidents from both political parties have adopted many of the most salient themes in this part of his vision. Ryn argues that ideas similar to those expressed by Reagan have had a profound influence upon what he calls neo-Jacobin political thinking in the United States.[27] The appeal of ideas like Reagan's is understandable. A world in which peace could be achieved on the terms Reagan suggests would be a place in which most Americans would like to live. Nevertheless, Reagan's more prominent ideas about foreign policy and peace have been shown to suffer from serious weaknesses. Further, these ideas often have disappointing and even disastrous consequences when put into practice. Recent events in American foreign policy practice appear to confirm this conclusion. If Americans truly desire a more humble foreign policy, one in which they are not engaged in seemingly perpetual warfare around the world, then, among other things, they would need to abandon their admiration for ideas that draw strength from this part of Reagan's vision.

Reagan's intuitions of progress, peace, religion, and America's role in the world are intimately connected to his visions of human nature and politics. Reagan imagined the American people as industrious, entrepreneurial, free, optimistic, patriotic, pious, commonsensical, and morally good. Reagan's vision of the American people and human nature has much in common with the ideas of American figures such as Thomas Jefferson and with modern political theorists such as John Locke and Jean-Jacques Rousseau. The predominant side of Reagan's intuitive sense of the American people and human nature contrasts sharply with the ideas of other leading early Americans such as John Adams, with the ideas of Publius in *The Federalist*, and with other and kindred political thinkers such as Edmund Burke. In the context of Reagan's religious sensibilities, his notions of human nature are also deeply at odds with the mainstream of Christian political thought, as represented by St. Augustine and Thomas Aquinas.

Reagan's view of Americans and of human nature is ethically monistic rather than dualistic. He often downplays or ignores the roles selfishness, deceit, and cruelty play in the choices human beings make every day. Hence, he locates the source of political and social disorder not in man but in an abstraction he calls "government." Reagan believed that the national government had grown well beyond the boundaries of the U.S. Constitution. He felt that the federal bureaucracy had inserted itself into too many aspects of American life. The results of these disconcerting developments in American politics were high taxes, high inflation, high unemployment, and low national morale. Reagan dedicated his presidency to reversing all these trends. As president he sought to reinvigorate the American people with confidence and to unleash them from the shackles of government that were holding them back, thwarting their best intentions, and making America miserable.

In Reagan's imagination there is a dichotomy between good human beings and incompetent or evil government. This view of the relationship between Americans and government resonates with similar ideas held by Jefferson and Paine. These historical figures celebrated democracy in the abstract, but they deeply distrusted actual governments, seeing them more often as threats to individual liberty than as protectors of freedom. In thinking about the relationship between politics and people in this manner, Reagan also reflects central elements of the political philosophy of Rousseau. Reagan's chimeric view of the relationship between people and government was not widely embraced by the American Framers. Drawing upon the broader tradition of Western political thought, the Framers generally considered government as an institution dedicated both to providing a secure environment in which citizens could use their freedom responsibly and to restraining individuals when they abused their liberty. In the minds of the Framers, a failure to recognize this perhaps unpopular but necessary role for government would be a sign of naiveté. Such dreaminess ultimately spells disaster in practical politics.

Not only did Reagan's chimeric imagination downplay the vital responsibility of government to protect citizens from their own worst inclinations, but it also dodged an issue that was deeply important to the Framers, Burke, Babbitt, and countless others in the Western tradition—the qualifications for leadership. In his Farewell Address and elsewhere, Reagan described himself as a citizen politician—i.e., as one of the countless Americans who simply felt the way he did. Presumably any American holding such views would have been as qualified to lead the United States as was Reagan. As president, Reagan often conveyed the sense that anyone could do what he was doing if they applied common sense and represented the American people rather than government. His tendency to romanticize the wisdom and virtue of the people had much in common with the political ideas of Rousseau. Like Rousseau, Reagan rarely asked questions about qualifications for political leaders. Burke, Babbitt, and many of the Framers, on the other hand, would have seen Reagan's frequent celebration of the divine average in America as an irresponsible and dangerous form of demagogic pandering. In his efforts to improve the morale of Americans, Reagan seems to have done them a long-term disservice by failing to provide them with a more comprehensive and accurate picture of the human condition and the nature of politics.

To some extent, Reagan's intuitions about human nature and the limits of politics were informed by his vision of the American past. He was deeply fond of the era of the American Revolution and the Founding fathers. In Reagan's mind, the Founding initiated a profound break with the human past. In documents such as the Declaration of Independence and the U.S. Constitution, Americans proclaimed new, revolutionary political ideas about equality, democracy, and liberty. The ideas and events of the Revolution also forged the American people and the American spirit and had global implications. Reagan's interest in the Revolution was not nostalgic. In his imagination, the Founding symbolized a living American past, capturing the essence of America's identity and political ideas. As president he referred to figures and events from this historical period to explain his own vision of America and its people and to articulate his ideas about domestic and foreign policy.

Reagan's vision of the Founding has much in common with the ideas of American historical figures such as Paine, Jefferson, and Lincoln. His intuitive grasp of the American past is also similar in important respects to the ideas of scholars such as Harry Jaffa and Allan Bloom. In his presidential speeches, Reagan celebrated radical conceptualizations of the meaning of the American Revolution put forth during the Founding era. He downplayed the mainstream, modest, historically rooted political expectations of the Framers and portrayed them instead as revolutionary apostles of universal democracy and freedom. He generally ignored the high degree of historical continuity between the political, religious, and social ideas of the Founding and the colonial period. Many components of his view of this era are both ahistorical and highly romantic.

Reagan's views about the American Revolution are very different from those expressed by historical American figures such as John Adams and scholars of the Founding era such as George Carey and Russell Kirk. Adams was a leader in the cause of American independence, and he certainly hoped for the success of the American Revolution. At the same time, he did not see these events as a profound break from the American or Western past. He observed a great deal of continuity between America's colonial and republican periods, and he saw a number of important similarities between America and England in the areas of political thought and practice. His understanding of politics and human nature also made him more aware than Paine and Jefferson of the fragility of the American experiment with republican government. From the point of view of Adams, the ideas of Paine and Jefferson about the events and meaning of the Founding were sentimental and expressed an unseemly degree of pride.

Scholars such as Carey and Kirk have further clarified what Adams and other figures from the Founding period actually believed. They have drawn attention to the modest goals of the American Revolution, which were to declare and establish a union of American States independent from England. As these scholars point out, the Revolution sought to reclaim what the Fundamental Orders of Connecticut described as decent and orderly government. With these objectives in mind, Kirk and Carey argue that most Americans did not invest their separation from Great Britain with the universal political pretensions of the French Revolution. In their views, the Americans did not see themselves as proclaiming an abstract blueprint for government; they did not see themselves as announcing to the world the only legitimate foundation for politics. In Kirk's mind, the American Revolution was primarily a conservative enterprise insofar as it pursued prudent political change consistent with America's historical traditions and experiences. He stressed the compatibility of American mores, history, and politics during the Founding era. If Reagan is conserving anything from the Founding period, it is its more questionable and less representative elements.

This study has also shed light upon two of the most important images in Reagan's mind—liberty and democracy. Reagan imagined liberty in terms that were expansive, ahistorical, and sentimental. His view of human beings as good by nature enabled him to avoid giving serious consideration to the moral challenges of freedom and the ethical prerequisites for individual liberty. Thus, whether liberty was proclaimed in America or around the world, Reagan believed that it was an unqualified good for human beings. His understanding of liberty is similar to those of Rousseau, Locke, and Jefferson. John Adams, Publius, and Burke all had markedly different understandings of freedom. From their points of view, an intuition of liberty like Reagan's, one that fails to take into account the ethical duality of human beings, would be grievously deficient and dangerous for practical politics.

Burke, Publius, and Adams would have drawn the same conclusions about Reagan's notion of democracy. Reagan considered democracy to be an unqualified good for all human beings. In his view, regardless of differences in religion, culture, history, or social traditions, the people of the world are entitled to live in a democracy, consisting of a host of specific political, economic, and social institutions, in which all citizens are equal and free. As with his vision of liberty, Reagan did not consider for any substantial length of time the moral challenges and ethical preconditions for practicing responsible democratic government. For him, democracy would function well so long as it was arranged correctly, preferably in a written constitution similar to the U.S. Constitution. In holding such views, he reflects once again ideas about democracy expressed by figures such as Paine, Jefferson, Rousseau, and Locke.

Reagan's sanguine view of democracy stands in particularly stark contrast to the one held by Plato, but is also quite different from the notions expressed by such thinkers as Babbitt and Ryn. Plato contemptuously describes democracy as the worst form of government except for tyranny. In his mind, democracy has little or no moral and political order; its citizens have little or no restraint. Whatever the inadequacies of Plato's understanding of democracy, he provides timeless insight into the ways in which democracy of a certain kind can degenerate into disorder and tyranny. His political anthropology—i.e., his sense that the order of the state and the soul reflect and reinforce one another—reveals important truths about politics and democracy that are generally overlooked by Reagan.

Babbitt and Ryn stress the ethical preconditions for responsible democratic government. They defend what they call constitutional democracy. For both thinkers, this form of democracy provides an environment in which individuals and communities can pursue the moral life and experience meaningful freedom. In order for this possibility to be realized, first, citizens must exhibit a great degree of moral responsibility and restraint. Second, in a constitutional democracy, government must place strong restraints upon the spontaneous desires and actions of the people. In their views, only a constitutionally evolved majority that has withstood thoughtful scrutiny can be described as the will of the people. Only the will of a constitutional majority deserves to be translated into law.

Ryn and Babbitt both examine another form of democracy that is often associated with the political philosophy of Rousseau and can be called plebiscitary or direct democracy. This type of popular government promises the maximum in freedom and adherence to the unfiltered will of the people. Whereas constitutional democracy at its best is compatible with the aims of the ethical life because it takes the weakness of human nature into account, direct democracy ignores those weaknesses. Overall, Reagan expresses a vision of democracy much closer to the spirit of plebiscitary democracy than that of constitutional democracy. His sense of the sources of democratic political order is simplistic and utopian. His chimeric sensibilities militate against the very political order he seeks to support.

Here another conclusion about the overarching quality of Reagan's imagination can be drawn. Reagan is often considered to be the perfect embodiment of conservatism in America. The word "conservative" is rather difficult to define and has become increasingly confusing in the United States over the last few decades. Nevertheless, if one uses a loose, very general standard of measurement, this claim is at least plausible. In the United States, the word "conservative" is often used as a synonym for a member of the Republican Party. The word is often used to describe a person who claims to revere the American past, especially the Founding era, and is committed to specific axioms and abstract understandings of ideas and issues such as liberty, democracy, limited government, free markets, a hawkish U.S. foreign policy, low taxes, anticommunism, and moral values. Reagan was a member of the Republican Party for most of his adult life, and he apparently had much in common with other so-called conservatives on a number of political issues and ideas. Writers such as Dinesh D'Souza, Alfred Regnery, and Russell Kirk have described Reagan as a conservative.

But the specific, concrete meanings of words like the ones just listed are what decide the ideological affinities of a person, and Reagan's meaning has been carefully examined. The result is that the designation of Reagan as a conservative is difficult to maintain. He hardly fits under any historically and philosophically informed definition of conservatism. Here it is worthwhile to reiterate some words previously quoted from Peter Viereck that attempt to summarize the elements of a genuine conservatism:

> The conservative principles *par excellence* are proportion and measure; self-expression through self-restraint; preservation through reform; humanism and classical balance; a fruitful nostalgia for the permanent beneath the flux; and a fruitful obsession for unbroken historic continuity. These principles together create freedom, a freedom built

not on the quicksand of adolescent defiance but on the bedrock of ethics and law.[28]

Viereck is here summarizing a long Western tradition, the conservation and development of which has been the distinctive mark of modern conservatism, starting with Burke.

This type of conservatism is present in varying degrees in the writings and ideas from figures such as Adams, Burke, Publius, Brownson, Plato, Aquinas, and St. Augustine and from scholars such as Babbitt, Ryn, Carey, Voegelin, Kirk, Gamble, and McDougall. On almost every subject covered in this work, these are figures and scholars with whom Reagan ultimately has little in common, although they may happen to agree with him on particular practical issues. It is true that Reagan often refers to the American and broader Western past, but especially when searching for past resonances for his vision of democracy, liberty, and human nature, Reagan gravitates toward the least conservative figures from the Founding era, particularly Paine and Jefferson. His understanding of this era is very similar to those expressed by two scholars who cannot reasonably be associated with conservatism as just defined—Jaffa and Bloom. Reagan shares much with some of the least conservative thinkers in the modern era, such as Locke and Rousseau. If figures and scholars like Adams, Burke, Ryn, Kirk, and Babbitt are generally representative of conservatism, then, whatever else he might be, Reagan is not a conservative.

At this point, some readers might be wondering if an important issue has not been overlooked. Especially those who consider themselves Reagan's admirers might admit that his imagination had certain flaws, but that they were not very serious. That Reagan quoted frequently from Paine and Jefferson, that he expressed ideas more in tune with Rousseau than Burke, might not be an issue of great concern. Were those references not largely window dressing? Could these flaws not be overlooked or excused insofar as they *worked*, that is, were the basis for Reagan's presidential accomplishments? Did they not reinvigorate Americans with optimism and confidence at a time when both were desperately needed and in low supply? It is certainly true that Reagan's intuitive leaning shaped his foreign and domestic policy practices and achievements. Reagan often told Americans that he was appealing to their hopes, rather than their fears, and it cannot be disputed that his vision increased American morale and raised the national mood during the 1980s.

Yet the short-term practical successes of Reagan's presidency and the short-term effects of his vision upon the confidence and optimism of the American people do not obviate the important theoretical and imaginative dangers of his vision. Politics may be able to a considerable extent to sacrifice the true to the expedient, but philosophy seeks only that which is true, whether or not it is convenient. This work has described Reagan's imagination as predominantly chimeric. As defined in the introduction to this study, a chimeric imagination contains a mixture of hope, optimism, naiveté, and illusion. This study has identified and analyzed the manifold illusory elements of Reagan's imagination. The characteristics of a chimeric imagination have been shown to be strongly present in all the major aspects of Reagan's view of the world. It is true that Reagan expressed his vivid and powerful intuitions about human life and the possibilities of politics with confidence and that it helped marshal support for his policies. Countless Americans have taken to heart his message, and they have grown to love deeply the "American spirit" that Reagan seemed to embody. These facts do not make his vision any more grounded in reality or make it any less dangerous. To repeat an earlier point, the imagination always gives a unity of sorts, but it does not always give reality. After having taken the full measure of Reagan's chimeric imagination, there is little choice but to conclude that his vision is too far removed from a tenable understanding of human nature and politics to be accepted as a guide to and inspiration for practical action. In the end, despite its enduring power and popularity, Americans would do better relinquishing this kind of vision.

The purpose of this study has not been to provide an alternative to Reagan's imaginative vision, although the ideas and broader theoretical visions from figures and scholars such as Adams, Burke, Publius, St. Augustine, Voegelin, Ryn, and Babbitt suggest what such a vision might include. This work has sought to illuminate the nature and components of Reagan's chimeric imagination and has revealed its dubious and even dangerous character. It seems clear that there is a palpable need for a reorientation of the American imagination. This is a task for what Burke, Babbitt, and others have described as the moral imagination, an imagination that is rooted in a down-to-earth assessment of what life is really like. Realigning the intuitive sensibilities of Americans with the moral imagination could be neither quick, nor easy. Parting with a cherished imaginative vision, no matter how deeply flawed, is always difficult. This study is but a step in the large project of weaning Americans off an addiction to chimeric imagination and reintroducing them to the best elements in the American and Western political traditions. Equipped with a much improved understanding of the actual content of the chimeric imagination, Americans will be better able to resist its appeal as they search for imaginative vision consistent with the human condition as well as the particular circumstances of the present.

Notes

NOTES TO THE INTRODUCTION

1. Lou Cannon, "Why Reagan Was the 'Great Communicator,'" *USA Today*, 7 June 2004, p. 21A, http://www.lexisnexis.com.proxycu.wrlc.org/us/lnacademic/results/docview/docview.do?docLinkInd = true&risb = 21_T8981255756&format = GNBFI&sort = RELEVANCE&startDocNo = 1&resultsUrlKey = 29_T898125 5759&cisb = 22_T8981255758&treeMax = true&treeWidth = 0&csi = 8213& docNo = 15 (accessed 12 May 2007).
2. "National Cathedral Funeral Service," on *Ronald Reagan: An American President: The Official Reagan Library Tribute*, DVD (Beverly Hills, CA: Twentieth Century Fox Home Entertainment, 2004).
3. Brian Mulroney, "Eulogy at National Cathedral Funeral Service for Ronald Reagan, 11 June 2004," *CTV News*, http://www.ctv.ca/servlet/ArticleNews/story/CTVNews/1086969805692_82379005 (accessed 2 April 2007).
4. Margaret Thatcher, "Eulogy at National Cathedral Funeral Service for Ronald Reagan, 11 June 2004," *BBC News*, http://news.bbc.co.uk/go/pr/fr/-/1/hi/world/americas/3797947.stm (accessed 3 April 2007).
5. Ibid.
6. George W. Bush, "Eulogy at the National Funeral Service for President Ronald Reagan, June 11, 2004," in *Public Papers of the Presidents of the United States: George W. Bush, 2004 (in Three Books), Book I—January 1 to June 30, 2004* (Washington, DC: U.S. Government Printing Office, 2007), 1031.
7. Ibid., 1033.
8. "Comments on Ronald Reagan's Death, Legacy," *Los Angeles Times*, 9 June 2004, http://www.latimes.com/news/nationworld/politics/scotus/wire/sns-ap-reagan-quotes,1,2955312.story?coll = sns-ap-scotus-headlines (accessed 1 April 2007).
9. Ibid.
10. Rene Sanchez, "A Nation and the World Pay Tribute to Reagan; Body to Lie in State at Capitol; State Funeral Set for Friday," *Washington Post*, 7 June 2004, A01, http://www.lexisnexis.com.proxycu.wrlc.org/us/lnacademic/results/docview/docview.do?docLinkInd = true&risb = 21_T8981268017&format = GNBFI&sort = RELEVANCE&startDocNo = 1&resultsUrlKey = 29_T8981268020&cisb = 22_T8981268019&treeMax = true&treeWidth = 0&csi = 8075&docNo = 5 (accessed 14 August 2011).
11. Ronald Reagan, "Inaugural Address, January 20, 1981," in *Public Papers of the Presidents of the United States: Ronald Reagan: 1981, January 20 to December 31, 1981* (Washington, DC: U.S. Government Printing Office, 1982), 1.
12. Ibid., 2.

13. Ibid., 3.
14. Ibid., 4.
15. Ronald Reagan, "Farewell Address to the Nation, January 11, 1989," in *Public Papers of the Presidents of the United States: Ronald Reagan: 1988–89 (in Two Books), Book II—July 2, 1988 to January 19, 1989* (Washington, DC: U.S. Government Printing Office, 1991), 1720.
16. Lou Cannon, "Actor, Governor, President, Icon," *Washington Post*, 6 June 2004, A28, http://www.lexisnexis.com.proxycu.wrlc.org/us/lnacademic/results/docview/docview.do?docLinkInd = true&risb = 21_T8981271390&format = GNBFI&sort = RELEVANCE&startDocNo = 1&resultsUrlKey = 29_T8981271396&cisb = 22_T8981271395&treeMax = true&treeWidth = 0&selRCNodeID = 12&nodeStateId = 411en_US,1,9&docsInCategory = 9&csi = 8075&docNo = 5 (accessed 3 April 2007).
17. Ronald Reagan, *Speaking My Mind: Selected Speeches* (New York: Simon and Schuster, 1989), 14.
18. Representative examples of the diversity of books on Reagan written by journalists, scholars, and former Reagan administration members include Lou Cannon, *President Reagan: The Role of a Lifetime* (New York: PublicAffairs, 2000) and *Governor Reagan: His Rise to Power* (New York: PublicAffairs, 2003); Paul D. Erickson, *Reagan Speaks: The Making of an American Myth* (New York: New York UP, 1985); Robert Dallek, *Ronald Reagan: The Politics of Symbolism* (Cambridge, MA: Harvard UP, 1999); Paul Kengor, *God and Ronald Reagan: A Spiritual Life* (New York: HarperCollins, 2004); Edmund Morris, *Dutch: A Memoir of Ronald Reagan* (New York: Random House, 1999); David M. Abshire, *Saving the Reagan Presidency: Trust Is the Coin of the Realm* (College Station: Texas A&M UP, 2005); Peggy Noonan, *When Character Was King: A Story of Ronald Reagan* (New York: Viking, 2001); Garry Wills, *Reagan's America: Innocents at Home* (New York: Doubleday, 1987; Reprint, New York: Penguin Putnam, 2000); Michael Weiler and W. Barnett Pearce, eds., *Reagan and Public Discourse in America* (Tuscaloosa: U of Alabama P, 1992).
19. See Robert C. Rowland and John M. Jones, *Reagan at Westminster: Foreshadowing the End of the Cold War* (College Station: Texas A&M UP, 2010); Thomas W. Evans, *The Education of Ronald Reagan: The General Electric Years and the Untold Story of His Conversion to Conservatism* (New York: Columbia UP, 2006); Joseph A. McCartin, *Collision Course: Ronald Reagan, the Air Traffic Controllers, and the Strike That Changed America* (New York: Oxford UP, 2011); Frances FitzGerald, *Way Out There in the Blue: Ronald Reagan, Star Wars, and the End of the Cold War* (New York: Simon and Schuster, 2000); Douglas Brinkley, *The Boys of Pointe du Hoc: Ronald Reagan, D-Day, and the U.S. Army 2nd Ranger Battalion* (New York: William Morrow, 2005); Paul Kengor, *The Crusader: Ronald Reagan and the Fall of Communism* (New York: HarperCollins, 2006).
20. See Gil Troy, *Morning in America: How Ronald Reagan Invented the 1980s* (Princeton, NJ: Princeton UP, 2005); Toby Glenn Bates, *The Reagan Rhetoric: History and Memory in the 1980s* (DeKalb: Northern Illinois UP, 2011); Michael Schaller, *Reckoning with Reagan: America and Its President in the 1980s* (New York, Oxford UP, 1992); Wills, *Reagan's America*.
21. See Dinesh D'Souza, *Ronald Reagan: How an Ordinary Man Became an Extraordinary Leader* (New York: Touchstone, 1999); John Patrick Diggins, *Ronald Reagan: Fate, Freedom, and the Making of History* (New York: W. W. Norton, 2007); Ted V. McAllister, "Reagan and the Transformation of American Conservatism," in *The Reagan Presidency: Pragmatic Conservatism and Its Legacies*, eds. W. Elliot Brownlee and Hugh David Graham (Lawrence:

UP of Kansas, 2003); Lee Edwards, *The Essential Ronald Reagan: A Profile in Courage, Justice, and Wisdom* (Lanham, MD: Rowman & Littlefield, 2005); Hugh Heclo, "Ronald Reagan and the American Public Philosophy," in Brownlee and Graham, *Reagan Presidency*; Paul Kengor, *The Crusader* and *God and Ronald Reagan*; Peter Schweizer, *Reagan's War: The Epic Story of His Forty-Year Struggle and Final Triumph over Communism* (New York: Anchor Books, 2003).

22. See Charles W. Dunn, ed., *The Enduring Reagan* (Lexington: UP of Kentucky, 2009); Brownlee and Graham, *Reagan Presidency*; Lou Cannon and Carl M. Cannon, *Reagan's Disciple: George W. Bush's Troubled Quest for a Presidential Legacy* (New York: PublicAffairs, 2008); Michael J. Gerson, *Heroic Conservatism: Why Republicans Need to Embrace America's Ideals (And Why They Deserve to Fail If They Don't)* (New York: HarperCollins, 2007; Harper One, 2008); Sean Wilentz, *The Age of Reagan: A History: 1974–2008* (New York: HarperCollins, 2008); Will Bunch, *Tear Down This Myth: How the Reagan Legacy Has Distorted Our Politics and Haunts Our Future* (New York: Free Press, 2009); William Kleinknecht, *The Man Who Sold the World: Ronald Reagan and the Betrayal of Main Street America* (New York: Nation Books, 2009); Alfred Regnery, *Upstream: The Ascendance of American Conservatism* (New York: Threshold Editions, 2008).
23. Reagan, *Speaking My Mind*, 59.
24. Claes G. Ryn, "The Imaginative Origins of Modernity: Life as Daydream and Nightmare," *Humanitas* 10, no. 2 (1997): 42.
25. Ibid., 43.
26. "The First Presidential Debate" (Oxford, MS: 26 September 2008, http://elections.nytimes.com/2008/president/debates/transcripts/first-presidential-debate.html (accessed 3 December 2008); and Barack Obama, "The American Moment: Remarks to the Chicago Council on Global Affairs" (Chicago, IL: 23 April 2007), http://www.barackobama.com/2007/04/23/the_american_moment_remarks_to.php (accessed 3 December 2008).
27. Shailagh Murray, "Obama's Reagan Comparison Sparks Debate, January 17, 2008," *Washington Post*, http://blog.washingtonpost.com/44/2008/01/17/obamas_reagan_comparison_spark_1. html (accessed 14 May 2008).

NOTES TO CHAPTER 1

1. Peggy Noonan, *When Character Was King: A Story of Ronald Reagan* (New York: Viking, 2001), 245–46.
2. Ronald Reagan with Richard G. Hubler, *Where's the Rest of Me? The Autobiography of Ronald Reagan* (New York: Karz, 1981), 13–14.
3. Ibid., 13. On the relationship between Reagan's small-town upbringing and his professional and political ambitions, see Alonzo L. Hamby, *Liberalism and Its Challengers: From F.D.R. to Bush* (New York: Oxford UP, 1992), 341.
4. Lou Cannon, *Governor Reagan: His Rise to Power* (New York: PublicAffairs, 2003), 11.
5. Reagan, *Where's the Rest of Me?* 8. It is worth noting that *Birth of a Nation* was released just after Reagan turned four.
6. Ronald Reagan, *An American Life* (New York: Simon and Schuster, 1990), 30.
7. About the influence of Jack Reagan upon Ronald Reagan's early views on politics, Michael Schaller writes, "After the election of Franklin D. Roosevelt in 1933, the unemployed Jack Reagan found work with a New Deal work-relief program. In appreciation, [Reagan] became a fervent supporter of Roosevelt, memorizing many of the president's speeches and doing FDR impersonations

for friends. Although Roosevelt always remained in Reagan's pantheon, it was as an inspirational hero rather than as the architect of the New Deal and the modern welfare state." See Michael Schaller, *Reckoning with Reagan: America and Its President in the 1980s* (New York: Oxford UP, 1992), 6.

8. Reagan, *Where's the Rest of Me?* 7–8.
9. Paul Kengor, *God and Ronald Reagan: A Spiritual Life* (New York: HarperCollins, 2004), 10–16.
10. Reagan, *An American Life*, 20–21.
11. Kengor, *God and Ronald Reagan*, 11.
12. Garry Wills, *Reagan's America: Innocents at Home* (New York: Doubleday, 1987; Reprint, New York: Penguin Putnam, 2000), 27.
13. Kengor, *God and Ronald Reagan*, 11–12.
14. Ibid., 16.
15. Ibid.
16. Reagan, *An American Life*, 29, 32.
17. Harold Bell Wright, *That Printer of Udell's* (Washington, DC: Regnery, 1999), 13.
18. Ibid., 37.
19. Ibid., 59.
20. Kengor, *God and Ronald Reagan*, 25.
21. Wright, *That Printer of Udell's*, 462–63.
22. Ronald Reagan, "Letter to Mrs. Jean B. Wright, March 13, 1984," in *Reagan: A Life in Letters*, eds. Kiron K. Skinner, Annelise Anderson, and Martin Anderson (New York: Free Press, 2003), 6.
23. Wright, *That Printer of Udell's*, 461.
24. Ronald Reagan, "Address at Commencement Exercises at Eureka College in Illinois, May 9, 1982," in *Public Papers of the Presidents of the United States: Ronald Reagan: 1982 (in Two Books), Book I—January 1 to July 2, 1982* (Washington, DC: U.S. Government Printing Office, 1983), 581.
25. Kengor, *God and Ronald Reagan*, 41–42.
26. Reagan, *Where's the Rest of Me?* 26.
27. Cannon, *Governor Reagan*, 25.
28. For a more thorough treatment of the Eureka College strike, including Reagan's role in the event, see Wills, *Reagan's America*, especially chapters 4 and 5.
29. Reagan, *Where's the Rest of Me?* 26.
30. Ibid., 28–29.
31. Wills, *Reagan's America*, 59.
32. Reagan, *An American Life*, 72–73.
33. Wills, *Reagan's America*, 145.
34. Ibid., 144.
35. John Kenneth White, *The New Politics of Old Values*, 2nd ed. (Hanover, NH: UP of New England, 1990), 8–9.
36. Reagan, *Where's the Rest of Me?* 67.
37. Ibid., 139.
38. Reagan, *An American Life*, 105.
39. Reagan, *Where's the Rest of Me?* 139.
40. Ibid., 141.
41. Ibid.
42. Ibid., 142.
43. For a concise account of the development of Reagan's antipathy toward communism, see Robert C. Rowland and John M. Jones, *Reagan at Westminster: Foreshadowing the End of the Cold War* (College Station: Texas A&M UP, 2010), 25–33.
44. Ronald Reagan, *An American Life*, 115.

45. Reagan, *Where's the Rest of Me?* 145–46.
46. Reagan, *An American Life*, 107–9.
47. Reagan, *Where's the Rest of Me?* 155–57.
48. Ibid., 174.
49. Kengor, *God and Ronald Reagan*, 77.
50. Whittaker Chambers, *Witness* (Washington, DC: Regnery, 1952), 7.
51. Ibid., 164.
52. Ibid., 195.
53. Ibid., 80.
54. Ibid., 84.
55. Ibid., 16.
56. Ibid., 17.
57. Ibid., 9.
58. Ibid., 25.
59. Ibid., 10. Emphasis in original.
60. Ronald Reagan, "The President's News Conference, January 29, 1981," in *Public Papers of the Presidents of the United States: Ronald Reagan: 1981, January 20 to December 31, 1981* (Washington, DC: U.S. Government Printing Office, 1982), 57.
61. Ronald Reagan, "Remarks at the Conservative Political Action Conference Dinner, March 20, 1981," in *Public Papers: 1981*, 278.
62. Quoted from Reagan, *Where's the Rest of Me?* 268. Emphasis in original. For original quotation, see Chambers, *Witness*, 741.
63. Thomas W. Evans argues that Reagan's tenure at General Electric played a central role in the development of his political thinking. He claims GE executive Lemuel Boulware served as an ideological mentor to Reagan, educating him on topics such as economics, tax policy, and foreign policy. See Thomas W. Evans, *The Education of Ronald Reagan: The General Electric Years and the Untold Story of His Conversion to Conservatism* (New York: Columbia UP, 2006).
64. Reagan, *Where's the Rest of Me?* 261.
65. About Reagan's long-standing antipathy toward national tax policies, Gil Troy writes, "Since the 1950s, Ronald Reagan had been preaching against high taxes squelching Americans' desire to work." See Gil Troy, *Morning in America: How Ronald Reagan Invented the 1980s* (Princeton, NJ: Princeton UP, 2005), 39.
66. Reagan, *An American Life*, 135.
67. Dinesh D'Souza, *Ronald Reagan: How an Ordinary Man Became an Extraordinary Leader* (New York: Touchstone, 1999), 52.
68. Noonan, *When Character Was King*, 66.
69. Cannon, *Governor Reagan*, 83.
70. Ronald Reagan, " 'America the Beautiful,' June, 1952," in *Actor, Ideologue, Politician: The Public Speeches of Ronald Reagan*, ed. Davis W. Houck and Amos Kiewe (Westport, CT: Greenwood, 1993), 5.
71. Ibid., 6.
72. Ronald Reagan, "Commencement Address at Eureka College, June 7, 1957," PBS, http://www.pbs.org/wgbh/amex/presidents/40_reagan/psources/ps_eureka.html (accessed 4 March 2010).
73. Ibid.
74. Ibid.
75. Ibid.
76. Kengor, *God and Ronald Reagan*, 89.
77. Ibid., 95.
78. Quoted from Peter Schweizer, *Reagan's War: The Epic Story of His Forty-Year Struggle and Final Triumph over Communism* (New York: Anchor Books, 2003), 44.

79. Reagan, *An American Life*, 143.
80. Ronald Reagan, "Televised Nationwide Address on Behalf of Senator Barry Goldwater, October 27, 1964," in *Speaking My Mind: Selected Speeches* (New York: Simon and Schuster, 1989), 26, 33.
81. Ibid., 26.
82. Ibid., 36.

NOTES TO CHAPTER 2

1. Henry David Thoreau, *A Week on the Concord and Merrimack Rivers* (New York: Quality Paperback Book Club, 1997), 365.
2. M. H. Abrams, *The Mirror and the Lamp: Romantic Theory and the Critical Tradition* (New York: Oxford UP, 1953), 161.
3. Ibid., 37–39.
4. Ibid., 48–53.
5. Ibid., 57.
6. Ibid., 167–77.
7. Benedetto Croce, *Æsthetic as Science of Expression and General Linguistic*, trans. Douglas Ainslie (New Brunswick, NJ: Transaction, 1995), 13.
8. Ibid., 4.
9. Ibid., 22.
10. Claes G. Ryn, *Will, Imagination, and Reason: Irving Babbitt and the Problem of Reality* (Washington, DC: Regnery Books, 1986), 186.
11. Croce, *Æsthetic*, 51–52.
12. For a better sense of this unrealized possibility in Croce's later philosophy, see *Guide to Aesthetics*, trans. Patrick Romanell, 2nd rev. ed. (Indianapolis, IN: Hackett, 1995), especially page 64.
13. Ryn, *Will, Imagination, and Reason*, 148.
14. Ibid., 147.
15. Irving Babbitt, *Democracy and Leadership* (Indianapolis, IN: Liberty Fund, 1979), 36.
16. For a more complete account of this type of historical rationality, see Ryn, *Will, Imagination, and Reason*, especially chapter 4.
17. For a thorough treatment of the relationship between imagination and reason, including the ways in which reason can be misled by dubious types of intuitive vision, see Ryn, *Will, Imagination, and Reason*, especially chapters 9 and 10.
18. Babbitt, *Democracy and Leadership*, 258.
19. Ibid., 37.
20. Ibid., 47.

NOTES TO CHAPTER 3

1. George F. Will, "How Reagan Changed America," *Newsweek*, 9 January 1989, 13, http://www.lexisnexis.com.proxycu.wrlc.org/us/lnacademic/results/docview/docview.do?docLinkInd=true&risb=21_T9106281404&format=GNBFI&sort = BOOLEAN&startDocNo = 1&resultsUrlKey = 29_T9106281407&cisb = 22_T9106281406&treeMax = true&treeWidth = 0&csi = 5774&docNo = 2 (accessed 23 February 2007).
2. Ronald Reagan, "Remarks at the Republican National Convention in New Orleans, Louisiana, August 15, 1988," in *Public Papers of the Presidents of the United States: Ronald Reagan: 1988–89 (in Two Books), Book II—July 2,*

1988 to January 19, 1989 (Washington, DC: U.S. Government Printing Office, 1991), 1085.

3. Toby Glenn Bates, *The Reagan Rhetoric: History and Memory in 1980s America* (DeKalb: Northern Illinois UP, 2011), 15.

4. Ronald Reagan, "Remarks to the Reagan Administration Executive Forum, January 20, 1982," in *Public Papers of the Presidents of the United States: Ronald Reagan: 1982 (in Two Books), Book I—January 1 to July 2, 1982* (Washington, DC: U.S. Government Printing Office, 1983), 47.

5. Ibid.

6. Ibid., 48.

7. Ibid.

8. Ibid.

9. Ibid.

10. Lou Cannon, *Governor Reagan: His Rise to Power* (New York: PublicAffairs, 2003), 13.

11. Ronald Reagan, *An American Life* (New York: Simon and Schuster, 1990), 28.

12. Ibid., 205.

13. Ibid., 205–6. In *FDR and Reagan*, John Sloan writes the following about Carter's inadvertent contribution to Reagan's ascendency to the presidency: "If Carter had been planted as a mole in his own administration by conservative Republicans to deliberately wreck his presidency and prepare the way for Reagan's political successes, he could hardly have been more effectively in accomplishing that feat." See John W. Sloan, *FDR and Reagan: Transformative Presidents with Clashing Visions* (Lawrence: UP of Kansas, 2008), 44.

14. Reagan, *An American Life*, 219.

15. Ronald Reagan, "Remarks at Kansas State University at the Alfred M. Landon Lecture Series on Public Issues, September 9, 1982," in *Public Papers of the Presidents of the United States: Ronald Reagan: 1982 (in Two Books), Book II—July 3 to December 31, 1982* (Washington, DC: U.S. Government Printing Office, 1983), 1119.

16. Ibid., 1119–20.

17. Ronald Reagan, "Remarks at the Conservative Political Action Conference Dinner, March 20, 1981," in *Public Papers of the Presidents of the United States: Ronald Reagan: 1981, January 20 to December 31, 1981* (Washington, DC: U.S. Government Printing Office, 1982), 278.

18. Ronald Reagan, "Address before a Joint Session of the Congress on the Program for Economic Recovery, April 28, 1981," in *Public Papers: 1981*, 394.

19. Ibid.

20. Ronald Reagan, "Remarks at the Annual Convention of the National Association of Counties in Baltimore, Maryland, July 13, 1982," in *Public Papers: 1982, Book II*, 921.

21. Ronald Reagan, "Remarks at a Mount Vernon, Virginia, Ceremony Commemorating the 250th Anniversary of the Birth of George Washington, February 22, 1982," in *Public Papers: 1982, Book I*, 200.

22. Ronald Reagan, "Remarks at the Mathews-Dickey Boys' Club in St. Louis, Missouri, July 22, 1982," in *Public Papers: 1982, Book II*, 963.

23. Ronald Reagan, "Remarks at the Annual Meeting of the National Association of Towns and Townships, September 12, 1983," in *Public Papers of the Presidents of the United States: Ronald Reagan: 1983 (in Two Books), Book II—July 2 to December 31, 1983* (Washington, DC: U.S. Government Printing Office, 1985), 1254.

24. Ronald Reagan, "Address before a Joint Session of the Congress on the State of the Union, January 25, 1984," in *Public Papers of the Presidents of the United*

States: Ronald Reagan: 1984 (in Two Books), Book I—January 1 to June 29, 1984 (Washington, DC: U.S. Government Printing Office, 1986), 87.

25. Ronald Reagan, "Remarks Accepting the Presidential Nomination at the Republican National Convention in Dallas, Texas, August 23, 1984," *Public Papers of the Presidents of the United States: Ronald Reagan: 1984 (in Two Books), Book II—June 30 to December 31, 1984* (Washington, DC: U.S. Government Printing Office, 1987), 1176.

26. Gil Troy, *Morning in America: How Ronald Reagan Invented the 1980s* (Princeton, NJ: Princeton UP, 2005), 5.

27. Dinesh D'Souza, *Ronald Reagan: How an Ordinary Man Became an Extraordinary Leader* (New York: Touchstone, 1999), 74.

28. Garry Wills, *Reagan's America: Innocents at Home* (New York: Doubleday, 1987; Reprint, New York: Penguin Putnam, 2000), ix.

29. As evidence of this claim, Cannon provides the following representative example: " '[Reagan] really isn't like a Republican,' said Vincent Rakowitz, a retired brewery worker in San Antonio. 'He's more like an American, which is what we really need.' " Lou Cannon, *President Reagan: The Role of a Lifetime* (New York: PublicAffairs, 2000), 435.

30. Will, "How Reagan Changed America," 13.

31. Paul D. Erickson, *Reagan Speaks: The Making of an American Myth* (New York: New York UP, 1985), 61.

32. Cannon, *President Reagan*, 190.

33. Ibid., 189–90.

34. Lou Cannon, *Governor Reagan*, 74.

35. Gil Troy provides a succinct summary of the major elements of the Iran-Contra affair when he writes, "First, despite talking tough, Reagan had engaged in negotiations to free Americans held hostage by terrorists in Lebanon and authorized arms transfers to Iran to ransom the captives, violating an arms embargo against Iran. Word of the ransom in November 1986 undermined Reagan's credibility. Legal questions arose when the White House admitted that profits from the Iranian arms shipments funded the Nicaraguan 'Contras.' Congress had outlawed any funding for the Nicaraguan insurgents." See Troy, *Morning in America*, 238–39.

36. Ronald Reagan, "Address to the Nation on the Iran Arms and *Contra* Aid Controversy, March 4, 1987," in *Public Papers of the Presidents of the United States: Ronald Reagan: 1987 (in Two Books), Book I—January 1 to July 3, 1987* (Washington, DC: U.S. Government Printing Office, 1989), 209. Emphasis added.

37. Cannon, *President Reagan*, 190.

NOTES TO CHAPTER 4

1. Walt Whitman, "I Hear America Singing," in *Leaves of Grass and Other Writings*, ed. Michael Moon (New York: W. W. Norton, 2002), 12.

2. Ronald Reagan, "Empire of Ideals, August 17, 1992," in *The Greatest Speeches of Ronald Reagan* (West Palm Beach, FL: Newsmax.com, 2001), 276.

3. Ronald Reagan, "Televised Nationwide Address on Behalf of Senator Barry Goldwater, October 27, 1964," in *Speaking My Mind: Selected Speeches* (New York: Simon and Schuster, 1989), 26.

4. Ronald Reagan, "Inaugural Address, January 20, 1981," in *Public Papers of the Presidents of the United States: Ronald Reagan: 1981, January 20 to December 31, 1981* (Washington, DC: U.S. Government Printing Office, 1982), 1–2.

5. Ronald Reagan, "Address at Commencement Exercises at the University of Notre Dame, May 17, 1981," in *Public Papers: 1981*, 433.

6. Ronald Reagan, "Remarks to Students and Faculty at Thomas Jefferson High School of Science and Technology in Fairfax County, Virginia, February 7, 1986," in *Public Papers of the Presidents of the United States: Ronald Reagan: 1986 (in Two Books), Book I—January 1 to June 27, 1986* (Washington, DC: U.S. Government Printing Office, 1988), 177. Emphasis in original.
7. Ronald Reagan, "Remarks at a White House Briefing on the State of Small Business, March 1, 1982," in *Public Papers of the Presidents of the United States: Ronald Reagan: 1982 (in Two Books), Book I—January 1 to July 2, 1982* (Washington, DC: U.S. Government Printing Office, 1983), 235.
8. Ronald Reagan, "Remarks at a Spirit of America Rally in Atlanta, Georgia, January 26, 1984," in *Public Papers of the Presidents of the United States: Ronald Reagan: 1984 (in Two Books), Book I—January 1 to June 29, 1984* (Washington, DC: U.S. Government Printing Office, 1986), 98.
9. Ronald Reagan, "Remarks at the Opening Ceremonies of the Statue of Liberty Centennial Celebration in New York, New York, July 3, 1986," in *Public Papers of the Presidents of the United States: Ronald Reagan: 1986 (in Two Books), Book II—June 28 to December 31, 1986* (Washington, DC: U.S. Government Printing Office, 1989), 919.
10. Reagan, "Inaugural Address, January 20, 1981," 2, 3.
11. Ronald Reagan, "Remarks at the Annual Convention of the National Association of Evangelicals in Orlando, Florida, March 8, 1983," in *Public Papers of the Presidents of the United States: Ronald Reagan: 1983 (in Two Books), Book I—January 1 to July 1, 1983* (Washington, DC: U.S. Government Printing Office, 1984), 360.
    See also Thomas Jefferson, *A Summary View of the Rights of British America*, in *The Portable Thomas Jefferson*, ed. Merrill D. Peterson (New York: Viking, 1975), 21.
12. Ronald Reagan, "Remarks at an Ecumenical Prayer Breakfast in Dallas, Texas, August 23, 1984," in *Public Papers of the Presidents of the United States: Ronald Reagan: 1984 (in Two Books), Book II—June 30 to December 31, 1984* (Washington, DC: U.S. Government Printing Office, 1987), 1167.
13. Ronald Reagan, "Farewell Address to the Nation, January 11, 1989," in *Public Papers of the Presidents of the United States: Ronald Reagan: 1988–89 (in Two Books), Book II—July 2, 1988 to January 19, 1989* (Washington, DC: U.S. Government Printing Office, 1991), 1721.
14. Ronald Reagan, "Remarks to Marine Corps Basic Training Graduates in Parris Island, South Carolina, June 4, 1986," in *Public Papers: 1986, Book I*, 720.
15. Ronald Reagan, "Remarks Accepting the Presidential Nomination at the Republican National Convention in Dallas, Texas, August 23, 1984," in *Public Papers: 1984, Book II*, 1181.
16. About the general aim of Reagan's speeches during the 1984 presidential campaign, Gil Troy writes, "In 1984 Ronald Reagan again made it clear that he preferred to be the Wizard of America's Id than lead a new American revolution. Reagan wanted Americans to feel good, not think too hard." See Gil Troy, *Morning in America: How Ronald Reagan Invented the 1980s* (Princeton, NJ: Princeton UP, 2005), 148–49.
17. Ronald Reagan, "Remarks at the Annual Meeting of the National Alliance of Business, October 5, 1981," in *Public Papers: 1981*, 883.
18. Ibid., 884.
19. In his presidential speeches, Reagan often contrasted the good and simple American people with blundering or dangerous social and political "elites." See Paul D. Erickson, *Reagan Speaks: The Making of an American Myth* (New York: New York UP, 1985), 61.
20. Ronald Reagan, "Letter to Philip, Undated, pre-presidential," in *Reagan: A Life in Letters*, eds. Kiron K. Skinner, Annelise Anderson, and Martin Anderson

(New York: Free Press, 2003), 258. Formatting in original. It is unlikely that Jefferson ever said or wrote this phrase, although it does capture a key idea about human nature in Jefferson's political thought.

21. Ronald Reagan, "Address to the Nation on the Economy, February 5, 1981," in *Public Papers: 1981*, 79.

22. Ibid.

23. Ibid., 83.

24. Ronald Reagan, "Remarks at the Annual Dinner of the Conservative Political Action Conference, March 1, 1985," in *Public Papers of the Presidents of the United States: Ronald Reagan: 1985 (in Two Books), Book I—January 1 to June 28, 1985* (Washington, DC: U.S. Government Printing Office, 1988), 227.

25. Jefferson, *A Summary View*, 21.

26. Thomas Jefferson, "The Declaration of Independence, July 4, 1776," in *The Portable Thomas Jefferson*, 235.

27. Thomas Jefferson, "Letter to Peter Carr, August 10, 1787," in *The Portable Thomas Jefferson*, 424–25.

28. Thomas Jefferson, "Letter to Maria Cosway, October 12, 1786," in *The Portable Thomas Jefferson*, 409.

29. Jefferson, "Letter to Peter Carr," 425.

30. Thomas Jefferson, "Letter to John Jay, August 23, 1785," in *The Portable Thomas Jefferson*, 384.

31. Thomas Jefferson, *Notes on the State of Virginia*, in *The Portable Thomas Jefferson*, 217.

32. Ibid.

33. John Locke, *Second Treatise of Government*, ed. C. B. Macpherson (Indianapolis, IN: Hackett, 1980), 9. Formatting in original.

34. Ibid., 21–22. Formatting in original.

35. Ibid., 26–27.

36. Jean-Jacques Rousseau, *Emile, or On Education*, trans. Allan Bloom (New York: Basic Books, 1979), 92.

37. Jean-Jacques Rousseau, "Discourse on the Origin of Inequality," in *The Basic Political Writings*, trans. Donald A. Cress (Indianapolis, IN: Hackett, 1987), 64, 80.

38. Ibid., 55.

39. Jean-Jacques Rousseau, "Discourse on the Sciences and the Arts," in *Basic Political Writings*, 21.

40. Jean-Jacques Rousseau, "Essay on the Origin of Languages," in *The Discourses and Other Early Political Writings*, ed. and trans. Victor Gourevitch (New York: Cambridge UP, 1997; Reprint, 2001), 253.

41. Rousseau, "Discourse on the Origin of Inequality," 42, 54.

42. Irving Babbitt, *Democracy and Leadership* (Indianapolis, IN: Liberty Fund, 1979), 261.

43. John Adams, *Discourses on Davila*, in *The Political Writings of John Adams*, ed. George W. Carey (Washington, DC: Regnery, 2000), 357.

44. John Adams, "Letters to John Taylor of Caroline, Virginia," in *Political Writings of John Adams*, 369.

45. "Federalist No. 6," in *The Federalist*, The Gideon Edition, Alexander Hamilton, John Jay, and James Madison, ed. George W. Carey (Indianapolis, IN: Liberty Fund, 2001), 21; and "Federalist No. 10," in *The Federalist*, 43, 44.

46. "Federalist No. 55," in *The Federalist*, 291.

47. John Adams, "Letter to Samuel Adams, October 18, 1790," in *Political Writings of John Adams*, 668.

48. Edmund Burke, *Reflections on the Revolution in France*, ed. J.G.A. Pocock (Indianapolis, IN: Hackett, 1987), 7.

49. Edmund Burke, "A Letter to a Member of the National Assembly, May, 1791," in *Further Reflections on the Revolution in France*, ed. Daniel E. Ritchie (Indianapolis, IN: Liberty Fund, 1992), 69.
50. Claes G. Ryn, *Democracy and the Ethical Life: A Philosophy of Politics and Community*, 2nd ed. (Washington, DC: CUA Press, 1990), 65.
51. Ibid., 66.
52. Ibid., 62.

NOTES TO CHAPTER 5

1. Abraham Lincoln, "First Inaugural Address, March 4, 1861," in *Abraham Lincoln: His Speeches and Writings*, ed. Roy P. Basler (New York: Da Capo, 1990), 588.
2. Ronald Reagan, "Remarks at the Bicentennial Observance of the Battle of Yorktown in Virginia, October 19, 1981," in *Public Papers of the Presidents of the United States: Ronald Reagan: 1981, January 20 to December 31, 1981* (Washington, DC: U.S. Government Printing Office, 1982), 969.
3. Ronald Reagan, "Address before a Joint Session of the Alabama State Legislature in Montgomery, March 15, 1982," in *Public Papers of the Presidents of the United States: Ronald Reagan: 1982 (in Two Books), Book I—January 1 to July 2, 1982* (Washington, DC: U.S. Government Printing Office, 1983), 292.
4. Lee Edwards, *The Essential Ronald Reagan: A Profile in Courage, Justice, and Wisdom* (Lanham, MD: Rowman & Littlefield, 2005), 146.
5. Paul Kengor, *God and Ronald Reagan: A Spiritual Life* (New York: HarperCollins, 2004), 227.
6. Dinesh D'Souza, *Ronald Reagan: How an Ordinary Man Became an Extraordinary Leader* (New York: Touchstone, 1999), 74.
7. John Patrick Diggins, *Ronald Reagan: Fate, Freedom, and the Making of History* (New York: W. W. Norton, 2007), 1–2.
8. Ronald Reagan, "Address at Commencement Exercises at the University of Notre Dame, May 17, 1981," in *Public Papers: 1981*, 433.
9. Reagan, "Remarks at the Bicentennial Observance," 970.
10. Ibid., 968.
11. Ronald Reagan, "Remarks Announcing America's Economic Bill of Rights, July 3, 1987," in *Public Papers of the Presidents of the United States: Ronald Reagan: 1987 (in Two Books), Book I—January 1 to July 3, 1987* (Washington, DC: U.S. Government Printing Office, 1989), 740.
12. Ronald Reagan, "Message on the Observance of Independence Day, July 3, 1981," in *Public Papers: 1981*, 594.
13. Reagan, "Remarks at the Bicentennial Observance," 970.
14. Ronald Reagan, "Address to the Nation on Independence Day, July 4, 1986," in *Public Papers of the Presidents of the United States: Ronald Reagan: 1986 (in Two Books), Book II—June 28 to December 31, 1986* (Washington, DC: U.S. Government Printing Office, 1989), 922–23.
15. Ronald Reagan, "Remarks on Signing the Bill of Rights Day and Human Rights Day and Week Proclamation, December 9, 1983," in *Public Papers of the Presidents of the United States: Ronald Reagan: 1983 (in Two Books), Book II—July 2 to December 31, 1983* (Washington, DC: U.S. Government Printing Office, 1985), 1674.
16. Reagan, "Remarks at the Bicentennial Observance," 968.
17. Ibid.
18. Ibid.
19. Ibid.

20. Ibid., 968–69.
21. Ronald Reagan, "Remarks at the 'We the People' Bicentennial Celebration in Philadelphia, Pennsylvania, September 17, 1987," in *Public Papers of the Presidents of the United States: Ronald Reagan: 1987 (in Two Books), Book II—July 4 to December 31, 1987* (Washington, DC: U.S. Government Printing Office, 1989), 1041–42.
22. Ibid., 1042.
23. Ronald Reagan, "Address before a Joint Session of Congress on the State of the Union, January 27, 1987," in *Public Papers: 1987, Book I*, 60.
24. Ibid.
25. Ibid.
26. Ibid.
27. Ronald Reagan, "Remarks at a Flag Day Ceremony in Baltimore, Maryland, June 14, 1985," in *Public Papers of the Presidents of the United States: Ronald Reagan: 1985 (in Two Books), Book I—January 1 to June 28, 1985* (Washington, DC: U.S. Government Printing Office, 1988), 769.
28. Ibid.
29. Ibid.
30. Ibid.
31. Ibid.
32. Ibid.
33. Ibid., 770.
34. Ronald Reagan, "Remarks at a Mount Vernon, Virginia, Ceremony Commemorating the 250th Anniversary of the Birth of George Washington, February 22, 1982," in *Public Papers: 1982, Book I*, 199.
35. Ibid., 200.
36. Ibid.
37. Ibid.
38. Thomas Jefferson, "First Inaugural Address, March 4, 1801," in *The Portable Thomas Jefferson*, ed. Merrill D. Peterson (New York: Viking, 1975), 290, 292.
39. Thomas Jefferson, "Letter to Dr. Joseph Priestley, March 21, 1801," in *The Portable Thomas Jefferson*, 484.
40. Thomas Jefferson, "Letter to Major John Cartwright, June 5, 1824," in *The Portable Thomas Jefferson*, 578.
41. Thomas Jefferson, "Letter to Diodati, August 3, 1789," in *The Portable Thomas Jefferson*, 443.
42. Thomas Jefferson, "Letter to Roger C. Weightman, June 24, 1826," in *The Portable Thomas Jefferson*, 585.
43. Thomas Paine, *Common Sense*, in *The Thomas Paine Reader*, eds. Michael Foot and Isaac Kramnick (New York: Penguin Books, 1987), 109.
44. Thomas Paine, *The Rights of Man: Part Two*, in *The Thomas Paine Reader*, 263.
45. Ibid., 265.
46. Thomas Paine, "Letter to the Abbé Raynal, 1782," in *The Thomas Paine Reader*, 163, 165.
47. Abraham Lincoln, "Letter to H.L. Pierce and Others, April 6, 1859," in *Abraham Lincoln: His Speeches and Writings*, 489.
48. Reagan, "Remarks on Signing the Bill of Rights Day," 1674.
49. Abraham Lincoln, "Address in Independence Hall, Philadelphia, February 22, 1861," in *Abraham Lincoln: His Speeches and Writings*, 577.
50. Ronald Reagan, "Remarks to Students from Hine Junior High School on Abraham Lincoln, February 12, 1987," in *Public Papers: 1987, Book I*, 136.
51. Ibid.
52. Abraham Lincoln, "Fragment: The Constitution and the Union [1860?]," in *Abraham Lincoln: His Speeches and Writings*, 513. Emphases in original.

53. Ibid. Emphases in original.
54. Harry Jaffa, "Equality as a Conservative Principle," in *How to Think about the American Revolution: A Bicentennial Cerebration* (Durham, NC: Carolina Academic Press, 1978), 16.
55. For a critical analysis of Jaffa's vision of the Founding, see Barry Alan Shain, "Harry Jaffa and the Demise of the Old Republic," *Modern Age* 49, no. 4 (Fall 2007).
56. Allan Bloom, *The Closing of the American Mind* (New York: Simon and Schuster, 1988), 158.
57. Ibid., 246.
58. Ibid., 158.
59. Ibid.
60. Ibid., 55.
61. Ibid., 27.
62. Reagan, "Remarks Announcing America's Economic Bill of Rights," 744.
63. John Adams, *A Defence of the Constitutions of Government of the United States of America*, in *The Political Writings of John Adams*, ed. George W. Carey (Washington, DC: Regnery, 2000), 115.
64. Ibid., 255.
65. John Adams, "Letters to John Taylor of Caroline, Virginia," in *Political Writings of John Adams*, 398.
66. Adams, *A Defence of the Constitutions*, 224.
67. Ibid., 124.
68. Adams, "Letters to John Taylor," 388. Emphasis in original.
69. Willmoore Kendall and George W. Carey, *The Basic Symbols of the American Political Tradition* (Baton Rouge: Louisiana State UP, 1970), 75. Emphases in original.
70. Ibid., 83.
71. "Fundamental Orders of Connecticut, January 14, 1639," in *The American Republic*, ed. Bruce Frohnen (Indianapolis, IN: Liberty Fund, 2002), 12.
72. Kendall and Carey, *Basic Symbols of the American Political Tradition*, 88–89.
73. Ibid., 94.
74. Russell Kirk, *The Sword of Imagination: Memoirs of a Half-Century of Literary Conflict* (Grand Rapids, MI: Wm. B. Eerdmans, 1995), 454.
75. Russell Kirk, *The Politics of Prudence* (Wilmington, DE: ISI Books, 1998), 150.
76. Ibid., 152.
77. Kirk, *Sword of Imagination*, 454.
78. Russell Kirk, *The Roots of American Order* (Wilmington, DE: ISI Books, 2004), 411. Emphasis in original.
79. Russell Kirk, *Rights and Duties: Reflections on Our Conservative Constitution*, ed. Mitchell S. Muncy (Dallas, TX: Spence, 1997), 48–49.
80. Kirk, *Roots of American Order*, 414. Emphasis added.
81. Kirk, *Rights and Duties*, 110.
82. Kirk, *Roots of American Order*, 416.
83. Ibid.
84. Ibid.
85. Edmund Burke, *Reflections on the Revolution in France*, ed. J.G.A. Pocock (Indianapolis, IN: Hackett, 1987), 69.
86. Ibid., 67, 28.
87. Ibid., 27, 27–28. Emphases in original.
88. Thomas Paine, *The Rights of Man: Part One*, in *The Thomas Paine Reader*, 220.
89. Ibid., 221.
90. Ronald Reagan, "Remarks and a Question-and-Answer Session with Area Junior High School Students, November 14, 1988," in *Public Papers of the*

Presidents of the United States: Ronald Reagan: 1988–89 (in Two Books), Book II—July 2, 1988 to January 19, 1989 (Washington, DC: U.S. Government Printing Office, 1991), 1501.
91. Burke, *Reflections on the Revolution in France*, 4.

NOTES TO CHAPTER 6

1. Ronald Reagan, "Remarks at the Annual Convention of the United States Jaycees in San Antonio, Texas, June 24, 1981," in *Public Papers of the Presidents of the United States: Ronald Reagan: 1981, January 20 to December 31, 1981* (Washington, DC: U.S. Government Printing Office, 1982), 555.
2. Ronald Reagan, "Inaugural Address, January 20, 1981," in *Public Papers: 1981*, 1.
3. Ronald Reagan, *An American Life* (New York: Simon and Schuster, 1990), 232.
4. Ibid., 196.
5. Thomas Jefferson, "First Inaugural Address, March 4, 1801," in *The Portable Thomas Jefferson*, ed. Merrill D. Peterson (New York: Viking, 1975), 293.
For examples of Reagan approvingly referring to this passage from Jefferson's speech, see Reagan, *An American Life*, 134, and Ronald Reagan, "Statement on the 239th Anniversary of the Birth of Thomas Jefferson, April 13, 1982," in *Public Papers of the Presidents of the United States: Ronald Reagan: 1982 (in Two Books), Book I—January 1 to July 2, 1982* (Washington, DC: U.S. Government Printing Office, 1983), 457.
6. Ronald Reagan, "Letter to Mr. and Mrs. Richard A. Stanton, February 10, 1982," in *Reagan: A Life in Letters*, eds. Kiron K. Skinner, Annelise Anderson, and Martin Anderson (New York: Free Press, 2003), 341.
7. Reagan's commitments to federalism and limited government could find very poor expression at times. See Toby Glenn Bates, *The Reagan Rhetoric: History and Memory in 1980s America* (DeKalb: Northern Illinois UP, 2011), 18–43.
8. Reagan, *An American Life*, 197.
9. Ibid., 198.
10. Thomas Jefferson, "Opinion on the Constitutionality of a National Bank, February 15, 1791," in *The Portable Thomas Jefferson*, 262.
11. Thomas Jefferson, "The Kentucky Resolutions," in *The Portable Thomas Jefferson*, 281.
12. Reagan, *An American Life*, 160. Emphasis in original.
13. Ibid., 234.
14. Woodrow Wilson, article from "The International Review, August 1879," in *The Politics of Woodrow Wilson: Selections from His Speeches and Writings*, ed. August Heckscher (New York: Harper & Row, 1970), 13.
15. Woodrow Wilson, "Constitutional Government in the United States, 1908," in *The Politics of Woodrow Wilson*, 21.
16. Garry L. Gregg, "Whiggism and Presidentialism: American Ambivalence toward Executive Power," in *The Presidency: Then and Now*, ed. Phillip G. Henderson (Lanham, MD: Rowman & Littlefield, 2000), 82.
17. Reagan, *An American Life*, 69.
18. Ibid., 101.
19. Ibid., 120.
20. Reagan, "Remarks at the Annual Convention of the United States Jaycees," 555.
21. Reagan, "Inaugural Address, January 20, 1981," 1.
22. Ronald Reagan, "Address to the Nation on the Economy, February 5, 1981," in *Public Papers: 1981*, 81.
23. Ibid.

24. Ronald Reagan, "Remarks at the Annual Convention of the National Association of Counties in Baltimore, Maryland, July 13, 1982," in *Public Papers of the Presidents of the United States: Ronald Reagan: 1982 (in Two Books), Book II—July 3 to December 31, 1982* (Washington, DC: U.S. Government Printing Office, 1983), 918.
25. Ibid.
26. Ibid.
27. Ibid.
28. Ibid.
29. Ibid.
30. About the practical results of Reagan's efforts to reconfigure the relationship among national, state, and local government, Michael Schaller writes, "As a presidential candidate, Ronald Reagan pledged to shrink the scope of the federal government by returning greater authority and responsibility to the states. In practice, the Reagan administration shifted costs, not power, to local government. Under the so-called 'new federalism,' Washington burdened state, county, and city governments with many new, expensive-to-administer regulations—such as monitoring pollution, removing asbestos from schools, and supervising nursing homes—but provided less federal money than before." See Michael Schaller, *Reckoning with Reagan: America and Its President in the 1980s* (New York: Oxford UP, 1992), 71.
31. Ronald Reagan, "Radio Address to the Nation on Welfare Reform, February 15, 1986," in *Public Papers of the Presidents of the United States: Ronald Reagan: 1986 (in Two Books), Book I—January 1 to June 27, 1986* (Washington, DC: U.S. Government Printing Office, 1988), 215.
32. Ronald Reagan, "Remarks at the Annual Convention of the National Association of Evangelicals, March 8, 1983," in *Public Papers of the Presidents of the United States: Ronald Reagan: 1983 (in Two Books), Book I—January 1 to July 1, 1983* (Washington, DC: U.S. Government Printing Office, 1984), 361.
33. Ibid.
34. Ibid.
35. Ibid.
36. Reagan, *An American Life*, 333.
37. Alonzo Hamby notes that Reagan's desire to cut taxes reflected long-standing Republican policy desires and writes, "The major policy objective of supply-side economics, lower taxes, came naturally to most Republicans; for all their traditional talk about budget balancing, they long had lunged at any opportunity to cut taxes, assuming that lower revenues would sooner or later whittle down the size and functions of government." See Alonzo L. Hamby, *Liberalism and Its Challengers: From F.D.R. to Bush* (New York: Oxford UP, 1992), 358.
38. Reagan, "Address to the Nation on the Economy," 81.
39. Ibid., 82–83.
40. Ibid., 83.
41. About the deeper symbolic meaning of Reagan's economic policies, Robert Dallek argues, "Although advertised as an economic program, Reaganomics was, in fact, a form of symbolic politics, a means of liberating middle-class Americans from government tyranny and eliminating 'immoral' deficits and the government's perceived preferential treatment of the needs of minorities." See Robert Dallek, *Ronald Reagan: The Politics of Symbolism* (Cambridge, MA: Harvard UP, 1999), 64.
42. Contrasting the early months of the Carter and Reagan presidencies, John Sloan writes, "While Carter had squandered his first hundred days (his honeymoon period) by overwhelming Congress with a barrage of legislative proposals,

Reagan immediately established his strategic priorities: a three-year tax cut, budget reductions, and a major defense buildup." See John W. Sloan, *FDR and Reagan: Transformative Presidents with Clashing Visions* (Lawrence: UP of Kansas, 2008), 224.

43. Reagan, *An American Life*, 287–88.
44. Ronald Reagan, "Remarks in Atlanta, Georgia, at the Annual Convention of the National Conference of State Legislatures, July 30, 1981," in *Public Papers: 1981*, 680.
45. Jefferson, "The Kentucky Resolutions," 287–88.
46. Thomas Jefferson, "Letter to Edward Carrington, January 16, 1787," in *The Portable Thomas Jefferson*, 414.
47. Thomas Jefferson, "Response to the Citizens of Albemarle, February 12, 1790," in *The Portable Thomas Jefferson*, 260.
48. Jefferson, "First Inaugural Address, March 4, 1801," 293.
49. Jean-Jacques Rousseau, "Discourse on the Origin of Inequality," in *The Basic Political Writings*, trans. Donald A. Cress (Indianapolis, IN: Hackett, 1987), 67.
50. Jean-Jacques Rousseau, "The Social Contract," in *Basic Political Writings*, 141.
51. Irving Babbitt, *Rousseau and Romanticism* (New Brunswick, NJ: Transaction, 2002), 130.
52. Irving Babbitt, *Democracy and Leadership* (Indianapolis, IN: Liberty Fund, 1979), 277.
53. Ibid., 104.
54. John Adams, *A Defence of the Constitutions of the United States*, in *The Political Writings of John Adams*, ed. George W. Carey (Washington, DC: Regnery, 2000), 251.
55. Ibid., 231.
56. Ibid., 243–44.
57. "Federalist No. 51," in *The Federalist*, The Gideon Edition, Alexander Hamilton, John Jay, and James Madison, ed. George W. Carey (Indianapolis, IN: Liberty Fund, 2001), 268–69.
58. "Federalist No. 10," in *The Federalist*, 43.
59. Ibid., 46.
60. Ibid.
61. "Federalist No. 63," in *The Federalist*, 327.
62. "Federalist No. 71," in *The Federalist*, 370.
63. Ibid., 371.
64. Edmund Burke, *Reflections on the Revolution in France*, ed. J.G.A. Pocock (Indianapolis, IN: Hackett, 1987), 43.
65. Babbitt, *Democracy and Leadership*, 288.
66. Burke, *Reflections on the Revolution in France*, 44.

NOTES TO CHAPTER 7

1. Ronald Reagan, "Address to Members of the British Parliament, June 8, 1982," in *Public Papers of the Presidents of the United States: Ronald Reagan: 1982 (in Two Books), Book I—January 1 to July 2, 1982* (Washington, DC: U.S. Government Printing Office, 1983), 748.
2. Ronald Reagan, "Remarks at Kansas State University at the Alfred M. Landon Lecture Series on Public Issues, September 9, 1982," in *Public Papers of the Presidents of the United States: Ronald Reagan: 1982 (in Two Books), Book II—July 3 to December 31, 1982* (Washington, DC: U.S. Government Printing Office, 1983), 1120.

3. Ronald Reagan, "Address to the Nation and Other Countries on United States-Soviet Relations, January 16, 1984," in *Public Papers of the Presidents of the United States: Ronald Reagan: 1984 (in Two Books), Book I—January 1 to June 29, 1984* (Washington, DC: U.S. Government Printing Office, 1986), 44.

4. Gil Troy explains that Reagan came up with the story of Ivan, Anya, Jim, and Sally on his own. The version of the story Reagan told in the January 1984 speech was more or less the one he had originally written. See Gil Troy, *Morning in America: How Ronald Reagan Invented the 1980s* (Princeton, NJ: Princeton UP, 2005), 242.

5. Ronald Reagan, "Address before the 38th Session of the United Nations General Assembly in New York, New York, September 26, 1983," in *Public Papers of the Presidents of the United States: Ronald Reagan: 1983 (in Two Books), Book II—July 2 to December 31, 1983* (Washington, DC: U.S. Government Printing Office, 1985), 1350.

6. Ronald Reagan, "Remarks and a Question-and-Answer Session with the Students and Faculty at Moscow State University, May 31, 1988," in *Public Papers of the Presidents of the United States: Ronald Reagan: 1988 (in Two Books), Book I—January 1 to July 1, 1988* (Washington, DC: U.S. Government Printing Office, 1990), 687.

7. Reagan, "Address to Members of the British Parliament," 745, 748.

8. Ibid., 746.

9. Ibid.

10. For an insightful and concise account of the tense international and domestic circumstances in which Reagan delivered his address to the British Parliament, see Robert C. Rowland and John M. Jones, *Reagan at Westminster: Foreshadowing the End of the Cold War* (College Station: Texas A&M UP, 2010), 54–64.

11. Ronald Reagan, *An American Life* (New York: Simon and Schuster, 1990), 265, 588.

12. Ronald Reagan, "Address to the Nation on the Upcoming Soviet-United States Summit Meeting in Geneva, November 14, 1985," in *Public Papers of the Presidents of the United States: Ronald Reagan: 1985 (in Two Books), Book II—June 29 to December 31, 1985* (Washington, DC: U.S. Government Printing Office, 1988), 1389.

13. Ronald Reagan, "Remarks at a Spirit of America Festival in Decatur, Alabama, July 4, 1984," in *Public Papers of the Presidents of the United States: Ronald Reagan: 1984 (in Two Books), Book II—June 30 to December 31, 1984* (Washington, DC: U.S. Government Printing Office, 1987), 1002.

14. Ronald Reagan, "Christmas Day Radio Address to the Nation, December 25, 1982," in *Public Papers: 1982, Book II*, 1643.

15. Ronald Reagan, "Address at Commencement Exercises at the University of Notre Dame, May 17, 1981," in *Public Papers of the Presidents of the United States: Ronald Reagan: 1981, January 20 to December 31, 1981* (Washington, DC: U.S. Government Printing Office, 1982), 434; and Reagan, "Address to Members of the British Parliament," 747.

16. Reagan, *An American Life*, 556.

17. Ronald Reagan, "Address to the Nation on the Meetings with Soviet General Secretary Gorbachev in Iceland, October 13, 1986," in *Public Papers of the Presidents of the United States: Ronald Reagan: 1986 (in Two Books), Book II—June 28 to December 31, 1986* (Washington, DC: U.S. Government Printing Office, 1989), 1369.

18. Ronald Reagan, "Address before a Joint Session of the Congress on Central America, April 27, 1983," in *Public Papers of the Presidents of the United States: Ronald Reagan: 1983 (in Two Books), Book I—January 1 to July 1, 1983* (Washington, DC: U.S. Government Printing Office, 1984), 602.

19. Ronald Reagan, "Address to the Nation on Events in Lebanon and Grenada, October 27, 1983," in *Public Papers: 1983, Book II*, 1519.
20. Ibid., 1520.
21. Ibid.
22. Ibid., 1521.
23. Although the intervention in Grenada was popular in the United States, some suggest that the constitutionality of Reagan's decision to send troops to the island is questionable. Alonzo Hamby writes, "Reagan's one major coup, the invasion of the tiny island of Grenada and the displacement of a pro-Castro regime there was possible only because he acted without congressional authorization and met no significant military resistance." See Alonzo L. Hamby, *Liberalism and Its Challengers: From F.D.R. to Bush* (New York: Oxford UP, 1992), 380.
24. Ronald Reagan, "Remarks at the Annual Dinner of the Conservative Political Action Conference, March 1, 1985," in *Public Papers of the Presidents of the United States: Ronald Reagan: 1985 (in Two Books), Book I—January 1 to June 28, 1985* (Washington, DC: U.S. Government Printing Office, 1988), 228.
25. Reagan, *An American Life*, 457. Capitalized text in the original.
26. Reagan, "Remarks at the Conservative Political Action Conference," 228–29.
27. Lou Cannon, *President Reagan: The Role of a Lifetime* (New York: PublicAffairs, 2000), 317.
28. Ronald Reagan, "Remarks at a Ceremony Commemorating the 40th Anniversary of the Normandy Invasion, D-day, June 6, 1984," in *Public Papers: 1984, Book I*, 819.
29. Ronald Reagan, "Address to the 42d Session of the United Nations General Assembly in New York, New York, September 21, 1987," in *Public Papers of the Presidents of the United States: Ronald Reagan: 1987 (in Two Books), Book II—July 4 to December 31, 1987* (Washington, DC: U.S. Government Printing Office, 1989), 1058.
30. Ibid., 1059.
31. Ibid.
32. Ibid.
33. Reagan, "Address on Central America before a Joint Session," 601.
34. Quoted from Ronald Reagan, "Remarks at the Annual Convention of the National Association of Evangelicals, March 8, 1983," in *Public Papers: 1983, Book I*, 364.
35. Ronald Reagan, "Remarks and a Question-and-Answer Session at the University of Virginia in Charlottesville, December 16, 1988," in *Public Papers of the Presidents of the United States: Ronald Reagan: 1988–89 (in Two Books), Book II—July 2, 1988 to January 19, 1989* (Washington, DC: U.S. Government Printing Office, 1991), 1638.
36. Reagan, "Address to the Nation on the Meetings with Soviet General Secretary Gorbachev," 1371.
37. Reagan, "Remarks at a Ceremony Commemorating the 40th Anniversary," 818.
38. Ronald Reagan, "Radio Address to the Nation and the World on the Upcoming Soviet-United States Summit Meeting in Geneva, November 9, 1985," in *Public Papers: 1985, Book II*, 1363.
39. Reagan, "Remarks at Kansas State University at the Alfred M. Landon Lecture Series," 1120.
40. Dinesh D'Souza, *Ronald Reagan: How an Ordinary Man Became an Extraordinary Leader* (New York: Touchstone, 1999), 28.
41. Ibid., 172.
42. Paul Kengor, *God and Ronald Reagan: A Spiritual Life* (New York: HarperCollins, 2004), 34.
43. Ibid., 98–99. Emphasis in original.

44. Robert Kagan, "Neocon Nation: Neoconservatism, c. 1776," *World Affairs Journal* 170, no. 4 (Spring 2008): 14–15.
45. Ibid., 16.
46. John Lukacs, *June 1941: Hitler and Stalin* (New Haven, CT: Yale UP, 2006), 9.
47. Herbert Butterfield, *The Whig Interpretation of History* (Reprint, London: G. Bell and Sons, 1968), 10.
48. John Quincy Adams, "Address of July 4, 1821," in *John Quincy Adams and American Continental Empire: Letters, Speeches and Papers*, ed. Walter Lafeber (Chicago: Quadrangle Books, 1965), 44. Emphasis in the original.
49. Ibid., 45. Emphasis in the original.
50. Orestes A. Brownson, *The American Republic: Its Constitution, Tendencies, and Destiny*, vol. 1 of *Orestes A. Brownson: Works on Political Philosophy*, series ed. Gregory S. Butler (Wilmington, DE: ISI Books, 2003), 120–21.
51. Richard M. Gamble, "Savior Nation: Woodrow Wilson and the Gospel of Service," *Humanitas* 14, no. 1 (2001): 7.
52. Ibid.
53. Ibid.
54. Ibid.
55. Ibid., 8.
56. Ibid., 14.
57. Ibid., 15.
58. Richard M. Gamble, *The War for Righteousness: Progressive Christians, the Great War, and the Rise of the Messianic Nation* (Wilmington, DE: ISI Books, 2003), 73.
59. Ibid., 176.
60. Ibid., 177.
61. Walter A. McDougall, *Promised Land, Crusader State: The American Encounter with the World since 1776* (New York: Houghton Mifflin, 1997), 4.
62. Ibid.
63. Ibid., 5.
64. Ibid., 20. Emphasis in original.
65. Ibid., 39.
66. Ibid., 40. Emphasis in original.
67. George Washington, "Farewell Address, September 19, 1796," in *Writings* (New York: Literary Classics of the United States, 1997), 974, 975. Emphasis in original.
68. McDougall, *Promised Land, Crusader State*, 111.
69. Ibid., 118.
70. Woodrow Wilson, "Address at Mobile, Alabama, October 27, 1913," in *The Politics of Woodrow Wilson: Selections from His Speeches and Writings*, ed. August Heckscher (New York: Harper & Row, 1970), 206.
71. Woodrow Wilson, "Address to Congress, August 27, 1913," in *The Politics of Woodrow Wilson*, 199.
72. Ibid.
73. McDougall, *Promised Land, Crusader State*, 131.
74. Ibid.
75. Woodrow Wilson, "Address at the Brooklyn Navy Yard, May 11, 1914," in *The Politics of Woodrow Wilson*, 240–41.
76. McDougall, *Promised Land, Crusader State*, 132.
77. Woodrow Wilson, "Gridiron Dinner Address, February 26, 1916," in *The Politics of Woodrow Wilson*, 257.
78. Ibid., 258.
79. Woodrow Wilson, "Address to the Congress, April 2, 1917," in *The Politics of Woodrow Wilson*, 277.
80. Ibid., 278.

81. Ibid., 279.
82. Woodrow Wilson, "Address at Baltimore, Maryland, April 6, 1918," in *The Politics of Woodrow Wilson*, 309.
83. Woodrow Wilson, "Address at Mount Vernon, July 4, 1918," in *The Politics of Woodrow Wilson*, 312.
84. Gamble, "Savior Nation," 21.
85. McDougall, *Promised Land, Crusader State*, 126.
86. Ibid., 146.
87. Gamble, "Savior Nation," 21.
88. Plato, *Republic*, trans. Desmond Lee (New York: Penguin Putnam, 2003), 277.
89. Ibid., 298.
90. Irving Babbitt, *Democracy and Leadership* (Indianapolis, IN: Liberty Fund, 1979), 273.
91. Claes G. Ryn, *Democracy and the Ethical Life: A Philosophy of Politics and Community*, 2nd ed. (Washington, DC: CUA Press, 1990), 18, 197.
92. Ibid., 13–14.
93. Ibid., 15.
94. Ibid., 15–16.
95. Ibid., 93.

NOTES TO CHAPTER 8

1. Ronald Reagan, "Address before the Bundestag in Bonn, Federal Republic of Germany, June 9, 1982," in *Public Papers of the Presidents of the United States: Ronald Reagan: 1982 (in Two Books), Book I—January 1 to July 2, 1982* (Washington, DC: U.S. Government Printing Office, 1983), 759.
2. Ronald Reagan, "Address to the Nation on National Security, February 26, 1986," in *Public Papers of the Presidents of the United States: Ronald Reagan: 1986 (in Two Books), Book I—January 1 to June 27, 1986* (Washington, DC: U.S. Government Printing Office, 1988), 272.
3. Ronald Reagan, "Remarks at the Annual Convention of the American Legion in Seattle, Washington, August 23, 1983," in *Public Papers of the Presidents of the United States: Ronald Reagan: 1983 (in Two Books), Book II—July 2 to December 31, 1983* (Washington, DC: U.S. Government Printing Office, 1985), 1192.
4. Ibid.
5. Ibid.
6. Ronald Reagan, "Address at Commencement Exercises at Eureka College in Illinois, May 9, 1982," in *Public Papers: 1982, Book I*, 583.
7. Ronald Reagan, "Address to the Nation and Other Countries on the United States-Soviet Relations, January 16, 1984," in *Public Papers of the Presidents of the United States: Ronald Reagan: 1984 (in Two Books), Book I—January 1 to June 29, 1984* (Washington, DC: U.S. Government Printing Office, 1986), 42.
8. Ronald Reagan, "Address to the Nation on the Upcoming Soviet-United States Summit Meeting in Geneva, November 14, 1985," in *Public Papers of the Presidents of the United States: Ronald Reagan: 1985 (in Two Books), Book II—June 29 to December 31, 1985* (Washington, DC: U.S. Government Printing Office, 1988), 1388.
9. Ibid., 1389.
10. Reagan made this argument about the inherent nonviolent nature of democracy in numerous presidential speeches, including his address to the British Parliament in 1982. See Robert C. Rowland and John M. Jones, *Reagan at Westmin-*

ster: *Foreshadowing the End of the Cold War* (College Station: Texas A&M UP, 2010), 113.

11. Ronald Reagan, "Address before a Joint Session of Congress on the State of the Union, February 4, 1986," in *Public Papers: 1986, Book I*, 129.
12. Reagan, "Address before the Bundestag in Bonn," 759.
13. Ronald Reagan, "Address to the 42d Session of the United Nations General Assembly in New York, New York, September 21, 1987," in *Public Papers of the Presidents of the United States: Ronald Reagan: 1987 (in Two Books), Book II—July 4 to December 31, 1987* (Washington, DC: U.S. Government Printing Office, 1989), 1059.
14. Ibid.
15. Ronald Reagan, "Address to the Nation on Defense and National Security, March 23, 1983," in *Public Papers of the Presidents of the United States: Ronald Reagan: 1983 (in Two Books), Book I—January 1 to July 1, 1983* (Washington, DC: U.S. Government Printing Office, 1984), 437.
16. Ibid., 441.
17. Ibid., 438.
18. Ibid., 442.
19. Ibid.
20. Ibid.
21. Ibid., 442–43.
22. Ibid., 443.
23. Reagan, "Address to the Nation on the Upcoming Soviet-United States Summit," 1388.
24. Ibid., 1390.
25. Ibid.
26. Ibid., 1388.
27. Ibid., 1391.
28. Michael Schaller explains that the Geneva Summit met these low expectations. He writes, "The Geneva summit improved 'atmospherics' but did not end the rivalry of the two superpowers." See Michael Schaller, *Reckoning with Reagan: America and Its President in the 1980s* (New York, Oxford UP, 1992), 172.
29. Ronald Reagan, *An American Life* (New York: Simon and Schuster, 1990), 12, 13.
30. Ibid., 14.
31. Ibid., 637.
32. Ibid., 665.
33. Ibid., 15.
34. Ibid., 676.
35. Ibid., 677.
36. Ibid.
37. John Patrick Diggins, *Ronald Reagan: Fate, Freedom, and the Making of History* (New York: W. W. Norton, 2007), 380.
38. Reagan, *An American Life*, 679.
39. Ronald Reagan, "Address to the Nation on Meetings with Soviet General Secretary Gorbachev in Iceland, October 13, 1986," in *Public Papers of the Presidents of the United States: Ronald Reagan: 1986 (in Two Books), Book II—June 28 to December 31, 1986* (Washington, DC: U.S. Government Printing Office, 1989), 1367, 1369.
40. Ibid., 1370.
41. Ibid.
42. Ibid.
43. Ibid., 1371.
44. Ronald Reagan, "Diary Entry, March 22, 1983," in *The Reagan Diaries*, ed. Douglas Brinkley (New York: HarperCollins, 2007), 139.

45. Lou Cannon, *President Reagan: The Role of a Lifetime* (New York: PublicAffairs, 2000), 288.

46. Paul Kengor, *The Crusader: Ronald Reagan and the Fall of Communism* (New York: HarperCollins, 2006), 177.

47. Frances FitzGerald, *Way Out There in the Blue: Ronald Reagan, Star Wars, and the End of the Cold War* (New York: Simon and Schuster, 2000), 22–23.

48. Cannon, *President Reagan*, 288.

49. Dinesh D'Souza, *Ronald Reagan: How an Ordinary Man Became an Extraordinary Leader* (New York: Touchstone, 1999), 177.

50. Reagan, *An American Life*, 608.

51. Ronald Reagan, "Address to Members of the British Parliament, June 8, 1982," in *Public Papers: 1982, Book I*, 746.

52. Eric Voegelin, "Liberalism and Its History," in *The Collected Works of Eric Voegelin*, vol. 11: *Published Essays 1953–1965*, ed. Ellis Sandoz (Columbia: U of Missouri P, 2000), 95–96.

53. Eric Voegelin, "Industrial Society in Search of Reason," in *Published Essays 1953–1965*, 186.

54. Claes G. Ryn, *A Common Human Ground: Universality and Particularity in a Multicultural World* (Columbia: U of Missouri P, 2003), 5.

55. Ibid., 21.

56. Ibid., 133.

57. Irving Babbitt, *Democracy and Leadership* (Indianapolis, IN: Liberty Fund, 1979), 248.

58. Ibid., 296.

59. Ronald Reagan, "Empire of Ideals, August 17, 1992," in *The Greatest Speeches of Ronald Reagan* (West Palm Beach, FL: Newsmax.com, 2001), 268.

60. Ronald Reagan, "Remarks at the Annual Washington Conference of the American Legion, February 22, 1983," in *Public Papers: 1983, Book I*, 265–66.

61. Ibid., 270.

62. Ronald Reagan, "Remarks at the 'We the People' Bicentennial Celebration in Philadelphia, Pennsylvania, September 17, 1987," in *Public Papers: 1987, Book II*, 1042.

NOTES TO CHAPTER 9

1. Ronald Reagan, "Remarks at a Spirit of America Festival in Decatur, Alabama, July 4, 1984," in *Public Papers of the Presidents of the United States: Ronald Reagan: 1984 (in Two Books), Book II—June 30 to December 31, 1984* (Washington, DC: U.S. Government Printing Office, 1987), 1001.

2. Ronald Reagan, "Empire of Ideals, August 17, 1992," in *The Greatest Speeches of Ronald Reagan* (West Palm Beach, FL: Newsmax.com, 2001), 274.

3. Ronald Reagan, "Address before a Joint Session of the Congress on the State of the Union, January 25, 1983," in *Public Papers of the Presidents of the United States: Ronald Reagan: 1983 (in Two Books), Book I—January 1 to July 1, 1983* (Washington, DC: U.S. Government Printing Office, 1984), 107.

4. Ronald Reagan, "Remarks at the Tuskegee University Commencement Ceremony in Alabama, May 10, 1987," in *Public Papers of the Presidents of the United States: Ronald Reagan: 1987 (in Two Books), Book I—January 1 to July 3, 1987* (Washington, DC: U.S. Government Printing Office, 1989), 489–90.

5. Ronald Reagan, "Remarks to Students and Faculty at Thomas Jefferson High School of Science and Technology in Fairfax County, Virginia, February 7, 1986," in *Public Papers of the Presidents of the United States: Ronald Reagan:*

1986 (in Two Books), Book I—January 1 to June 27, 1986 (Washington, DC: U.S. Government Printing Office, 1988), 177.

6. Ronald Reagan, "Radio Address to the Nation on the Quality of Life in America, October 15, 1983," in *Public Papers of the Presidents of the United States: Ronald Reagan: 1983 (in Two Books), Book II—July 2 to December 31, 1983* (Washington, DC: U.S. Government Printing Office, 1985), 1463.

7. Reagan, "Remarks to Students and Faculty at Thomas Jefferson High School," 177.

8. Ronald Reagan, "Remarks during a Visit to the Goddard Space Flight Center in Greenbelt, Maryland, August 30, 1984," in *Public Papers: 1984, Book II*, 1207.

9. Reagan, "Remarks at the Tuskegee University Commencement Ceremony," 490.

10. Ibid.

11. Reagan, "Remarks to Students and Faculty at Thomas Jefferson High School," 177.

12. Ronald Reagan, "Remarks at Edwards Air Force Base, California, on Completion of the Fourth Mission of the Space Shuttle *Columbia*, July 4, 1982," in *Public Papers of the Presidents of the United States: Ronald Reagan: 1982 (in Two Books), Book II—July 3 to December 31, 1982* (Washington, DC: U.S. Government Printing Office, 1983), 892.

13. Ibid.

14. Ibid.

15. Ronald Reagan, "Remarks at the Annual Convention of the National Association of Evangelicals in Orlando, Florida, March 8, 1983," in *Public Papers: 1983, Book I*, 362.

16. Ibid.

17. Ronald Reagan, "Radio Address to the Nation on Voluntarism, May 24, 1986," in *Public Papers: 1986, Book I*, 670.

18. Ibid.

19. Ronald Reagan, "Inaugural Address, January 21, 1985," in *Public Papers of the Presidents of the United States: Ronald Reagan: 1985 (in Two Books), Book I—January 1 to June 28, 1985* (Washington, DC: U.S. Government Printing Office, 1988), 57–58.

20. Ronald Reagan, "Address to the 42d Session of the United Nations General Assembly in New York, New York, September 21, 1987," in *Public Papers of the Presidents of the United States: Ronald Reagan: 1987 (in Two Books), Book II—July 4 to December 31, 1987* (Washington, DC: U.S. Government Printing Office, 1989), 1059.

21. Ibid.

22. Ibid.

23. Ibid.

24. Ronald Reagan, "Address before a Joint Session of Congress on the State of the Union, February 4, 1986," in *Public Papers: 1986, Book I*, 126.

25. About the cultural resonance of Reagan's vision of the recent American past, John Sloan writes, "By the end of the 1970s, liberal policies were seen as a major cause of high taxes, budget deficits, inflation, and stifling bureaucracies. Democrats were shocked that populist conservative allegations that a liberal elite was benefiting from policies that hindered social mobility were being accepted by a growing proportion of the electorate." See John W. Sloan, *FDR and Reagan: Transformative Presidents with Clashing Visions* (Lawrence: UP of Kansas, 2008), 49.

26. Ronald Reagan, "Address to the Nation on the Economy, February 5, 1981," *Public Papers of the Presidents of the United States: Ronald Reagan: 1981,*

January 20 to December 31, 1981 (Washington, DC: U.S. Government Printing Office, 1982), 82–83. Emphasis added.

27. Ronald Reagan, "Address before a Joint Session of the Congress on the State of the Union, February 6, 1985," in *Public Papers: 1985, Book I*, 130. Emphasis added.

28. Reagan, "Remarks during a Visit to the Goddard Space Flight Center," 1208.

29. Ronald Reagan, "Address at Commencement Exercises at the United States Air Force Academy in Colorado Springs, Colorado, May 30, 1984," in *Public Papers of the Presidents of the United States: Ronald Reagan: 1984 (in Two Books), Book I—January 1 to June 29, 1984* (Washington, DC: U.S. Government Printing Office, 1986), 760.

30. Ibid.

31. Ibid., 761.

32. Ibid.

33. Ibid.

34. Ibid.

35. Ronald Reagan, "Address before a Joint Session of the Congress on the State of the Union, January 25, 1984," in *Public Papers: 1984, Book I*, 90.

36. Ibid.

37. Ronald Reagan, "Remarks at the Unveiling of the Knute Rockne Commemorative Stamp at the University of Notre Dame in Indiana, March 9, 1988," in *Public Papers of the Presidents of the United States: Ronald Reagan: 1988 (in Two Books), Book I—January 1 to July 1, 1988* (Washington, DC: U.S. Government Printing Office, 1990), 309.

38. Ronald Reagan, "Radio Address to the Nation on the Space Program, January 28, 1984," in *Public Papers: 1984, Book I*, 108, 109.

39. Ronald Reagan, "Remarks at a White House Ceremony Commemorating the Bicentennial Year of Air and Space Flight, February 7, 1983," in *Public Papers: 1983, Book I*, 198.

40. Reagan, "Remarks during a Visit to the Goddard Space Flight Center," 1209.

41. Ronald Reagan, "Remarks at the Opening Ceremonies for the Knoxville International Energy Exposition (World's Fair) in Tennessee, May 1, 1982," in *Public Papers of the Presidents of the United States: Ronald Reagan: 1982 (in Two Books), Book I—January 1 to July 2, 1982* (Washington, DC: U.S. Government Printing Office, 1983), 547.

42. Reagan, "Remarks at the Unveiling of the Knute Rockne Commemorative Stamp," 309.

43. Ibid., 310.

44. Ibid.

45. Ibid.

46. Ibid.

47. Robert Nisbet, *The Quest for Community: A Study in the Ethics of Order and Freedom* (San Francisco, CA: ICS Press, 1990), 8–9.

48. Ibid., 18.

49. Ibid., 19.

50. Wilhelm Röpke, *A Humane Economy: The Social Framework of the Free Market*, 3rd ed. (Wilmington, DE: ISI Books, 1998), 41.

51. Ibid., 89.

52. Irving Babbitt, *Democracy and Leadership* (Indianapolis, IN: Liberty Fund, 1979), 265.

53. Ibid., 266.

54. Irving Babbitt, *Literature and the American College: Essays in Defense of the Humanities* (Washington, DC: National Humanities Institute, 1986), 104.

55. Babbitt, *Democracy and Leadership*, 25.

56. Ibid.
57. Irving Babbitt, *Rousseau and Romanticism* (New Brunswick, NJ: Transaction, 2002), 366.
58. Ibid., 217.
59. Ibid., 350.
60. Babbitt, *Democracy and Leadership*, 254.
61. Ibid., 25.
62. Babbitt, *Rousseau and Romanticism*, 346.
63. Nathaniel Hawthorne, "Earth's Holocaust," in *Nathaniel Hawthorne's Tales*, ed. James McIntosh (New York: W. W. Norton, 1987), 144.
64. Ibid.
65. Ibid., 153.
66. Ibid., 158–59.
67. Russell Kirk, "What is Conservatism?" in *The Essential Russell Kirk: Selected Essays*, ed. George A. Panichas (Wilmington, DE: ISI Books, 2007), 6.
68. Ibid., 7.
69. Ibid.
70. Ibid.
71. Babbitt, *Democracy and Leadership*, 138.
72. Edmund Burke, *Reflections on the Revolution in France*, ed. J.G.A. Pocock (Indianapolis, IN: Hackett, 1987), 19.
73. Ibid., 30.
74. Ibid., 29.
75. Peter Viereck, *Conservatism Revisited: The Revolt against Ideology*, introduction by Claes G. Ryn (New Brunswick, NJ: Transaction, 2005), 70.
76. Peter Viereck, *Unadjusted Man in the Age of Overadjustment: Where History and Literature Intersect* (New Brunswick, NJ: Transaction, 2004), 35.
77. Ronald Reagan, "The New Republican Party, Fourth Annual Conservative Political Action Conference, February 6, 1977," in *Greatest Speeches of Ronald Reagan*, 53, 54.

NOTES TO CHAPTER 10

1. Ronald Reagan, "Remarks at the Opening Ceremonies of the Statue of Liberty Centennial Celebration in New York, New York, July 3, 1986," in *Public Papers of the Presidents of the United States: Ronald Reagan: 1986 (in Two Books), Book II—June 28 to December 31, 1986* (Washington, DC: U.S. Government Printing Office, 1989), 919.
2. Ronald Reagan, "Remarks at the Annual Conservative Political Action Conference Dinner, March 2, 1984," in *Public Papers of the Presidents of the United States: Ronald Reagan: 1984 (in Two Books), Book I—January 1 to June 29, 1984* (Washington, DC: U.S. Government Printing Office, 1986), 289.
3. Irving Babbitt, *Democracy and Leadership* (Indianapolis, IN: Liberty Fund, 1979), 23.
4. See Paul Kengor, *God and Ronald Reagan: A Spiritual Life* (New York: HarperCollins, 2004); and Hugh Heclo, "Ronald Reagan and the American Public Philosophy," in *The Reagan Presidency: Pragmatic Conservatism and Its Legacies*, eds. W. Elliot Brownlee and Hugh David Graham (Lawrence: UP of Kansas, 2003).
5. Ronald Reagan, "Remarks at a Conference on Religious Liberty, April 16, 1985," in *Public Papers of the Presidents of the United States: Ronald Reagan: 1985 (in Two Books), Book I—January 1 to June 28, 1985* (Washington, DC: U.S. Government Printing Office, 1988), 437.

6. Ibid., 437–38.
7. Ibid., 438.
8. Rom. 13:1 KJV.
9. Gelasius I, "The Bond of Anathema," in *From Irenaeus to Grotius: A Sourcebook in Christian Political Thought 100–1625*, eds. Oliver O'Donovan and Joan Lockwood O'Donovan (Grand Rapids, MI: William B. Eerdmans, 1999), 179.
10. St. Thomas Aquinas, *On Politics and Ethics*, trans. and ed. Paul E. Sigmund (New York: W. W. Norton, 1988), 39.
11. Ibid., 27, 28.
12. John 18:36 KJV.
13. Claes G. Ryn, "The Things of Caesar: Toward the Delimitation of Politics," in *Essays on Christianity and Political Philosophy*, eds. George W. Carey and James V. Schall (Reprint, Lanham, MD: UP of America and the Intercollegiate Studies Institute, 1984), 108.
14. Reagan, "Remarks at the Opening Ceremonies of the Statue of Liberty Centennial Celebration," 919.
15. Ronald Reagan, "Proclamation 4897—National Day of Prayer, February 12, 1982," in *Public Papers of the Presidents of the United States: Ronald Reagan: 1982 (in Two Books), Book I—January 1 to July 2, 1982* (Washington, DC: U.S. Government Printing Office, 1983), 171.
16. Ronald Reagan, "Proclamation 5017—National Day of Prayer, January 27, 1983," in *Public Papers of the Presidents of the United States: Ronald Reagan: 1983 (in Two Books), Book I—January 1 to July 1, 1983* (Washington, DC: U.S. Government Printing Office, 1984), 130.
17. Ronald Reagan, "Remarks at Kansas State University at the Alfred M. Landon Lecture Series on Public Issues, September 9, 1982," in *Public Papers of the Presidents of the United States: Ronald Reagan: 1982 (in Two Books), Book II—July 3 to December 31, 1982* (Washington, DC: U.S. Government Printing Office, 1983), 1121.
18. Ronald Reagan, "Remarks at the Annual Convention of the National Association of Evangelicals in Orlando, Florida, March 8, 1983," in *Public Papers: 1983, Book I*, 362.
19. Ronald Reagan, "Remarks in New York City on Receiving the Charles Evans Hughes Gold Medal of the National Conference of Christians and Jews, March 23, 1982," in *Public Papers: 1982, Book I*, 357.
20. Ibid., 357–58.
21. Ibid., 361.
22. About Reagan's understanding of his religious role as president, see Paul D. Erickson, *Reagan Speaks: The Making of an American Myth* (New York: New York UP, 1985), 72–93.
23. Ronald Reagan, "Interview with the Knight-Ridder News Service on Foreign and Domestic Issues, February 13, 1984," in *Public Papers: 1984, Book I*, 207.
24. Ibid.
25. Ronald Reagan, "Remarks at the Republican National Convention in New Orleans, Louisiana, August 15, 1988," in *Public Papers of the Presidents of the United States: Ronald Reagan: 1988–89 (in Two Books), Book II—July 2, 1988 to January 19, 1989* (Washington, DC: U.S. Government Printing Office, 1991), 1081.
26. Reagan, "Remarks in New York City on Receiving the Charles Evans Hughes Gold Medal," 358.
27. Ronald Reagan, "Remarks at the Annual Meeting of the American Bar Association in Atlanta, Georgia, August 1, 1983," in *Public Papers of the Presidents of the United States: Ronald Reagan: 1983 (in Two Books), Book II—July 2*

to December 31, 1983 (Washington, DC: U.S. Government Printing Office, 1985), 1111.

28. Ibid.
29. Luke 10:25–37 KJV.
30. James 1:22 KJV.
31. Matthew 7:20 KJV.
32. Ronald Reagan, "Remarks at the Annual Convention of the National Religious Broadcasters, February 9, 1982," in *Public Papers: 1982, Book I*, 159.
33. Reagan, "Remarks in New York City on Receiving the Charles Evans Hughes Gold Medal," 359–60.
34. Matthew 25:14–30 KJV.
35. 1 Cor. 12:4, 12:8–9 KJV.
36. Ronald Reagan, "Radio Address to the Nation on Small Business, May 14, 1983," in *Public Papers: 1983, Book I*, 705.
37. Ibid.
38. Ronald Reagan, "Remarks at a Spirit of America Festival in Decatur, Alabama, July 4, 1984," in *Public Papers of the Presidents of the United States: Ronald Reagan: 1984 (in Two Books), Book II—June 30 to December 31, 1984* (Washington, DC: U.S. Government Printing Office, 1987), 1001.
39. Ronald Reagan, "Inaugural Address, January 21, 1985," in *Public Papers: 1985, Book I*, 58.
40. Ibid.
41. Reagan, "Remarks at a Spirit of America Festival," 1001.
42. Ronald Reagan, "Remarks at the 'We the People' Bicentennial Celebration in Philadelphia, Pennsylvania, September 17, 1987," in *Public Papers of the Presidents of the United States: Ronald Reagan: 1987 (in Two Books), Book II—July 4 to December 31, 1987* (Washington, DC: U.S. Government Printing Office, 1989), 1042.
43. Reagan, "Remarks at Kansas State University at the Alfred M. Landon Lecture Series," 1120.
44. Ibid.
45. Ronald Reagan, "Remarks Following a Meeting with Pope John Paul II in Vatican City, June 7, 1982," in *Public Papers: 1982, Book I*, 737.
46. Ibid.
47. Reagan, "Remarks at the Annual Convention of the National Association of Evangelicals," 364.
48. Ronald Reagan, "Remarks at the Conservative Political Action Conference Dinner, March 20, 1981" in *Public Papers of the Presidents of the United States: Ronald Reagan: 1981, January 20 to December 31, 1981* (Washington, DC: U.S. Government Printing Office, 1982), 278; and Ronald Reagan, "Address to Members of the British Parliament, June 8, 1982," in *Public Papers: 1982, Book I*, 747.
49. About Reagan's thinking on the logic of history and the inevitable demise of communism, see Robert C. Rowland and John M. Jones, *Reagan at Westminster: Foreshadowing the End of the Cold War* (College Station: Texas A&M UP, 2010), 63–88.
50. Ronald Reagan, "Remarks to Religious Leaders at the Danilov Monastery in Moscow, May 30, 1988," in *Public Papers of the Presidents of the United States: Ronald Reagan: 1988 (in Two Books), Book I—January 1 to July 1, 1988* (Washington, DC: U.S. Government Printing Office, 1990), 674–75.
51. Ronald Reagan, "Remarks to Soviet Dissidents at Spaso House in Moscow, May 30, 1988," in *Public Papers: 1988, Book I*, 675–76.
52. Ibid., 676–77.
53. Isaiah 2:4 KJV.

54. Ronald Reagan, "Address to the 42d Session of the United Nations General Assembly in New York, New York, September 21, 1987," in *Public Papers: 1987, Book II*, 1059.
55. Ronald Reagan, "Remarks to the Student Congress on Evangelism, July 28, 1988," in *Public Papers: 1988–89, Book II*, 991.
56. Ronald Reagan, "Remarks at the Annual Convention of the National Association of Evangelicals in Columbus, Ohio, March 6, 1984," in *Public Papers: 1984, Book I*, 306.
57. Thomas Jefferson, "First Inaugural Address, March 4, 1801," in *The Portable Thomas Jefferson*, ed. Merrill D. Peterson (New York: Viking, 1975), 292.
58. John Adams, "Dissertation on the Canon and Feudal Law," in *The Political Writings of John Adams*, ed. George W. Carey (Washington, DC: Regnery, 2000), 8.
59. George Washington, "First Inaugural Address, April 30, 1789," in *Writings* (New York: Literary Classics of the United States, 1997), 733. Emphasis in original.
60. Jonathan Edwards, "The Latter-Day Glory Is Probably to Begin in America," in *God's New Israel: Religious Interpretations of American Destiny*, ed. Conrad Cherry (Chapel Hill: U of North Carolina P, 1998), 54.
61. John Winthrop, "A Modell of Christian Charity," in *God's New Israel: Religious Interpretations of American Destiny*, ed. Conrad Cherry (Chapel Hill: U of North Carolina P, 1998), 40. Spelling in original.
62. Jonathan Edwards, "A City on a Hill," in *Works of Jonathan Edwards Online*, vol. 19: *Sermons and Discourses 1734–1738*, ed. M. X. Lesser (New Haven, CT: Jonathan Edwards Center at Yale University, 2008), 540, http://edwards.yale.edu (accessed 19 August 2008). Emphasis in original.
63. Ibid., 545. Spelling in original.
64. Richard M. Gamble, *The War for Righteousness: Progressive Christians, the Great War, and the Rise of the Messianic Nation* (Wilmington, DE: ISI Books, 2003), 5.
65. Ernest Lee Tuveson, *Redeemer Nation: The Idea of America's Millennial Role* (Chicago: U of Chicago P, 1968; Midway Reprint, 1980), 34.
66. Ibid., 34.
67. Ibid., 18–19.
68. Ibid., 19.
69. Matthew 24:27 KJV.
70. 2 Peter 3:10 KJV.
71. 2 Peter 3:8 KJV.
72. Eusebius of Caesarea, "A Speech on the Dedication of the Holy Sepulchre Church," in O'Donovan and O'Donovan, *From Irenaeus to Grotius*, 58–59.
73. St. Augustine, *The City of God against the Pagans*, ed. and trans. R. W. Dyson (New York: Cambridge UP, 2005), 227.
74. Ibid., 223.
75. St. Augustine, *The City of God*, ed. Vernon J. Bourke, trans. Gerald G. Walsh, Demetrius B. Zema, Grace Monahan, and Daniel J. Honan (New York: Doubleday, 1958), 398.
76. Ibid., 446–47.
77. Eric Voegelin, *The New Science of Politics: An Introduction* (Chicago: U of Chicago P, 1987), 122.
78. Ibid.
79. Ibid.
80. Eric Voegelin, *Science, Politics, and Gnosticism*, in *The Collected Works of Eric Voegelin*, vol. 5: *Modernity without Restraint: The Political Religions; The New Science of Politics; and Science, Politics, and Gnosticism*, ed. Manfred Henningsen (Columbia: U of Missouri P, 2000), 297–98.

81. Voegelin, *The New Science of Politics*, 129.
82. Eric Voegelin, *Order and History*, vol. 1: *Israel and Revelation* (Baton Rouge: Louisiana State UP, 1994), 451.
83. Ibid., 452.
84. Ibid., 453.
85. Ibid.
86. Ibid., 454.
87. Eric Voegelin, "Man in Society and History," in *The Collected Works of Eric Voegelin*, vol. 11: *Published Essays 1953–1965*, ed. Ellis Sandoz (Columbia: U of Missouri P, 2000), 205.
88. Ibid., 204.
89. Eric Voegelin, "*The Origins of Totalitarianism*," in *Published Essays 1953–1965*, 22.
90. Ibid.
91. Karl Marx, *The German Ideology*, in *Karl Marx: Selected Writings*, ed. David McLellan (New York: Oxford UP, 1977), 169.
92. David Walsh, *After Ideology: Recovering the Spiritual Foundations of Freedom* (New York: HarperCollins, 1990), 192.
93. Eric Voegelin, "Immortality: Experience and Symbol," in *The Collected Works of Eric Voegelin*, vol. 12: *Published Essays 1965–1985*, ed. Ellis Sandoz (Baton Rouge: Louisiana State UP, 1990), 78.
94. Edmund Burke, *Reflections on the Revolution in France*, ed. J. G. A. Pocock (Indianapolis, IN: Hackett, 1987), 86.
95. For a more extensive treatment of criticisms of Voegelin's views on Christianity, see Michael P. Federici, *Eric Voegelin: The Restoration of Order* (Wilmington, DE: ISI Books, 2002), especially pp. 166–82. For a critique of the notion of radical transcendence, see Claes G. Ryn, "Leo Strauss and History: The Philosopher as Conspirator," *Humanitas* 18, nos. 1–2 (2005), especially pp. 43–49. For a more complete analysis of the relationship between universality and history, see Claes G. Ryn, *A Common Human Ground: Universality and Particularity in a Multi-cultural World* (Columbia: U of Missouri P, 2003), especially chapters 8 and 9.
96. Heclo, "Ronald Reagan and the American Public Philosophy," 35.
97. Ryn, "The Things of Caesar," 126.
98. Ibid., 124. Emphasis in original.
99. Babbitt, *Democracy and Leadership*, 311.
100. Ibid., 312.
101. Ibid., 313.

NOTES TO THE CONCLUSION

1. Ronald Reagan, "Farewell Address to the Nation, January 11, 1989," in *Public Papers of the Presidents of the United States: Ronald Reagan: 1988–89 (in Two Books), Book II—July 2, 1988 to January 19, 1989* (Washington, DC: U.S. Government Printing Office, 1991), 1720.
2. Will Bunch, *Tear Down This Myth: How the Reagan Legacy Has Distorted Our Politics and Haunts Our Future* (New York: Free Press, 2009), 10–13.
3. William J. Clinton, "Address before a Joint Session of the Congress on the State of the Union, January 23, 1996," in *Public Papers of the Presidents of the United States: William J. Clinton: 1996 (in Two Books) Book I—January 1 to June 30, 1996* (Washington, DC: Government Printing Office, 1997), 79.
4. See Bunch, *Tear Down This Myth*.
5. See William Kleinknecht, *The Man Who Sold the World: Ronald Reagan and the Betrayal of Main Street America* (New York: Nation Books, 2009).

6. See Hugh Heclo, "The Mixed Legacies of Ronald Reagan," in *The Enduring Reagan*, ed. Charles W. Dunn (Lexington: UP of Kentucky, 2009).
7. See Alfred S. Regnery, *Upstream: The Ascendance of American Conservatism* (New York: Threshold Editions, 2008).
8. See Lou Cannon and Carl M. Cannon, *Reagan's Disciple: George W. Bush's Troubled Quest for a Presidential Legacy* (New York: PublicAffairs, 2008).
9. See Michael J. Gerson, *Heroic Conservatism: Why Republicans Need to Embrace America's Ideals (And Why They Deserve to Fail If They Don't)* (New York: Harper One 2008).
10. Reagan, "Farewell Address to the Nation," 1719.
11. Ibid.
12. Ibid.
13. Ibid.
14. Ibid., 1720.
15. Ibid.
16. Ibid.
17. Ibid.
18. Ibid., 1721.
19. Ibid., 1720.
20. Ibid.
21. Ibid., 1721.
22. Ibid.
23. Ibid., 1722. Formatting in original.
24. Ibid.
25. Ibid.
26. Ibid.
27. In *America the Virtuous* and in other places, Claes G. Ryn has carefully examined a common contemporary American ideology and political modality that he calls the new Jacobinism. Like the French Jacobins, the new American Jacobins see their country as destined to spread universal principles in the world. According to Ryn, the neo-Jacobins believe that America must play a crucial role in establishing freedom and democracy where they do not yet exist. He argues that these new Jacobins have been rather successful in spreading their political ideas in the United States in part because "they contend that America needs an infusion of 'moral values' and a return to its 'Founding principles.' That their interpretation of those values and principles make them virtually indistinguishable from the French Jacobins is easily overlooked by people who are anxious for any kind of defense of America. It does not occur to most individuals to inquire into just what kind of America is being defended." See Claes G. Ryn, *America the Virtuous: The Crisis of Democracy and the Quest for Empire* (New Brunswick, NJ: Transaction, 2003), 111.
28. Peter Viereck, *Conservatism Revisited: The Revolt against Ideology*, introduction by Claes G. Ryn (New Brunswick, NJ: Transaction, 2005), 70.

Selected Bibliography

PRIMARY SOURCES

Reagan, Ronald. *Actor, Ideologue, Politician: The Public Speeches of Ronald Reagan.* Edited by Davis W. Houck and Amos Kiewe. Westport, CT: Greenwood, 1993.
———. *An American Life.* New York: Simon and Schuster, 1990.
———. *The Greatest Speeches of Ronald Reagan.* West Palm Beach, FL: Newsmax. com, 2001.
———. *Public Papers of the Presidents of the United States: Ronald Reagan, 1981–89.* 15 vols. Washington, DC: U.S. Government Printing Office, 1982–1991.
———. *Reagan: A Life in Letters.* Edited by Kiron K. Skinner, Annelise Anderson, and Martin Anderson. New York: Free Press, 2003.
———. *The Reagan Diaries.* Edited by Douglas Brinkley. New York: HarperCollins, 2007.
———. *Reagan: In His Own Hand.* Edited by Kiron K. Skinner, Annelise Anderson, and Martin Anderson. New York: Free Press, 2001.
———. *Reagan's Path to Victory: The Shaping of Ronald Reagan's Vision.* Edited by Kiron K. Skinner, Annelise Anderson, Martin Anderson, and George P. Schultz. New York: Free Press, 2004.
———. *Speaking My Mind: Selected Speeches.* New York: Simon and Schuster, 1989.
Reagan, Ronald, with Richard G. Hubler. *Where's the Rest of Me?* New York: Karz, 1981.

SECONDARY SOURCES

Abrams, M. H. *The Mirror and the Lamp: Romantic Theory and the Critical Tradition.* New York: Oxford UP, 1953.
Abshire, David M. *Saving the Reagan Presidency: Trust Is the Coin of the Realm.* College Station: Texas A&M UP, 2005.
Adams, John. *The Political Writings of John Adams.* Edited by George W. Carey. Washington, DC: Regnery, 2000.
Adams, John Quincy. *John Quincy Adams and American Continental Empire: Letters, Speeches and Papers.* Edited by Walter Lafeber. Chicago: Quadrangle Books, 1965.
Babbitt, Irving. *Democracy and Leadership.* Indianapolis, IN: Liberty Fund, 1979.
———. *Literature and the American College: Essays in Defense of the Humanities.* Washington, DC: National Humanities Institute, 1986.
———. *Rousseau and Romanticism.* New Brunswick, NJ: Transaction, 2002.
Bates, Toby Glenn. *The Reagan Rhetoric: History and Memory in 1980s America.* DeKalb: Northern Illinois UP, 2011.

Bloom, Allan. *The Closing of the American Mind.* New York: Simon and Schuster, 1987. First Touchstone Edition, 1988.

Brinkley, Douglas. *The Boys of Pointe du Hoc: Ronald Reagan, D-Day, and the U.S. Army Ranger 2nd Battalion.* New York: William Morrow, 2005.

Brownlee, W. Elliot, and Hugh David Graham, eds. *The Reagan Presidency: Pragmatic Conservatism and Its Legacies.* Lawrence: UP of Kansas, 2003.

Brownson, Orestes A. *The American Republic: Its Constitution, Tendencies, and Destiny.* Vol. 1 of *Orestes A. Brownson: Works on Political Philosophy.* Series edited by Gregory S. Butler. Wilmington, DE: ISI Books, 2003.

Bunch, Will. *Tear Down This Myth: How the Reagan Legacy Has Distorted Our Politics and Haunts Our Future.* New York: Free Press, 2009.

Burke, Edmund. *Further Reflections on the Revolution in France.* Edited by Daniel E. Ritchie. Indianapolis, IN: Liberty Fund, 1992.

———. *Reflections on the Revolution in France.* Edited by J.G.A. Pocock. Indianapolis, IN: Hackett, 1987.

Bush, George W. *Public Papers of the Presidents of the United States: George W. Bush, 2004 (in Three Books), Book I—January 1 to June 30, 2004.* Washington, DC: U.S. Government Printing Office, 2007.

Butterfield, Herbert. *The Whig Interpretation of History.* Reprint, London: G. Bell and Sons, 1968.

Cannon, Lou. *Governor Reagan: His Rise to Power.* New York: PublicAffairs, 2003.

———. *President Reagan: The Role of a Lifetime.* New York: PublicAffairs, 2000.

Cannon, Lou, and Carl M. Cannon. *Reagan's Disciple: George W. Bush's Troubled Quest for a Presidential Legacy.* New York: PublicAffairs, 2008.

Carey, George W. *The Federalist: Design for a Constitutional Republic.* Urbana: U of Illinois P, 1989.

———. *In Defense of the Constitution.* Revised and expanded edition. Indianapolis, IN: Liberty Fund, 1995.

Chambers, Whittaker. *Witness.* Washington, DC: Regnery, 1952.

Cherry, Conrad, ed. *God's New Israel: Religious Interpretations of American Destiny.* Revised and updated edition. Chapel Hill: U of North Carolina P, 1998.

Clinton, William J. *Public Papers of the Presidents of the United States: William J. Clinton, 1996 (in Two Books), Book I—January 1 to June 30, 1996.* Washington, DC: U.S. Government Printing Office, 1997.

Croce, Benedetto. *Æsthetic as Science of Expression and General Linguistic.* Translated by Douglas Ainslie. New introduction by John McCormick. New Brunswick, NJ: Transaction, 1995.

———. *Guide to Aesthetics.* Translated by Patrick Romanell. 2nd revised edition. Indianapolis, IN: Hackett, 1995.

Dallek, Robert. *Ronald Reagan: The Politics of Symbolism.* Cambridge, MA: Harvard UP, 1999.

Diggins, John Patrick. *Ronald Reagan: Fate, Freedom, and the Making of History.* New York: W. W. Norton, 2007.

D'Souza, Dinesh. *Ronald Reagan: How an Ordinary Man Became an Extraordinary Leader.* New York: Touchstone, 1999.

Dunn, Charles W., ed. *The Enduring Reagan.* Lexington: UP of Kentucky, 2009.

Edwards, Jonathan. *Works of Jonathan Edwards Online.* Vol. 19: *Sermons and Discourses, 1734–1738.* Edited by M. X. Lesser. New Haven, CT: Jonathan Edwards Center at Yale University, 2008. http://edwards.yale.edu (accessed 19 August 2008).

Edwards, Lee. *The Essential Ronald Reagan: A Profile in Courage, Justice, and Wisdom.* Lanham, MD: Rowman & Littlefield, 2005.

Erickson, Paul D. *Reagan Speaks: The Making of an American Myth.* New York: New York UP, 1985.

Evans, Thomas W. *The Education of Ronald Reagan: The General Electric Years and the Untold Story of His Conversion to Conservatism.* New York: Columbia UP, 2006.

Federici, Michael P. *Eric Voegelin: The Restoration of Order.* Wilmington, DE: ISI Books, 2002.

FitzGerald, Frances. *Way Out There in the Blue: Ronald Reagan, Star Wars, and the End of the Cold War.* New York: Simon and Schuster, 2000.

Frohnen, Bruce, ed. *The American Republic.* Indianapolis, IN: Liberty Fund, 2002.

Gamble, Richard M. "Savior Nation: Woodrow Wilson and the Gospel of Service." *Humanitas* 14, no. 1 (2001): 4–22.

———. *The War for Righteousness: Progressive Christians, the Great War, and the Rise of the Messianic Nation.* Wilmington, DE: ISI Books, 2003.

Gerson, Michael J. *Heroic Conservatism: Why Republicans Need to Embrace America's Ideals (And Why They Deserve to Fail If They Don't).* New York: HarperCollins, 2007; Harper One, 2008.

Hamby, Alonzo L. *Liberalism and Its Challengers: From F.D.R. to Bush.* 2nd edition. New York: Oxford UP, 1992.

Hamilton, Alexander, John Jay, and James Madison. *The Federalist.* The Gideon Edition. Edited by George W. Carey and James McClellan. Indianapolis, IN: Liberty Fund, 2001.

Hawthorne, Nathaniel. *Nathaniel Hawthorne's Tales.* Edited by James McIntosh. New York: W. W. Norton, 1987.

Henderson, Phillip G., ed. *The Presidency: Then and Now.* Lanham, MD: Rowman & Littlefield, 2000.

Jaffa, Harry. *How to Think about the American Revolution: A Bicentennial Cerebration.* Durham, NC: Carolina Academic Press, 1978.

Jefferson, Thomas. *The Portable Thomas Jefferson.* Edited by Merrill D. Peterson. New York: Viking, 1975.

Kagan, Robert. "Neocon Nation: Neoconservatism c. 1776." *World Affairs Journal* 170, no. 4 (Spring 2008): 13–35.

Kendall, Willmoore, and George W. Carey. *The Basic Symbols of the American Political Tradition.* Baton Rouge: Louisiana State UP, 1970.

Kengor, Paul. *The Crusader: Ronald Reagan and the Fall of Communism.* New York: HarperCollins, 2006.

———. *God and Ronald Reagan: A Spiritual Life.* New York: HarperCollins, 2004.

Kirk, Russell. *The Conservative Mind: From Burke to Eliot.* 7th revised edition. Washington, DC: Regnery, 1999.

———. *The Essential Russell Kirk: Selected Essays.* Edited by George A. Panichas. Wilmington, DE: ISI Books, 2007.

———. *The Politics of Prudence.* 3rd printing. Wilmington, DE: ISI Books, 1998.

———. *Rights and Duties: Reflections on Our Conservative Constitution.* Edited by Mitchell S. Muncy. Dallas, TX: Spence, 1997.

———. *The Roots of American Order.* Hardcover edition. Wilmington, DE: ISI Books, 2004.

———. *The Sword of Imagination: Memoirs of a Half-Century of Literary Conflict.* Grand Rapids, MI: Wm. B. Eerdmans, 1995.

Kleinknecht, William. *The Man Who Sold the World: Ronald Reagan and the Betrayal of Main Street America.* New York: Nation Books, 2009.

Kristol, William, and Robert Kagan. "Toward a Neo-Reaganite Foreign Policy." *Foreign Affairs* 75, no. 4 (July/August 1996): 18–32.

Lincoln, Abraham. *Abraham Lincoln: His Speeches and Writings.* Edited by Roy P. Basler. New York: Da Capo, 1990.

Locke, John. *Second Treatise of Government.* Edited by C. B. Macpherson. Indianapolis, IN: Hackett, 1980.

Lukacs, John. *Democracy and Populism: Fear and Hatred*. New Haven, CT: Yale UP, 2005.

———. *June 1941: Hitler and Stalin*. New Haven, CT: Yale UP, 2006.

Marx, Karl. *Karl Marx: Selected Writings*. Edited by David McLellan. New York: Oxford UP, 1977.

McDougall, Walter A. *Promised Land, Crusader State: The American Encounter with the World since 1776*. New York: Houghton Mifflin, 1997.

Morris, Edmund. *Dutch: A Memoir of Ronald Reagan*. New York: Random House, 1999.

Nisbet, Robert. *Conservatism: Dream and Reality*. New Brunswick, NJ: Transaction, 2002.

———. *The Present Age: Progress and Anarchy in Modern America*. Indianapolis, IN: Liberty Fund, 1988.

———. *The Quest for Community: A Study in the Ethics of Order and Freedom*. San Francisco: ICS Press, 1990.

———. *Twilight of Authority*. Indianapolis, IN: Liberty Fund, 2000.

Noonan, Peggy. *When Character Was King: A Story of Ronald Reagan*. New York: Viking, 2001.

O'Donovan, Oliver, and Joan Lockwood O'Donovan, ed. *From Irenaeus to Grotius: A Sourcebook in Christian Political Thought 100–1625*. Grand Rapids, MI: William B. Eerdmans, 1999.

Paine, Thomas. *The Thomas Paine Reader*. Edited by Michael Foot and Isaac Kramnick. New York: Penguin Putnam, 1987.

Plato. *Republic*. Translated by Desmond Lee. New York: Penguin Putnam, 2003.

Regnery, Alfred S. *Upstream: The Ascendance of American Conservatism*. New York: Threshold, 2008.

Röpke, Wilhelm. *A Humane Economy: The Social Framework of the Free Market*. 3rd edition. Wilmington, DE: ISI Books, 1998.

Rousseau, Jean-Jacques. *The Basic Political Writings*. Translated by Donald A. Cress. Indianapolis, IN: Hackett, 1987.

———. *Discourses and Other Early Political Writings*. Edited and translated by Victor Gourevitch. New York: Cambridge UP, 1997. Reprint, 2001.

———. *Emile, or On Education*. Translated by Allan Bloom. New York: Basic Books, 1979.

———. *Letter to Beaumont, Letters Written from the Mountain, and Related Writings*. Edited by Eve Grace and Christopher Kelly. Translated by Judith R. Bush and Christopher Kelly. Collected Writings of Rousseau, vol. 9. Hanover, NH: UP of New England, 2001.

———. *Reveries of the Solitary Walker*. Translated by Peter France. New York: Penguin Books, 1979.

Rowland, Robert C., and John M. Jones. *Reagan at Westminster: Foreshadowing the End of the Cold War*. College Station: Texas A&M UP, 2010.

Ryn, Claes G. *America the Virtuous: The Crisis of Democracy and the Quest for Empire*. New Brunswick, NJ: Transaction, 2003.

———. *A Common Human Ground: Universality and Particularity in a Multicultural World*. Columbia: U of Missouri P, 2003.

———. *Democracy and the Ethical Life: A Philosophy of Politics and Community*. 2nd edition. Washington, DC: CUA Press, 1990.

———. "The Imaginative Origins of Modernity: Life as Daydream and Nightmare." *Humanitas* 10, no. 2 (1997): 41–60.

———. "Leo Strauss: The Philosopher as Conspirator." *Humanitas* 18, nos. 1–2 (2005): 31–58.

———. "The Things of Caesar: Toward the Delimitation of Politics." In *Essays on Christianity and Political Philosophy*. Edited by George W. Carey and James

V. Schall. Reprint, Lanham, MD: UP of America and the Intercollegiate Studies Institute, 1984.

——. *Will, Imagination, and Reason: Irving Babbitt and the Problem of Reality.* Washington, DC: Regnery Books, 1986.

Schaller, Michael. *Reckoning with Reagan: America and Its President in the 1980s.* New York: Oxford UP, 1992.

Schweizer, Peter. *Reagan's War: The Epic Story of His Forty-Year Struggle and Final Triumph over Communism.* New York: Anchor Books, 2003.

Sloan, John M. *FDR and Reagan: Transformative Presidents with Clashing Visions.* Lawrence: UP of Kansas, 2008.

St. Augustine of Hippo. *The City of God.* Edited by Vernon J. Bourke. Translated by Gerald G. Walsh, Demetrius B. Zema, Grace Monahan, and Daniel J. Honan. New York: Doubleday, 1958.

——. *The City of God against the Pagans.* Edited and translated by R. W. Dyson. New York: Cambridge UP, 2005.

——. *The Political Writings of St. Augustine.* Edited by Henry Paolucci. Chicago: H. Regnery, 1962. Reprint, Washington, DC: Regnery, 2002.

St. Thomas Aquinas. *On Politics and Ethics.* Translated and edited by Paul E. Sigmund. New York: W. W. Norton, 1988.

Thoreau, Henry David. *A Week on the Concord and Merrimack Rivers.* New York: Quality Paperback Book Club, 1997.

Troy, Gil. *Morning in America: How Ronald Reagan Invented the 1980s.* Princeton, NJ: Princeton UP, 2005.

Tulis, Jeffrey K. *The Rhetorical Presidency.* Princeton, NJ: Princeton UP, 1987.

Tuveson, Ernest Lee. *Redeemer Nation: The Idea of America's Millennial Role.* Chicago: U of Chicago P, 1968. Midway Reprint, 1980.

Viereck, Peter. *Conservatism Revisited: The Revolt against Ideology.* Introduction by Claes G. Ryn. New Brunswick, NJ: Transaction, 2005.

——. *Unadjusted Man in the Age of Overadjustment: Where History and Literature Intersect.* New Brunswick, NJ: Transaction, 2004.

Voegelin, Eric. *The Collected Works of Eric Voegelin.* Vol. 5: *Modernity without Restraint: The Political Religions; The New Science of Politics; and Science, Politics, and Gnosticism.* Edited by Manfred Henningsen. Columbia: U of Missouri P, 2000.

——. *The Collected Works of Eric Voegelin.* Vol. 11: *Published Essays 1953–1965.* Edited by Ellis Sandoz. Columbia: U of Missouri P, 2000.

——. *The Collected Works of Eric Voegelin.* Vol. 12: *Published Essays 1965–1985.* Edited by Ellis Sandoz. Baton Rouge: Louisiana State UP, 1990.

——. *The Collected Works of Eric Voegelin.* Vol. 16: *Order and History Vol. III: Plato and Aristotle.* Edited by Dante Germino. Columbia: U of Missouri P, 2000.

——. *The New Science of Politics: An Introduction.* Chicago: U of Chicago P, 1987.

——. *Order and History.* Vol. 1: *Israel and Revelation.* Baton Rouge: Louisiana State UP, 1994.

Walsh, David. *After Ideology: Recovering the Spiritual Foundations of Freedom.* New York: HarperCollins, 1990.

——. "Voegelin's Response to the Disorder of the Age." *Review of Politics* 46, no. 2 (1984): 266–87.

Washington, George. *Writings.* New York: Literary Classics of the United States, 1997.

Weiler, Michael, and W. Barnett Pearce, eds. *Reagan and Public Discourse in America.* Tuscaloosa: U of Alabama P, 1992.

White, John Kenneth. *The New Politics of Old Values.* 2nd edition. Hanover, NH: UP of New England, 1990.

Whitman, Walt. *Leaves of Grass and Other Writings*. Edited by Michael Moon. New York: W. W. Norton, 2002.

Wilentz, Sean. *The Age of Reagan: A History: 1974–2008*. New York: HarperCollins, 2008.

Wills, Garry. *Reagan's America: Innocents at Home*. New York: Doubleday, 1987. Reprint, New York: Penguin Putnam, 2000.

Wilson, Woodrow. *The Politics of Woodrow Wilson: Selections from His Speeches and Writings*. Edited by August Heckscher. New York: Harper & Row, 1970.

Wright, Harold Bell. *That Printer of Udell's*. Washington, DC: Regnery, 1999.

Index